Ken Hutchinson
London   1958

# of ARCHAEOLOGY

C. W. CERAM

310 illustrations in photogravure
16 plates in full colour

THAMES AND HUDSON LONDON

Jacket and typographic design by
GEORGE A. ADAMS

Translated from the German by
RICHARD and CLARA WINSTON

A PICTURE HISTORY OF ARCHAEOLOGY

CONTENTS

WHEN I WAS WRITING my first book about the history of archaeology, I discovered to my surprise that although there were any number of picture books which show the riches of past civilizations as revealed by archaeology – the bookseller sets them on his shelves under the general heading of "art books" – there was not a single book whose subject was the history of archaeology itself. One reason for this is apparent enough: the archaeologist's work on a site, or in the interior of tombs and pyramids tends to yield little of pictorial value. Or rather, the picture is always the same: a few men with picks and spades staring at some barely recognizable object or at the remnants of walls which – at least in the state in which they are found – are pictorially most unattractive. And yet archaeology, considered in its full import as the study of antiquity, includes far more than is immediately evident under the excavator's spade. Every find is followed by the far more important process of *interpretation*. And in the course of interpretation there takes place that methodical re-creation of the past which our civilization alone has practiced and which makes it clear that archaeology is among the "conquering sciences of the nineteenth century" (to borrow a phrase from Adolf Michaelis, who was first to deal with the history of archaeology). Taking archaeology, therefore, in this larger sense as a complete science of which excavation is but a part, and seeking such illustrative material, we find not a paucity but a wealth of fascinating pictures. And only in the rarest cases are these merely of a "man with a spade".

How our view of the ancient world was born, how it changed, and how it is still changing – that, then, is the real theme of this book. (The reader will find a small selection of essential texts on this subject in the introduction to the list of sources.)

In devising a format for this book I soon realized that the time-honoured method of assembling a collection of pretty pictures with such captions as, "No. 17; carved cosmetic palette; Late Predynastic period; height $3^1/_2$ inches", would be useless for the sort of book I had in mind. Similarly, the manner of

most picture-books, of referring the reader to the appendix for additional information, has always seemed to me something less than encouraging. In fact it is
the fate of such collections of pictures to be merely skimmed through (except by
interested professionals, of course); they are seldom looked at intently. Similarly,
their texts are not particularly readable. I therefore chose a format in which picture and text are so welded together that the one cannot stand without the other.
If the result has been a picture-book which can be read – it is not my province to
judge – then I have achieved my aim.

The pattern of the book deliberately follows the structure of *Gods, Graves, and
Scholars* because I have sought to trace the historical, cultural continuity which
extends from Sumeria through Babylonia, Assyria, Crete, Greece and Rome
down to our own times. This, to me, is a more natural presentation of the facts
than any attempt to draw in the overall archaeological scene. The excursion into
Middle America is justified only as an express and conscious digression. For
the reader who wishes to apprehend at least the outlines of the general scene, the
chronological tables offer a chart high-lighting the major events in the history of
archaeology, from the first stirrings of interest in antiquity to the present-day
triumphs of scores of specialists.

Many of the illustrations are reproduced here for the first time. Several of the
quotations are here published from manuscript for the first time; many others
are reprinted here for the first time after having fallen into oblivion for two,
three or four hundred years.

In regard to the choice of illustrations, I have been forced to cull boldly from
more than two thousand pictures. Specialists will be quick to see how much
has had to be omitted. The Egyptologist would wish for, say, more precise
references to Greaves's *Pyramidographia* – a book whose very title may be unfami-
liar to the classical archaeologist. Perhaps the orientalist will find the absence of
a certain Amarna letter a painful lacuna, whereas the specialist in American
archaeology may not be in the least aware of its importance. I can only ask forbearance of the specialists. Perhaps the general critic will observe the material
that has been presented here in this particular order for the first time.

The three hundred and twenty-six pictures have for the most part been reproduced anew, from the originals. Similarly, all the quotations in the text have
been drawn from the sources. Wherever translations were necessary, they have

been done anew; condensations and cuts have been noted in every case. Thus the material in this book is documentary in the strict sense. A detailed list of sources, which like the text contains numerous bibliographical references, will enable the interested reader to pursue various subjects farther.

A word of explanation: This book – like *Gods, Graves, and Scholars* or my book on the discovery of the Hittite Empire – has nothing to do with "popular science". I am not a scientist, but a writer, and in my presentation of a scientific development I have acted upon a literary principle: reality seen through a temperament. In this book on the history of archaeology, then, I am simply following the method which guided the naturalistic novelists when they described the world of priests, bankers or coal miners, subjecting themselves to the exceedingly earnest obligation of studying very closely, before writing, theology and Church history, the stock exchange, or the social conditions of miners.

In conclusion, my expressions of gratitude, which ordinarily are but a matter of custom, are here a necessity. It is due only to the patience and labours of the publisher, Walter Neurath, and his associates at Thames and Hudson that this book, technically so difficult to produce, and requiring years of preparation, can be made accessible to a larger public. The readiness of museums, libraries and many scholars to aid in the production of this book was extraordinary.

I owe particular thanks to the following institutions: American Museum of Natural History, New York; Ashmolean Museum, Oxford; British Museum, London; Germanisches Museum, Nuremberg; Griffith Institute, Oxford; Kunsthistorisches Museum, Vienna; Metropolitan Museum, New York; Musée du Louvre, Paris; Musée de l'Homme, Paris; Museum am Kupfergraben, Staatliche Museen, Berlin-Dahlem; Museum für Völkerkunde, Vienna; Museo Nacional de Historia, Mexico; Museo Regional de Oaxaca, Mexico; Peabody Museum, Harvard University, Cambridge, Mass.; Staatliche Kunstsammlungen, Weimar; Vorderasiatisches Museum, Berlin; Victoria and Albert Museum, London; Biblioteca Palatina, Parma; Biblioteca Laurenziana, Florence; Biblioteca Nazionale, Naples; Biblioteca Nazionale Centrale, Florence; Biblioteca Vaticana, the Vatican; Bodleian Library, Oxford; Newberry Library, Chicago; British School at Athens; Université Saint Joseph, Beirut; Warburg Institute, London.

For assistance in assembling the pictures I am indebted to: Professor C. W.

Blegen, M. Philippe Diolé; I.E.S. Edwards, Esq.; Dr. Johannes Friedrich; Dr. Zakaria Goneim; Dr. Siegfried Grotefend; Mrs. Seton Lloyd; Professor Amadeo Maiuri; Dr. Ernst Meyer; the executors of the estate of Sir Arthur Evans; and Miss Ann Petrie, who also gave permission for the inclusion of a paragraph from the book by her father, Sir Flinders Petrie: *Pyramids and Temples of Gizeh*.

September 1958   C.W.C.

I

Book I

WINCKELMANN

PATER PIAGGIO

FRANÇOIS MAZOIS

SCHLIEMANN

WILHELM DÖRPFELD

ARTHUR EVANS

AMADEO MAIURI

MICHAEL VENTRIS

ab urbe lapidem : biduo post dela-
tum est in capitolium maximo po-
puli concursu iussu conservatorum
urbis .

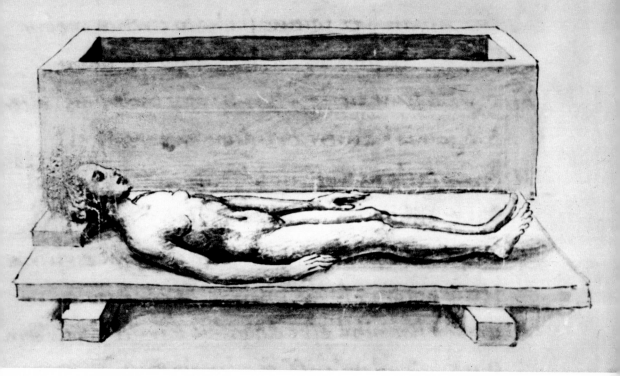

On Rome's Via Appia, in April 1485,

labourers uncovered a sarcophagus whose contents shook the minds of men. Exhibited in the Palazzo dei Conservatori in Rome two days later, the find attracted so vast a crowd "that it was as if indulgence from all sins were being given". Within the sarcophagus was the body of a girl of ancient Rome, well preserved and extraordinarily beautiful. After twenty thousand people had come to see it on a single day (lured also by the rumour that an oil lamp miraculously still alight had been found beside the body), Pope Innocent VIII issued an unusual order. The body was taken in the dead of night to a deserted spot outside the Porta Pinciana and there reburied in secrecy. Our picture is the only contemporary one that has survived; it is a tinted pen drawing appended to a letter written in Latin by a Florentine humanist to a friend of the famous Medici, Lorenzo the Magnificent. The letter reads:

"Bartolommeo Fonte greets his friend Francesco Sassetti ... You have asked me for tidings concerning the woman's body recently found on the Via Appia. I can but hope that my pen is equal to describing the beauty and charm of this body. Had we not all of Rome for witnesses, the story would indeed be incredible ... Close to the sixth milestone on the Via Appia labourers looking for marble were extracting a large block of the stone when they suddenly broke through a brick vault twelve feet deep. Here they found a marble sarcophagus. When they opened it, they discovered a body lying on its face, coated with a greasy but fragrant substance to the thickness of two fingers. When they cleared away the perfumed coating – they had begun at the head – they looked upon a pale face with features so clear that it seemed as if the girl might have been buried that very day. Her long black hair, which was still firmly attached to the scalp, was fastened in a knot and parted in a manner suitable to a maiden; it was also covered with a snood of silk and gold.

"Tiny ears, a delicate forehead, black eyebrows – and finally eyes of curious shape, with the whites showing below the lids. Even the nostrils were unimpaired, and so soft that they yielded to the slightest pressure of a finger. The lips were red and slightly parted, the teeth small and white, the tongue scarlet almost to the palate. Cheeks, chin, throat and neck seemed warm as life. The arms hung from the shoulders in such perfect state that they could be moved in any direction. On the lovely, long fingers of the outstretched hands, the fingernails were firmly rooted; no pulling could have detached them. Breast, abdomen and loins, however, had been pressed to one side, and disintegrated after removal of the aromatic coating. The back, hips and buttocks, on the other hand, had retained their shape and their wonderful curves; likewise thighs and legs, which during life must have displayed even greater beauties than the face.

"In short, here was a sublimely beautiful girl of noble family from the days when Rome stood at the pinnacle of her glory.

"Unfortunately, the imposing monument above this burial vault was destroyed many centuries ago, and the inscription was not preserved. The sarcophagus, too, bears no markings – we know neither this maiden's name, her origin nor her age ..."

This mummy, ripped from its grave in 1485 and a few days later returned to the earth at some unknown spot, is certainly not the one find from which we can date the beginning of archaeology – it was too haphazard for that. But up to that time such finds had kindled the imagination and aroused delight in only a few connoisseurs and collectors. Now, in the age of rebirth of interest in classical antiquity, people were learning to think, to feel, and to create anew in its spirit, though they sometimes misunderstood it. A wonder-struck populace stood ready to imbibe the very breath of remote times. Their excitement suggests that something new was truly in the air. The past of which the Roman maiden was ambassadress had come to life again and was to remould the culture of the West.

"When as a boy I was in Rome for the first time",

the aged sculptor Francesco da San-gallo recalled in 1567, "news was brought to the Pope of some remark-ably fine statues just discovered in a vineyard near Santa Maria Maggiore. Then the Pope sent forth a servant: 'Go and tell Giuliano da Sangallo to hasten to the place and look.' So my father went; but since Michelangelo Buonarotti was living with him, he asked him to come along ... When we reached the place where the statues were standing, my father said at once: 'This is the Laocoön mentioned by Pliny!' ... After we had seen what there was to see, we returned home for our supper."

Thus, we have a terse account of Michelangelo's confronting for the first time a work of art that was to exert the most powerful influence upon the sculptors of the Renaissance. Two centuries later the piece of sculpture could still inspire Gotthold Ephraim Lessing, the celebrated German critic, to write his *Laocoön, or the Limits of Painting and Poetry*. "Everyone in Rome considers it the most wonderful statue that was ever created", a contemporary of Sangallo wrote. And another: "So valuable was it reckoned by all who would possess it that the owner, Felice de' Freddi, kept it in his own room beside his bed."

The group was carved (according to Pliny) by the Rhodian sculptor Agesander and his sons Polydorus and Athenodorus (1st century B. C.). It represents the Trojan priest Laocoön (who warned the Trojans against drawing the wooden horse into their city) at the moment he was strangled by serpents rising out of the sea. The reception given to the *Laocoön* group is an excellent example of how a new consciousness of history tended to take up a single chance discovery and exaggerate its importance, with the result that a highly one-sided picture of an alien past is transmitted to succeeding centuries. The century of humanism (whose artistic manifestation was the "Renaissance") which turned so passionately toward pagan antiquity was nevertheless profoundly Christian. What it saw in antiquity was indubitably an ancient world, "but inwardly illuminated by the Christian Faith. That world never existed as they pictured it . . ." (Huizinga).

Naturally, at the time the *Laocoön* was found, other significant discoveries had already been made, as our chronological table shows. But none had such an instant and compelling effect. In spite of the efforts of a few persons genuinely interested in the art of antiquity, certain detestable practices long remained the rule. Fanatics broke the heads of newly unearthed statues because they were naked and pagan. Treasure-hunters pillaged and destroyed graves. Because Christianity needed churches, princes needed palaces, and vine-growers needed terraces, ancient buildings were used as quarries for worked stone.

The man who was to revolutionize the whole approach to antiquity was not born until 1717.

In the early days of archaeology

those who practiced it viewed all excavations as tasks requiring merely the application of sufficient force. In the drawing made by Giovanni Permoli in about 1760, a classical statue of Livia, wife of Emperor Augustus and mother of Tiberius, is being crudely raised with levers. The marble statue was found near the north Italian city of Parma in the early eighteenth century. Permoli intended his drawing as an illustration for a work that never reached print – on monuments "brought to light from the depths of the city of Velleia, with some reflections thereon". The manuscript, precious for its early and extremely vivid descriptions of archaeological finds, is now in the Palatine Library at Parma.

bring about his death, has been called "the Father of Archaeology". More accurately, Johann Joachim Winckelmann (1717–1768) was the father of archaeology insofar as it resurrected the *art* of antiquity. He brought order into the interpretation of art. Son of a German cobbler, he was the first to discriminate among styles. Only to this extent was he an archaeologist. A poet hid under his scholarly mantle. Some of his descriptions of ancient sculpture are close to ecstatic hymns. Phrases in his *Open Letters* and his *History of Ancient Art*, phrases such as "noble simplicity and tranquil grandeur", "noble harmony", and "men like gods", were taken up by his contemporaries and applied to the whole of Greek culture and civilization. Thus fundamental misunderstandings were propagated, and these persisted into the nineteenth century.

His work made him famous throughout Europe; after his conversion to Catholicism he was accorded high offices in Rome. At fifty-one he was murdered in an inn in the Adriatic port city of Trieste by a stranger with whom he had unwisely taken up.

This portrait, dated 1768, is signed by Anton von Maron. The cobbler's son was not only a scholar and poet; he was at times a conceited ass. "Mr. Hamilton", he wrote, "the English Minister at Naples, who is the greatest connoisseur of painting among living men, declares that he has never seen a handsomer head than mine; and he is right!"

Winckelmann is wearing his Russian wolf's pelt; in the background on the right is a bust of Homer – and before him on the table lies an engraving of the statue he loved best: that of Antinous.

"...Thence
he led me
with marked
gravity

to the gem of the collection, the head of Antinous, in low-relief, of white marble. Even an Iroquois, I reflected, would have to apprehend the beauty of this statue ... But how beautiful the entire relief must have been. For Winckelmann asserts that this is only the upper part; ... presumably the whole figure was represented as standing on a chariot. This he surmised, he said, from the preserved hands, of which the right seems to be holding one end and the left the other end of the reins. In restoration a bunch of flowers was placed in the left hand." (C. T. Weinlig in *Briefe über Rom* [Letters on Rome] 1782.)

The relief dates from the period between A. D. 130 and 138, the dates of the deaths of Antinous and Hadrian. The heavy-hearted boy from Claudiopolis was Emperor Hadrian's favourite companion. In a fit of melancholia, and perhaps also with the idea of making the supreme sacrifice for the Emperor, Antinous drowned himself in the Nile in A. D. 130. Hadrian caused him to be deified.

In 1735, when this Antinous was found in the Villa Hadriana, the first excavations near Naples were beginning. Within three years they had brought to light the wonderful discoveries which were to send Winckelmann into raptures. Herculaneum and Pompeii rose out of the graves in which they had lain for almost 1,700 years.

"Even for gods this was going too far",

said the poet Martial. On August 20 in the year A. D. 79 Vesuvius gave vent to a low growl; birds stopped singing, and the cattle tugged at the chains in their stalls. On August 24 a terrible thunderclap crashed into the peace of a radiant morning. The sun was suddenly obscured; the peak of Vesuvius split open; fire and smoke leaped toward the sky. Rain streamed down upon the rich cities of Pompeii and Herculaneum, and rivers of lava poured into the streets.

Herculaneum, in the midst of its bustling life, was overwhelmed and covered by a river of lava which in places congealed to a thickness of fifty feet. Pompeii was buried under hot ashes and lapilli, small fragments of volcanic stone. Dense fumes of sulphur descended on both cities, suffocating all living creatures. On the third day, when the sun rose again, the earth all around Vesuvius was covered by a vast shroud of white ashes under which the cities of Pompeii and Herculaneum had vanished.

We have here a photograph of a model of the excavated city of Pompeii as it was about 1900. In the foreground are the large and the small theatres, on the left the Forum Triangulare. The first successful excavations began in 1748 under the direction of Rocco Gioacchino de Alcubierre, an engineer in the service of King Charles III of Naples. On April 6 the first wall painting was found. From that date onward excavation has continued, with interruptions, to the present day. Three fifths of the city have been uncovered, and wonderful works of art brought to light.

In April 1943 Allied reconnaissance patrols flying over the city thought they detected a German panzer division hidden in the ruins. (There was none.) The first bomb struck the Forum. It was followed by 150 more bombs. Damage was enormous. The monuments and buildings which had been reconstructed with so much toil were once again demolished and buried.

unlike Pompeii under its soft pumice. For that reason General Emanuel Moritz, Prince d'Elboeuf, had enormous technical difficulties to overcome before he could make his way from a peasant's well-shaft into the darkness of the city. We may assume that he was actuated in equal degrees by love of art and greed for treasure. Among a variety of fragments he found first an inscription on marble, then three splendid classical statues of women. These were damaged, and parts were missing. Believing that only perfection could be valuable, he secretly removed the statues to Rome where second-rate sculptors restored them to their "ancient beauty" – without knowing in the slightest what such beauty was.

So began systematic archaeological restoration – a practice that only rarely served a useful purpose, and that usually led to the strangest reconstructions and misconceptions.

A still more amazing case of "restoration" occurred after the next sizable excavations in Herculaneum, under the direction of Alcubierre. Working at the Theatrum Herculanense (and thus following the trail of d'Elboeuf, who by chance or instinct had dug first shot into this storehouse of statues), Alcubierre came across numerous fragments of what had obviously been a mighty bronze horse. He reasoned that this had belonged to an extremely imposing quadriga, or four-horse chariot. The sculptor Joseph Canart, who was entrusted with the restoration, simply melted down many of the pieces. Either he thought them beyond using, or was unable to recognize them as belonging to a greater whole. From the metal so easily obtained he made chandeliers for chapels and a statue of the Madonna. Years later the rest of the pieces, which had meanwhile been scattered widely, were assembled and patched together into a single whole. The bronze horse here reproduced still stands in the National Museum at Naples, and looks to the casual eye as if it were from a single mold.

Since even Winckelmann saw nothing wrong with such treatment of fragments, let us glance into one of his favourite workshops.

**Naples gave
Winckelmann
nothing but trouble,**

and yet offered him the challenge that moved him to arrange the art of antiquity along rational lines of development. It was in 1756 that he made his first journey to the city – he was thirty-nine and not yet famous. But although he was known for his just-published, three-volume *Thoughts on the Imitation of Greek Works in Painting and Sculpture*, he encountered the most annoying barriers whenever he wanted to examine finds. The nineteenth-century concept of a museum – as a collection of beautiful and significant objects accessible to every-one – was quite absent in the eighteenth century. Charles III, who had accumu-lated a sizable collection, kept jealous watch over these works; to break the ban on uninvited visitors was to court severe penalties. Winckelmann, aggrieved and therefore crafty, succeeded in the course of time in inspecting many of these works of art. When he published his account of them, he fell into dis-favour in the highest quarters. A quotation from Weinlig, the German traveller who was at Portici in October 1768, summarizes the situation:
"It is scarcely permissible to look at an object long enough to form an impres-sion, let alone to take out a pencil. I had the bright idea of using the stem of my lorgnette to scratch a few of the patterns of the mosaic floor into the lining of my hat, and even this had to be done with great caution. I believe the custodian would have cut out the hat lining if he had noticed."
Winckelmann was on a friendly footing with a restorer, Bartolomeo Cavaceppi,

and had great faith in his skill and conscientiousness. Undoubtedly too great faith, as we can see today in the catalogue from which our picture was taken. The man in the foreground on the right, who is "restoring" a bust with the aid of a heavy mallet and a foot-long chisel, would horrify a contemporary restorer.

We shall return to the question of restorations, reconstruction and condition of finds in our section on Crete. For the present it is important to see, by a few examples, how the spirit of the age viewed these finds.

Probably the earliest picture of resurrected Pompeii

It shows the Via di Sallustio, which leads to the Herculaneum Gate, and is a pen drawing by Giovanni Battista Piranesi (1720–1778), a prolific sketcher of classical architecture. Piranesi was a romantic. His depiction of the Accademia of the Villa Hadriana at Tivoli (overleaf) shows an ancient world so overgrown by ivy and forest vegetation that it is a wonder the buildings still stand. This is a good example of the then dawning conception of classical architecture as "picturesque ruins". (Only a few decades later the custom arose of viewing the Colosseum at Rome by moonlight.)

(Francesco, who died in 1810), after a drawing by Desprez, contrasts by its clarity – although it is, if we will, the "clarity" of a Late Baroque tableau. It is amusing to see the groups of strollers among the ruins – people were already organizing Sunday afternoon outings to the world of classical antiquity. (The engraving shows the Temple of Isis adjacent to the theatre at Pompeii.)

It is astonishing that the numerous masters of architectural drawing in the period so completely missed the human aspect of many of the Pompeian finds. Where it was recognized, the artists indulged not in romanticism, but in the baser practice of romanticizing.

"The skeleton in the laundry"

This is a scene which might have formed the climax of a nineteenth-century *grand guignol* drama. It would be perfectly in order for the lady on the left to recognize, from an amulet, the skeleton of her murdered mother. Nevertheless, such spectacles were actually encountered at Pompeii. The English antiquary Sir William Hamilton, writing in 1777, narrates: "Skeleton of the washer-woman (for anatomists say it is that of a female); she seems to have been shut up in this vault, the staircase having been filled with rubbish, and to have waited for death with calm resignation, and true Roman fortitude, as the attitude of the skeleton really seems to indicate. It was at my instigation, that the bones were left untouched on the spot where they were found."

The next picture, a photograph, reveals the gulf between an early nineteenth-century artist's version and the unvarnished reality registered by the camera.

Here, crushed by lapilli and suffocated by sulphur fumes,

the first Pompeians collapsed. The figures on the right are a young girl and an older woman into whose arms she crept for refuge. During excavation arch-aeologists came across hollows which they recognized as the forms of bodies preserved by the petrified cinders. They poured plaster into these hollows – thus obtaining these reproductions of bodies dead 1,700 years but still imbued with a ghostly reality.

This technique of making plaster casts from hollows, incidentally, enabled archaeologists to determine that the palaestra, the great stadium of Pompeii, had been surrounded by tall plane trees before the disaster. The trees themselves had vanished completely, but the space left by their root systems could be filled, and the nature of the roots indicated the size and variety of the trees. The palaestra yielded nearly one hundred human skeletons. Among them was a doctor, for beside one body lay a remarkably well equipped bag of instruments.

Nor did the animals of Pompeii escape

the fate of the humans. Here is the plaster cast of a dog which had probably been on a chain. The body shows the convulsive effect of the poisonous fumes.

"Though slow, this is the best method

to proceed with an excavation, the work being done by women and children, who carry away the earth by small basketfuls. During the French occupation the government assigned a regiment of engineers to the work, and I saw as many as 1,500 soldiers employed. But they were so destructive that their activities had to be restricted to excavating the city wall and the amphitheatre. Nowadays the excavations are let to entrepreneurs for so much per double cubic yard. The disadvantages are plain; to mention but one, the heavy ox-carts moving constantly through the ruins cause disastrous cave-ins . . ."

These words were written by François Mazois (1783–1826), court painter at the short-lived Kingdom of Naples whose king was Napoleon's general Murat and whose queen was Marie Caroline Bonaparte. The engraving on the right comes from his book, *The Ruins of Pompeii*. Such was Mazois's passion for the ruins that he was able to stir the interest of the new and therefore enterprising royal couple. He persuaded them to finance extensive excavations. While he was in Paris, however, preparing publication of his first series of pictures, Napoleon was overthrown. Murat was shot by a firing squad, and the "Bonapartist" Mazois was not granted a passport to go back to Naples. In 1816 he thought of a stratagem by which he was able to return. The Neapolitan Bourbon prince had applied for a papal dispensation. Mazois managed to have himself appointed the carrier of this document. Thus highly honoured as a papal envoy, he returned to his beloved ruins.

34

Here, at the corner of the V

The excavator, never knowing what the earth will yield,

stumbles on a prize. In May 1925 this youth was brought to light – one of the finest copies of early Greek sculpture to be salvaged from the ashes of Pompeii. The statue is nearly five feet tall. The broken legs were easily restored; the bronze eyes were intact; iris and pupil had no doubt been inlaid in colour, but were missing. Various factors suggest that this statue, on which a high value must have been placed at the time, was moved at the beginning of the eruption from its original site in a garden to a semi-sheltered porch.

Stabiae and the Via dell' Abbondanza,

the Pompeians could buy themselves a bowl of steaming mulled wine before they went upstairs to be welcomed by Aegle, Maria and Smyrna, those charming ladies of easy virtue who were called "little donkeys" *(asinellae)*.

The bar had been marble-topped. Scattered on the floor were coins dropped by the last customers. The names of the girls were scratched into the wall.

"The talisman by which the archaeologist reanimates long-dead civilizations", writes that great antiquary Ernst Buschor, "is made of the tangible property left by men of the past . . . Such things run the entire scale of value, and are of varying significance, but to the eye of the true archaeologist each one has something to tell." Only in Pompeii and Herculaneum, however, is this "tangible property" still warm from men's hands, so to speak; only here do we feel so vividly the living presence of the human beings who inhabited these cities. To make a coherent story of the following pictures we may, for example, imagine a certain Mr. Pompeius. He has drunk his bowl of wine at the bar, exchanged a few words with the proprietor on the political situation . . .

and is prompted, after turning into the Via dell' Abbondanza

to pause in front of Trebius Valens' house, the wall of which is covered with inscriptions in red and black letters. They are election slogans – and no wonder, for Trebius is related to many politicians. Pompeius reads the candidates' names and the praises of their virtues (second rectangle from the left): *Q(uintum) Postumum modestum*; he reads (middle of the wall, and on the right) the announcement of gladiatorial combats and athletic games sponsored and paid for by Lucretius Satrius, who evidently hoped to win popularity in this way.

(The wall reproduced here is about thirteen feet long. It was excavated in 1913–14. Many houses would be covered with election slogans at the time of the annual elections in March. After elections a painter came along and covered the inscriptions with a coat of fresh whitewash.)

Mr. Pompeius walks on. Suddenly it occurs to him that he promised to drop in on Verecundus, the draper, and inquire about the long-promised blankets.

Marcus Caecilius Verecundus is by trade

(as the inscription on the lower frieze of a painted pillar advertises) a dealer in cloth and a manufacturer of wool and felt. If our friend Pompeius cares for painting, he will like looking at the large painted shop front. It represents Venus

39

Pompeiana, goddess of the city, bearing crown and sceptre and leaning against a tiller, the symbol of a coastal city. She rides in a chariot drawn by four elephants. On the left is Fortuna, scattering good luck, and rolling along with the globe; on the right is the Genius Coloniae with cornucopia and drinking bowl.

If our Pompeius is partial to modern Pompeian painting, he may by delighted by the deceptive realism with which the painter has done the apparently three-dimensional frame which separates the upper from the lower picture.

Pompeius enters the shop, whose activities we can reconstruct from the frieze. He watches the nimble fingers of the wool-carders who, seated on stools, the scraping-block between their feet, are working on the raw wool with big wooden combs and scrapers. They are demurely dressed in long, bright-coloured skirts, while the felters beside them are bared to the waist as they toil over their steaming vats. They dip the vinegar, which serves to bind the felt, from a basin and pour it into the two triangular tubs in which the felt is made by constant shaking and reheating. Arms outstretched, Master Verecundus shows the finished blanketing to Pompeius.

Before Pompeius goes home,

he may drop in at a friend's. Since he is a creation of ours, he cannot object to our making this friend stern Arrius Crescentius, whose private dining room *(triclinium)* we see here. Arrius has had this room inscribed with mottoes which must have seemed a little captious in gay Pompeii, so that archaeologists have called his home the Casa del Moralista (House of the Moralist). "If you cannot

refrain from quarrels and disputes, you had better go home'', we may read on the upper left. And in the panel to the far right he actually tells his guests to wash themselves and to keep their host's linen clean.

Arrius had room for four guests – since these are not benches but couches; the Romans, like the Greeks, ate and drank in a reclining position. Undoubtedly the stone was covered with cushions. The wall paintings – alternate red and black rectangles – are extremely plain; simple borders surrounding a small wreath or bird. Standing on the table are the utensils Arrius used: glass bottles and bronze jugs, a ladle, a lamp with a chain, and the big mixing bowl on its high bronze pedestal. The house was bombed in the Second World War.

Apparently a Greek named Zosimos

was the last owner of the splendid building (excavated 1909–10 and 1929–30) which we now call the Villa dei Misteri (Villa of the Mysteries). Let us have our imaginary Pompeius end his round of visits in its private chapel which contains one of the finest examples of classical painting we possess.

In twenty-nine life-size figures the fresco shows the initiation of a bride into the "Dionysian Mysteries" – a sectarian form of religious ceremony whose abuse led to such excesses that it was outlawed by the Roman Senate. The climax of the ceremony, the bride's hailing of the male symbol of fertility, is dimly depicted on the extreme right.

For the age of Winckelmann, Pompeian paintings were only sensational aesthetic discoveries. There was some discussion of their artistic form and mythological content but not of the questions which now concern us, such as the relationship of this ubiquitous painting to the Roman house as an architectural whole, and to its inhabitants. For this Roman painting was more than mere decoration. It fulfilled a new function in domestic architecture: it *extended* the house, "created aura and atmosphere" (Karl Kerényi), employed perspective devices to create the illusion of large spaces. In this, it was the true forerunner of the Renaissance.

Father Piaggio, who unrolled the charred papyrus rolls

with skillful hands and the aid of ingenious devices while Winckelmann looked on. These two men represented the meeting of two sciences which have ever since been indissolubly linked: the science of monuments and the science of documents.

In Herculaneum in 1753 a treasure trove of manuscripts was found in the villa that had

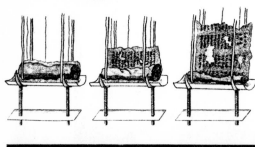

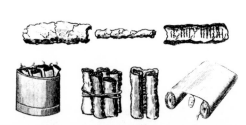

belonged to Philodemus, the philosopher. But the rolls of papyrus were all charred and gummed together. It seemed impossible to do anything with them. A certain Camillo Paderni undertook the work of salvage. He rolled up his sleeves, tied a rough apron around his waist, and with his Genoese razor went boldly at the papyri. Cutting a slash the length of the roll, he extracted the core, gutting the roll so completely that a single smooth sheet remained from the outer layer – all the rest was reduced to chips and was thrown away as rubbish.

Antonio Piaggio, the Franciscan father, proceeded differently. Outside Italy, little had been known about him, except for what Winckelmann had written: that he had made himself an ingenious apparatus (centre) by means of which he succeeded in unrolling the papyri with relatively little damage; that he must have been a rather crusty character – he spoke ill of the king and slanderously of Alcubierre, who did not sufficiently appreciate his work; and that to satisfy his spite he supplied the material for Winckelmann's *Open Letters*.

In the preparation of this book a letter of Sir William Hamilton's was found in the British Museum which at least enables us to calculate the year of his birth. "He is now 87", Hamilton writes in 1794, "and no longer able to work." We possess also a letter written to the Royal Society in 1755 which not only provides the first description of his technique, but also shows a proper appreciation for it.

"It is incredible to imagine what this man [Piaggio] contrived and executed. He made a machine with which, by the means of certain threads which, being gummed, stick to the back of the papyrus where there is no writing, begins by degrees to pull (with screws fitted into a horizontal bar above the scroll), while he loosens one leaf from the other with a sort of engraver's instrument (which is the most difficult part of all), and then makes a sort of lining to the back of the papyrus, with exceeding thin leaves ... and with some spirituous liquor, with which he wets the papyrus, by little and little he unfolds it. All this labour cannot be well comprehended without seeing. With patience superior to what man can imagine, this good father has unrolled a pretty large piece of papyrus ..."

The first papyrus Piaggio unrolled (shown here) was, in fact, the famous treatise on music, *De Musica*, by Philodemus.

The mysterious magic square

Professor Matteo Della Corte, one of the most successful Pompeian exca-vators of our century, found scratched upon one of the pillars of the palaestra a twenty-five letter inscription that yielded the same five words which ever way they were read. And the central word, TENET, formed a cross. Since the letters could also be so arranged to form the beginning of the Paternoster, the discoverer concluded that this had probably been the secret sign of a Christian sect. After all, a Christian cross had been found scratched into a wall in Herculaneum.

This is a controversial question. Whether the magic square really was intended to represent a Christian cross is not yet established. Heretofore, the oldest evidences of a Christian cross dated from the second century A.D. It is unlikely (but by no means impossible) that even before A.D. 79 there were Christians in Pompeii who used the sign of the cross.

The magic square has been the subject of endless discussion. Recently a new interpretation which seems reasonable has been presented. Hitherto, the word AREPO has always given trouble; no such word is known, whereas the others are common Latin words. Ludwig Diehl, studying the matter, suggest-ed that the square should be read *bustrophedon* ("as the ox plows" – the mode of writing employed by scribes of Hieroglyphic Hittite, for example) – in other words, the first line from right to left, the second from left to right, and so on. In this case the central word, TENET, must be read twice. The result is: SATOR OPERA TENET; TENET OPERA SATOR.

The meaningless word AREPO is thus eliminated. The translation, in spite of the repetition, has a convincing sound: "The great Sower [God] holds in his hand all works; all works the great Sower holds in his hand."

There have been other surprising minor finds at Pompeii, and no doubt there will be more in the future. In October 1938, in the so-called "House of the Four Styles", was found an ivory statuette of Lakshmi, the Hindu goddess of love.

**A new era
of intelligent
excavation**

began at last in 1861 under the direction of Giuseppe Fiorelli. Arrested during the revolution of 1848, and confined to prison, he wrote there the first pages of his description of Pompeii *(Pompeianarum antiquitatum historia)*. Jobless afterwards, he happened by chance to prevent the count of Syracuse from being swindled when he discovered that several "well preserved heads of antique bodies", which someone was about to sell the count, were fakes made of wax. Ultimately he obtained the appointment as director of excavations at Pompeii. Fiorelli introduced a number of important innovations in the technique of excavation. He not only dug; he protected. It was he who first had the hollows left by skeletons filled with plaster.

The work was finally placed upon a thoroughly modern scientific basis by Professor Amadeo Maiuri, who has been digging and conducting research in Pompeii and Herculaneum since 1911. (Our picture shows him looking at recently discovered Roman tombs.) He has made many significant finds, and published exemplary accounts of them. During the Second World War, with the troops advancing and the dangers of needless destruction and perhaps of pillaging daily mounting, he waged a stalwart defense of his life work. He remained at the site until he was within range of small arms, and finally fled on a bicycle, wounded by a machine-gun bullet.

Excavation continues in Pompeii and Herculaneum. Professor Maiuri now wants to install a cable railway to transport the highly fertile lava-ash, which has been removed from the ruins for more than two hundred years, to unfertile soil, thus enriching all the land around Naples.

47

Meditatively circling this curious hill

in the spring of 1869, the middle-aged man in European dress looked rather odd among the camels of this unpromising scrubland. This man, whose success equalled his energy, blazed new paths in archaeology, leading the way to such remarkable insights that professional colleagues refused to follow. "My claims are most modest", he was to say later – although he was in fact outlining a programme going far beyond the prevailing school of 'art archaeology'. "I do not hope to find works of plastic art. From the start the sole purpose of my excavations was to find Troy . . . I should be content if I have succeeded only, by my work, in penetrating into the profound obscurity of prehistoric times and in enriching science by the discovery of a few interesting pages from the most ancient history of the great Hellenic nation."

With the *Iliad* tucked under his arm (in striking contrast to all the other scientists of his day he regarded Homer's work as a precise description of actual events), and with a watch in his hand, he walked around the hill called Hissarlik. He needed the timepiece to determine whether it was humanly possible to circle the walls of the city three times, as Homer reported Achilles and Hector did in the heat of battle. These facts established, he pronounced the site to be that of ancient Troy – once more countering the general view that Troy, if it ever existed, should lie beneath a mound near Bunarbashi, which he had previously tested in the same manner.

Our picture is taken from a travel account by the Count of Choiseul-Gouffier (published in 1809), who until the beginning of the French Revolution was France's ambassador to the Sublime Porte.

I Zeus abducting Ganymede

II Greek Temples were Coloured

Heinrich Schliemann,

wholesale merchant of the Imperial Guild of St. Petersburg, hereditary honorary freeman, Judge of the St. Petersburg Commercial Court, and Director of the Imperial State Bank in St. Petersburg. (The photograph was taken around 1860.) This is the man who wrote to his father as early as 1854: "Here in Moscow I am considered the slyest, most cunning and most capable of merchants . . ." In 1868, a multi-millionaire at the height of his success, he retired from business to pursue the dream of his youth: to dig up Troy.

A simple-hearted pride speaks in the lines he wrote on June 24, 1870 to his son Serge, who was then at school: ". . . You ought to try to follow the example of your father who in whatever situation always proved what a man can accomplish by unflagging energy alone. During the four years in Amsterdam from 1842 to 1846 I truly performed wonders. My achievements there have never been equalled, and never will be equalled in the future. Later, when I became a wholesale merchant in St. Petersburg, I was the most brilliant and at the same time the most astute dealer on the stock exchange. When I began to travel, I was a traveller *par excellence*. No St. Petersburg merchant has ever written a learned book, but I have written one that has been translated into four languages, and generally commended. At the moment, as an archaeologist, I am the sensation of Europe and America because I have discovered ancient Troy, that Troy for which the archaeologists of the entire world have searched in vain during the past two thousand years . . ."

Schliemann the Entrepreneur

1822 Birth of Heinrich Schliemann, son of a poor pastor in Neu-Bukow, Mecklenburg, Germany. Until

1831 the family lives in the village of Ankershagen, around whose ruins, hills and ponds many ghost stories are told. These stimulate the child's imagination, as do his father's tales of the doom of Pompeii and the struggle of the heroes at Troy. In

1829 he receives the then popular *Universal History for Children* as a Christmas present. In it he finds a print depicting the mighty Scaean Gate of Troy, and expresses his opinion to his father that such monuments cannot possibly have vanished utterly. "And by and by we agreed", he says in his autobiography, "that some day I should excavate Troy."

1831 His mother dies, leaving seven children. The family came to know neglect and poverty.

1832 He writes his first Latin composition on Troy as a Christmas present for his father.

1836 Aged fourteen, he becomes an apprentice in a grocer's shop in the small town of Fürstenberg, north Germany. For five and a half years he works eighteen hours a day behind the counter and in the warehouse. His most momentous experience is an encounter with a down-at-heel student who in return for three glasses of brandy recites Homer in Greek to him.

1841 He has to give up this job because of illness. He goes to Hamburg on foot, is able to take only temporary jobs, and signs on as a cabin boy on the brig *Dorothea*. The ship is wrecked on the night of December 11 off the Dutch island of Texel. After nine perilous hours the crew is rescued.

1842 Destitute in Amsterdam, he finally finds a job in a merchant's office, and begins to devote every free minute to the systematical study of foreign languages.

"After three months I could with ease recite ... twenty printed pages of English prose word for word if I had read them through attentively three times." He learns English, French, Dutch, Spanish, Italian and Portugese – spending only six weeks on each of the last four languages.

1844 He enters the firm of B. H. Schröder & Co. as correspondent and book-keeper. He learns Russian.

1846 He goes to St. Petersburg as agent for his firm. Before the end of his first year he does so well in the indigo trade that in

1847 he is admitted to the guild of wholesalers.

1850 He goes to California in search of a missing brother. While he is there, the entrance of California into the Union automatically gives him American citizenship.

1852 He sets up a Moscow branch of his St. Petersburg company for wholesale trade in indigo.

1854 He learns Swedish and Polish. By now he has a fortune of 150,000 taler which he doubles in the course of the following year (during the Crimean War).

1856 At the age of thirty-four he learns modern Greek in six weeks, and ancient Greek in another three months, so that he can read Homer in the original. He reads exclusively ancient Greek literature. Meanwhile, his fortune keeps increasing, even during the depression of 1857.

1858 He perfects his knowledge of Latin, and decides to retire from business. Travels take him to Sweden, Denmark, Germany, Italy and Egypt as far as the second cataract of the Nile. "Here I made use of the favourable opportunity to learn Arabic." He travels on to Jerusalem and takes a quick look at Syria.

1859 He visits Smyrna, the Cyclades and Athens, falls ill, and because his business runs into difficulties without his guiding hand, has to return to St. Petersburg.

1860 The value of the goods he imports within six months amounts to over 850,000 pounds. Up to

1863 he makes a series of such remarkably profitable deals in cotton and tea that he finally decides to liquidate his companies completely and devote his time to his youthful dream of excavating Troy. First,

however, "in order to see more of the world", he embarks in

1864 on a tour of the world from Egypt through India, China and the United States. On the fifty-day crossing from Japan to San Francisco he writes his first book, *La Chine et le Japon* – in French.

1866 He settles down in Paris, as he says, "to devote myself permanently to the study of archaeology".

Schliemann the Excavator

1868 "At last I was able to realize the dream of my life, to visit with requisite leisure the realm of action and the homeland of the hereos whose adventures had delighted and sustained me in my childhood." Schliemann journeys through Ithaca, the native island of Ulysses. In December his book is published: *Ithaca. Archäologische Forschungen* (Ithaca. Archaeological Researches).

1869 He visits Troy, Mycenae and Tiryns, and in a new book announces his theory that the ruins of Troy lie beneath Hissarlik, and that the graves of the Atrides should be sought inside rather than outside the fortress wall. Nearing fifty, he marries an eighteen-year-old Greek girl, Sophia.

1870–3 Excavations in Troy, eleven and a half months in all, with 100 to 150 workmen. Schliemann discovers much evidence, especially in the form of ceramics, of a pre-Greek Aegean culture upon this site hitherto unknown to science. In the charred rubble of the second and third strata he believes he has found the Palace of Priam. In June 1873 he finds "Priam's treasure".

1874 First survey in Mycenae.

1875 Refusing to deliver half of his finds at Troy to Constantinople, he is fined 10,000 francs. Instead of paying the fine, he makes a gift of 50,000 francs to the Turkish government, and receives permission to continue digging. When in spite of this the local pasha obstructs his work, he writes a letter to *The Times* (July 24, 1876) "in which I submit the conduct of Ibrahim Pasha to the judgment of the civilized world." As a result of this publicity, the pasha is transferred by the central government.

1876 Besides his travels in Greece (where he keeps his journal in Greek), he goes to England, Germany and Italy, begins one excavation in Sicily which he abandons because the finds date *only* from the fifth century B.C., and another near the Sea of Marmora. In August he begins excavations in Mycenae; in November he finds five graves with skeletons bedecked with gold and jewels; he decides that these are the bodies of Agamemnon and his companions. The finds include types of art which have not been encountered in Troy; Schliemann has discovered true "Mycenaen" culture.

1877–8 Schliemann busies himself preparing

the publication of his book, *Mycenae*, in German, English and French.

1878–9 Resumption of excavations in Troy. Now fifty-six, Schliemann regularly every morning before sunrise rides out to the coast, a good hour away, takes a dip in the sea, and is back at the site of the excavations before his workmen have awakened. Rudolf Virchow, the famous physician and amateur student of pre-history, and the French scholar Emile Burnouf publicly come out in support of Schliemann's view; other scientists remain sceptical.

1880 Excavations in Orchomenus; discovery of the Treasury of Minyas.

1882 The young architect William Dörpfeld comes to assist Schliemann in digging at Troy. Henceforth deliberation and method rather than wild enthusiasm govern the procedure of the excavations. The patterns of the various Trojan strata are recognized.

1884–5 Uncovering of the Cyclopean palace walls of Tiryns. Small finds establish beyond any doubt the interrelationships of a pre-Greek culture around the Aegaean Sea, which we now call Minoan-Mycenaean.

1886–7 Schliemann goes to Cuba on business, then to Egypt.

1888 He makes a survey of Crete, but does no digging. However, he recognizes the "Palace of Minos", which is later excavated by Evans.

1890 Schliemann's last excavation at Troy. On Christmas Day Schliemann dies in Naples. He collapses in the street, and the bystanders wonder who is to pay for the cab to take him to the hospital – until someone recognizes the modestly dressed foreigner.

A double page from Schliemann's diary (April 14, 1873)

wherein he records that he employed 157 workers for digging that day, and discovered several small pots, ornamented urns whose resemblance to owls would make them emblems of the tutelary goddess of Troy. Among the decorative motifs he was most impressed by the ancient swastika which, raised once more to a symbol, was to gain a grim notoriety during the thirties and forties of the present century.

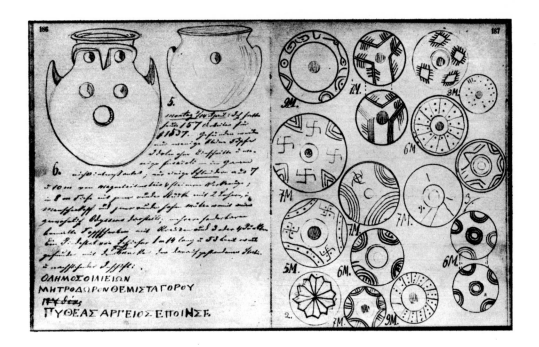

It is high time the nonsense about Schliemann's "dilettantism" were corrected. It is true that he made many mistakes – but what pioneer does not make them? The errors perpetrated by professional scientists, especially in regard to pre-Homeric Greece, fill far more volumes than Heinrich Schliemann wrote. Excavation of clay tablets such as was undertaken three decades later (when archaeological methods had been greatly refined) by the bona fide "scientific expert" Hugo Winckler, at Boghazköy, was an outright scandal compared to Schliemann's rough and ready work at Troy. The charge that Schliemann was no professional stems from that academic conceit which rates proper degrees, even if secured by the most mediocre minds, above genius. Schliemann, with his phenomenal memory and gift for languages, devoted four to five years to intensive study of antiquity (delving in museums and libraries, and conversing with the foremost scientists of his age) before he went to Troy. Moreover he was, although the fact is little known, legitimate holder of the title of doctor of philosophy. He received his degree from the University of Rostock, Mecklenburg, for an account of his travels in the Peloponnesus, and for a dissertation *written in classical Greek.*

The great Tower of Ilium

"There was and is at the site of Troy no sublimer place than this", wrote Schliemann in his earliest account of the excavations in 1874. Homer enthusiast that he was, his imagination immediately animated the ruins. "And I therefore presume that it was Ilium's great tower to which Andromache climbed because she had heard (*Iliad*, VI) that the Trojans were sore oppressed and that mighty was the power of the Achaeans." On the brow of the hill we see the barracks of Schliemann and his labourers; the nature of the excavation, as we may see on the lower left, suggests the work had its dangers. He made the find which stirred the world just one day before the end of the 1873 season. He was with his second wife, whom he had acquired in a highly curious manner.

Sophia Schliemann, née Engastromenos,

Schliemann's second wife, is here wearing the golden ornaments found in the second stratum at Troy. Schliemann's ardent imagination immediately made him decide that these jewels had belonged to that beauteous Helen whose face had launched a thousand ships. Since he considered the second stratum the Palace of Priam, he did not hesitate to speak of "Priam's treasure". The incredible accumulation of diadems, earrings, finger rings, buttons and so on – all in all, he and Sophia took a total of 8,750 small fragments of gold jewelry from under the dangerous overhanging rubble – certainly prompted the conclusion that he had discovered a mythic treasure-house.

To return to Sophia: his plan to marry a second time, after his first wife refused to follow him on his archaeological quests, was set forth in two letters of very different tempers. On May 18, 1869, he wrote to his father: "The Archbishop of Greece . . . has sent me the portraits of several Athenian women for me to choose from. Of these, I have selected Sophia Engastromenos as the most charming . . . It seems . . . that the Archbishop, before he was advanced to the higher clergy and while he still thought he would be able to remain a sinner, had intended to marry her. In any case I plan . . . to go to Athens in July to marry her . . . For since the growth of my passion for the Greek language,

I believe that I can be happy only with a Greek woman. I will take her, however, only if she has an interest in the sciences . . . A pretty young girl can love an old man in such a case only if she cares deeply for the sciences in which he is so far ahead of her."

To his brother-in-law, however, he wrote on July 30, 1869, a far more crass description of his enterprise: "I intend to go to Greece in a fortnight in order to look around for another wife, for there I have the tremendous advantage that the girls are as poor as church mice . . . Thus I can coldbloodedly and at leisure get to know the ladies there very well, and if I should find a Greek girl whose age still offers hope of progeny . . . and who moreover is enthusiastic about classical Greek language and literature, as well as ancient history, archaeology and geography . . . I shall marry her, but *only in that case*, and you may be sure that I will not be over-hasty . . . Thank God, the choice in Greece is large, and the girls as beautiful as the pyramids of Egypt!"

Strangely enough, the marriage proved an extremely happy one. Sophia actually became her husband's best assistant, and bore him two children: Agamemnon and Andromache.

Not far from the great Tower of Ilium

the foundation walls of a house, in places still ten feet high, were found in 1873. Schliemann could not at the time suspect that he would find "Priam's treasure" at this spot. But the walls alone sent him into transports because here for the first time he saw the outline of a Trojan house. He called it "the most interesting object I have been able to find in the past three years". This exultation at a purely scientific discovery should prove that Schliemann was anything but the gold-seeker so many critics later branded him. The first detail from a drawing by Lempesis (left) of the excavation gives some impression of the tremendous masses of earth Schliemann's men moved – with only picks, shovels and wheelbarrows for tools.

In the second detail from this drawing (top of preceding page) Dr. Schliemann is handing his wife a pot that has just come to light.

Here Schliemann is digging in Stratum II. Shortly after Schliemann's death Dörpfeld began to wonder whether this was actually the Homeric stratum. From 1932–8 Professor William T. Semple of the University of Cincinnati carried out another thorough study of the ruins. The results of this work were published after Semple's death (1950) by Professor Carl W. Blegen, the scientific director of the expedition. Our photograph shows one of the strata at the eastern wall. This is the level on which, it is now believed, Priam's fortress stood. The matter probably cannot be settled with absolute certainty. The Hissarlik mound has been thoroughly sifted, and affords no further information.

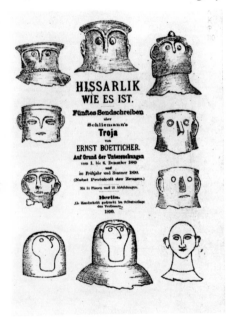

Foe and Friend

Schliemann's bitterest adversary, as obstinate and hidebound as they come, was a German army captain named Ernst Boetticher. He insisted that the finds at Hissarlik were the remains of an ancient crematorium – a view which even the most casual glance refuted. In 1889 Schliemann invited him to come to Troy to see for himself. Once on the site, the stubborn captain did not quite dare to oppose the verdict of the many scholars who were present. But no sooner

had he returned home than he published a new pamphlet repeating his old contentions. (See title page on left.) Schliemann's adviser in the battle with Boetticher was Wilhelm Dörpfeld (1853–1940), the staunch friend who moderated his sometimes excessive enthusiasm. Schliemann had met him at the site of the exemplary excavations at Olympia, and had promptly retained him as an architectural expert. Dörpfeld, who made priceless contributions to our knowledge of ancient architecture, continued the excavations at Troy in 1893–4, with financial support from Sophia Schliemann and the Kaiser. So energetically did he labour that Professor Semple whose 1932–8 expedition he advised, said: "By the time the 1894 season ended, all in all more than half of the mound had been excavated, and perhaps four fifths had been at least superficially investigated." (Our picture shows Wilhelm Dörpfeld between Professor Semple and Mrs. Semple in front of their house at Troy in 1935.) Before we leave Schliemann we must glance at his second important excavation: his equally sensational and scientifically still more rewarding exploration of the graves of Mycenae. For it pointed beyond the palace at Tiryns to the oldest leading culture of Europe, that of Crete.

Your Excellency's

kind letter of 9ᵗ Jany and Review of the famous Ethnological Essays is duly received and read with paramount interest. Yᵉ Exᶜ opinion that the Trojans spoke greek is now outborn by Professor M. Haug's ipekanisch translation of my Trojan inscriptions, one of which he has already published in the Augsburg gazette: Δειν Σίγιον. He has explained at the same time that this name (Sigo or Siko) is contained in the name of the Σκαιαῖ Πύλαι, of the Σκάμανδρος, and of Σίγειον. I would add that it is also in Σίγια, the site of Alexandria Troas, according to Strabo, and in Σερνόΐα, of which, according to the Iliad, Echepolos a Trojan and son of Anchises was king.

Professor Haug gives me the translation of 5 more of my inscriptions, all of which are written in ancient Cyprus characters, except one, which is in very primitive phoenician and reads: l'gotap or l'gotef (to gotap or gotef). The phoenician alphabet not being older than the 13ᵗ century B.C., and the phoenician inscription having been found in a depth of 10 metres or 33⅓ feet, Prof Haug declares the chronology of Troy's tragic fate in 1180 B.C. to be approximately right. In all other inscriptions occurs the name Sigo or Siko, which stands even twice on a coin. Very often on the Trojan antiquities Yᵉ Exᶜ sees the sign Ⅲ alone, with the meaning (according to Haug) of Si, the first syllable of Sigo, very much like the ΣΙ on the medal of Sigeum (Σίγειον). The inscription on the vase, translated by Mr Burnouf with the chinese alphabet, and at first declared by Max Müller and Haug to be no inscription at all, is now recognized by the latter to be in very primitive Cyprus characters, but he has not deciphered it yet. Neither has he succeeded yet in making out the inscription on Table 190, which is in phoenician. Prof Haug is going to publish a second article on the inscriptions. He acknowledges with immense enthusiasm the discovery of the Homeric Ilium.

Max Müller having provoked me in the Academy to prove that Juno had been a cowheaded monster (sic), I solicited from the ministry the permission to make excavations at Mycenae and without awaiting for an answer, which I have even not got until this hour, I started for the capital of Agamemnon where, under the pretext merely to make some drawings, I succeeded in exploring the premises thoroughly, to dig in 34 places in the acropolis and

both in the Comptes rendus des Séances de l'Institut and in the Moniteur Univers trust the thousands of different symbolic signs which I have published in my Trojan atlas will lead to some important discoveries.

I remain with profound respect Your Excellency's

constant admirer

H. Schliemann

To the Rt Honble W. E. Gladstone
London

This is one of Schliemann's first reports

on his excavations in Mycenae – a letter dated March 15, 1874, addressed to the British Prime Minister, Gladstone, who later wrote the foreword to the Schliemann book *Mycenae*. Parts of the original letter are reproduced here.

In Mycenae Schliemann uncovered a culture whose existence had hitherto been unsuspected by scholars – a culture exhibiting a wealth of artistic and architectural forms such as was developed *again* in Greece proper only a thousand years later (about 500 B.C.). By excavating the citadel of the Atrides (where Perseus, Atreus and Agamemnon ruled, where Aegisthos committed threefold murder, where Clytemnestra became an adulteress and Orestes a matricide), Schliemann threw archaeologists into the situation of a museum curator who, prepared to arrange a single room full of new acquisitions, suddenly finds a dozen vast halls confronting him.

61

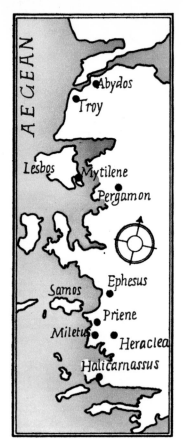

After preliminary investigations, the regular excavation

of Mycenae began in August, 1876. Schliemann had studied the account of the great Greek traveller Pausanias (second century A.D.), and had come up with a translation and interpretation that differed startlingly from the general opinion of scholars. He started digging directly behind the famous, long-known Lion Gate – a procedure his professional colleagues regarded as utterly futile. The result: at the outset he found five graves containing skeletons bedecked with jewelry. These he held to be the remains of Agamemnon and his companions; today we know that they are older, dating from the sixteenth century B.C. On the left we see the area after Schliemann's excavation; the illustration is taken from his book, *Mycenae*. Above is the same area seen from another angle in a photograph of its present state. By 1877–8 the Greek overseer Panagiotes Stamatakes had discovered a sixth vault; later Chrestos Tsountas carried on, sketching the first relatively realistic picture of Mycenaean culture.

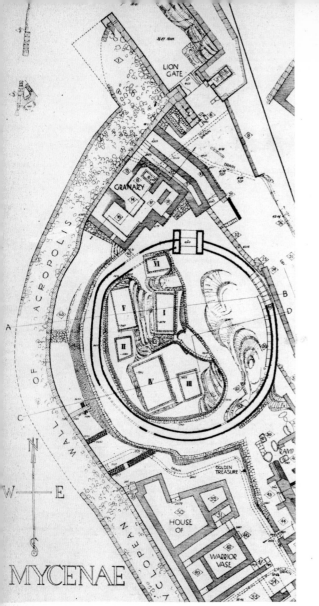

LION GATE

GRANARY

VI

V   I

III

IV   III

GOLDEN TREASURE

RAMP

HOUSE OF

WARRIOR VASE

WALL OF CYCLOPEAN

ACROPOLIS

A

B
D

C

N
W — E
S

MYCENAE

The area of the graves

mapped in 1923 by the British School at Athens. This plan clarified some of the obscurer riddles of the site, enabling scholars to read "from the stones" alone the history of a city which has not left us a single line of writing about itself. For we must not misunderstand Schliemann's use of the words "Homeric period", and imagine that ancient Troy knew the art of writing. *Homer was not the contemporary of his heroes.* He came along hundreds of years after their time to sum up the traditional accounts that had come down to him. The precise time and basis of the Homeric epics is still a subject of conjecture among scholars. The prevailing view nowadays is that Homer lived (and the *Iliad* and *Odyssey* were written) between 810 and 730 B.C.; the age of the Homeric heroes must be assigned to about 1200 B.C.

The first traces of human settlement in Mycenae date from between 3000 and 2800 B.C. "Golden Mycenae" grew during the second millennium B.C. It stood at the height of its power and cultural development probably between 1400 and 1150 B.C. At this time it had been richly impregnated by Cretan civilization, and we may say that European history began at this point. (Georg Karo and Alan B. Wace, in their recent researches, have provided us with the best account of the connections.)

III Vase Painting. Athene bearing Arms

IV Roman Woman playing the Cithara

Eloquent Treasures

The seventeen skeletons Schliemann unearthed in the citadel at Mycenae, had some thirty pounds of precious metal about them, most of it gold. This fact is not altogether without interest to archaeology, though for scholars the objects themselves and what they tell are of such great intrinsic value that the preciousness of their material becomes secondary.

The dagger above is a sample both of artistic mastery and technical skill. It demonstrates the treatment of metals of different colours, including alloys, by punching, engraving, cold hammering and riveting – more than 3,000 years ago. The scene shows a lion hunt.

The silver fragment of a drinking horn tells a story, if we examine its embossings closely: a saga of a battle before a towering citadel (above, on the left),

of terror-stricken women on the wall (right half, centre), of defenders making a sortie (only twelve can be seen on our fragment; they are fighting toward the four olive trees on the left), and of the use of catapults and bows. But there is another important factor: the outlines of the tower, mere primitive representation as it may seem to the layman, reveals to the scientific expert a similarity to the mosaics at Knossos in Crete.

Similar comment may be made on the stelae (some eleven were probably standing near the graves), the royal golden mask, which has the quality of an individual portrait (Schliemann thought it Agamemnon's mask), or the golden goblet with three lions, crouched to spring, around the rim. It is again of interest to science that the handle of the cup is riveted on in random fashion, right in the middle of a lion's back, without regard for aesthetic principles. Such disregard for finished artistic form – which no Egyptian or Greek artist of the classical period would have permitted himself – has its counterpart only in Hittite art, where what may be called "aesthetic nonchalance" is typical.

**A small, incredibly
short-sighted man**

who always carried a strong cane in order to feel his way along, turned up
toward the end of the 1870's almost everywhere in the Balkan countries that
antiquities were to be seen. And as correspondent of the *Manchester Guardian*
he gave active support to the Slavs in their struggle against Austrian occupation.

The above portrait of Arthur Evans (1851–1941), later Sir Arthur Evans, was
painted in 1907 by Sir William Richmond. Evans was destined to complete
the work which Schliemann had begun in Troy, Mycenae and Tiryns: the
unlocking of that pre-Homeric culture of the second millennium B. C. which
we may properly call the first *European* civilization. "... In its style, in which
man remained the measure of all things, it was free of the non-European

67

elements of giantism and bombast . . . Everything had a delicacy of structure, as does our continent compared to the mighty, oppressive land masses of Asia and Africa." (Ernst Sittig, co-decipherer of the Cretan hieroglyphs.)

In contrast to Schliemann, Evans was neither a self-made man nor a self-taught scholar. The scion of a wealthy manufacturing family in Nash Mills, England, he grew up in the atmosphere of Victorian learning and studied at Harrow, Oxford and Göttingen. His great interest was initially anthropology; in 1873-4 he travelled in Finland and Lapland, then in the southern Balkans. Traces of the Celts in the Balkans awakened his interest in archaeology. At first he concentrated on numismatics, the study of coins. He pursued this interest in Bosnia and Herze-govina. In 1878 he married Margaret Freeman. When in 1881 the Austrian authorities became aware of his activities on behalf of the Slav nationalists he was arrested as a troublesome foreigner and then deported from the Empire. By 1883 he was back in the Balkans with his wife – this time travelling in Greece. The finds at Mycenae fascinated him. While Margaret Evans and Sophia Schliemann chatted, Evans examined the ruins, and the question that was henceforth to dominate his life germinated: *Where* had all this come from, since it was neither Greek nor Oriental?

In 1893 he went to Crete for the first time. His essay, *Cretan Pictographics and Prae-Phoenician Script* (1896), indicates that he was beginning to be interested in inscriptions. And it was to find more of these that he returned to Crete in 1900 – but this time to dig for them. He dug up the so-called "Palace of King Minos".

Cretan-Mycenaean Culture

After more than fifty years of excavation, the following chronological system has been arrived at. It represents the sum of awe-inspiring labour, for it has been worked out exclusively from finds in the ground (often with gaps of cen-turies between them), supplemented by no written evidence.

3500–2600 B. C.: Transitional period from Stone Age to so-called Minoan I.

2600–2200: Early Minoan II and III.

2200–1550: Middle Minoan Ia, Ib; IIa, IIb; IIIa, IIIb.

1550–1100: Late Minoan Ia, Ib; II; IIIa, IIIb. This table, which distinguishes fourteen epochs in 1,500 years, is of course only an arrangement imposed by archaeologists. Periods and styles fuse into one another; all such boundaries are fluid. It is well to remember the quip of J. D. S. Pondlebury, for many years Evans's close associate. He said: "Nowhere do we read that Minos ever stated: I am now tired of this Middle Minoan Age Number III; let us move on to the Late Minoan Age."

In Troy a new mythological world

had been resurrected. In Knossos on Crete still another rose out of even denser and more distant darkness. Here Theseus had slain the Minotaur in the Labyrinth and made his escape by following Ariadne's thread. The ancient Cretan art which Evans brought to light, and quite quickly to the attention of the public, appeared to be the gay, cultivated form of expression of a highly civilized people. The Cretan architecture which he restored or reconstructed out of fragments had a bold, wholly original quality. People at the beginning of our century saw the Cretans as Evans saw them. But had he seen correctly?

The above photograph of the foundation walls of the western storehouse in the "Palace of Minos" at Knossos is one of the few pictures which affords us a view, *in situ*, that is, of Cretan stones left where they were found and as they were found. This is, therefore, authentic Cretan architecture. More and more archaeologists today are sharply questioning Evans's restorations. Thus one of the oldest problems of archaeology has again come to the fore.

Let us take a look at some of the issues involved in restoration and reconstruction, although we must limit ourselves to only a few examples.

Evans was no dilettante, as Schliemann

was always accused of being. Evans was also no robust pioneer. He applied and elaborated modern methods of excavation and reconstruction. But is this an Old Cretan colonnade? Are these Cretan women of the second millennium B. C., and are they really in an Old Cretan salon? For this is what Evans asserts in regard to this reconstruction in his *Palace of Minos at Knossos*.

The first sharp protest to his work was made in 1930. Camillo Praschniker, an Austrian archaeologist, called Evans's Knossos reconstruction "a movie city". There was no doubt Evans had permitted his imagination (or vision?) a freer range than the finds justified. For his reconstructions he put together elements of ancient buildings from various places; he used materials that were completely unknown to the Cretans.

To illustrate what strong words were used in this dispute, we quote Praschniker: "Recently this reporter had the opportunity to visit the palace once more, after a long interval, and unfortunately was compelled to recognize that his worst expectations had been far surpassed. There is so much new construction that it is scarcely possible to see old stones any longer; we walk through hypotheses of reinforced concrete which are not thereby made any less shaky."

71

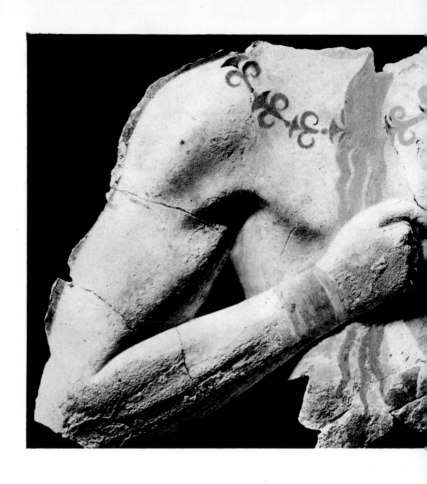

The Prince in the Field of Lilies,

actually the Priest-King, is one of the wall decorations which the painter Edouard Gillérion restored at the request of Evans. Another example of his work can be seen serving as background for the portrait of Evans on page 67. Here the elements ascribed to Cretan civilization are clearly present: fragility, noble form, serenity of expression, "charm", "Art Nouveau as decadence and snobbism" – words and concepts that had instant appeal at the beginning of the twentieth century when what was modern in art looked to the remote past for confirmation.

But what of the facts? Above left we see what the excavation yielded of the

Lily-Prince, above right we see the painted stucco relief after restoration.
Inset on page 70 are the few fragments which inspired Evans to that lavish
reconstruction. The question of what was genuinely Cretan, large as it looms
in the case of sizable objects, is almost as troublesome in the case of the smallest
finds, such as the Bull-Dancer and the Snake-Goddess.

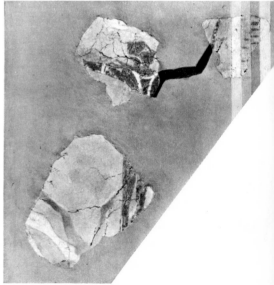

The Bull-Dancer poses one of the most interesting problems

of ancient Crete. Scholars still disagree as to whether what is depicted is sacrifice, sports, acrobatics or military training. The stone seal reproduced above, and the cup on the left, show this "dancer" motif, found frequently on Cretan artifacts, but rarely in clear form and unimpaired condition. Given these circumstances, it is plain how difficult and dubious are all restorations of the very badly damaged Cretan frescoes. Lower left are the remains of a fresco – one of the very few wherein a Cretan's head has been fully preserved.

The Snake-Goddess with the large, expressive eyes,

rich apparel and exposed breasts has been, perhaps even more than the Prince in the Field of Lilies, a key figure in our conception of ancient Crete – as evoked by Evans. From her came all the talk about the "Parisian charm" of Cretan women. It is amazing that a very few specimens of this kind have been able to form our whole concept of the culture. This picture, in particular, appeared everywhere, especially in histories of costume where it was used to represent women's fashions in Crete.

The drawings above allow us to see what was actually found. All the white portions in these drawings were reconstructed. Of the thing the painted clay figurine holds in its right hand only the upper part existed; it might have been anything *but* a snake. The small fragment found apart from the figurine (c) might be anything *but* a seated lion worn as a hat ornament. The entire face, the two forearms and the greater part of the body are hypothetical. At the right, front view of the Snake-Goddess, restored in glazed clay. The worn, round seal on the left, with the two dancing princesses, formed one of the few "proofs" of the style of exposed breasts. But – are these princesses? Perhaps they are temple prostitutes. To attempt to deduce a Cretan fashion from these "proofs" is more than daring.

Two comments by Ernst Buschor in his introduction to the *Handbuch der Archäologie* (1939), define the nature of the problem. "The falsification of monuments by deceptive restoration or reconstruction verges on the deliberate production of fake monuments, on forgery." But he also remarks: "Where only fragments of the object are preserved, or where it has been torn out of its vital context, scholarship is obligated to attempt to determine the original form. To leave everything in fragments would be to perpetrate a greater deception than the most unsuccessful reconstruction."

Yet the grace of this figure remains, for all that the tooth of time has gnawed it so cruelly. It leads us on to a few further examples of Cretan *objets d'art*.

77

Seals and votive figurines

of various materials display this people's
sense of life and decoration better, perhaps, than the fragmentary frescoes – because the smaller things are perfectly preserved, and therefore far more authentic.
Above, a stone seal in the form of an
owl. One of the oldest such seals to be
found, it dates from Early Minoan III,
between 2400 and 2200 B. C. Top left,
a bird with spread wings, looking
astonishingly modern in the manner in

which it tensely fills its space. This dates from the same age. Centre left, a jug under four crescent moons, from Middle Minoan I (2200–2000 B. C.). Then two wild goats browsing on a rocky hillside – Middle Minoan II (2000–1800 B. C.). Above right, finally, three clay votive figurines of women; although these appear to be much more primitive, more archaic than the seals, they belong to a more recent epoch, Late Minoan IIIb (1250–1100 B. C.).

Remnants of buildings, sculptures, even paintings so faded they can barely be made out, afford significant information. But true penetration into the life of an ancient civilization, into its customs, laws, social structure, ideas and organic development, and thus its history, can only be achieved through written documents. Evans had originally gone to Crete because he was interested in scripts. But the decipherment of Cretan script presented fearful difficulties, and the task is only now being accomplished.

so called from the site at which it was found, is a clear example of a very unusual style of hieroglyphics. It is a clay disc covered by inscriptions on both sides. Norbert Wiener, one of the most noted mathematicians and thinkers of our times, and developer of electronic calculators, wrote in *The Human Use of Human Beings*: "Probably much of the greatest ingenuity which has been shown in the breaking of ciphers appears not in the annals of the various secret services, but in the work of the epigrapher." (Page 124 of the Anchor edition.)

The story of the decipherment of Cretan hieroglyphics is a prime verification of this statement. For more than fifty years a dozen scholars wrestled with this problem, until finally Alice Kober, an American authority, declared resigned-ly in 1948: "Let us face the facts: An unknown language written in an un-known script cannot be deciphered, *with* or *without* a bilingual text."

Evans had discovered more than 2,000 clay tablets in the course of his first excavations. Helmuth T. Bossert (who recently deciphered Hieroglyphic Hittite), Piero Meriggi, Sundwall, and Ernst Sittig devoted years of their lives to studying this script – in vain. At last something happened which happens again and again in the history of archaeology: an outsider turned up and solved the problem that had defeated the specialists. This is the sort of triumph reserved

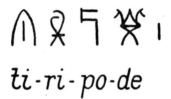

ti-ri-po-de

to the unbiased newcomer who leaps over the hurdles of conservatism at which the scholar shies.

Michael Ventris, the English amateur who succeeded in taking this leap, was an architect, a specialist in prefabricated school buildings and during the war he did service as a bomber navigator and cryptographer in the R.A.F. Studying Cretan scripts, especially the so-called Linear Script B, was his hobby. His first published speculations aroused nothing but benevolent forbearance among the professionals. But in 1953 he was fortunate enough to become

acquainted with a newly discovered clay tablet from Pylos. Here he found a tripod as a hieroglyphic sign, and the context was such that on the basis of his previous knowledge he felt encouraged to try the reading *ti-ri-po-de*, which suggested the Greek "tripod". After philological detail work of inordinate complexity, he ventured to take the leap which any professional would shudder at. Ancient Cretan, he maintained, had been a *Greek* dialect.

This assertion shook the structure of ancient history. It meant that Greek had been spoken on Crete six hundred years before Homer's time, whereas previously there had not been the slightest historical hint that this might be so. Quite the contrary. As far as scholars knew, around 1400 B. C., when Crete was flourishing, the Greeks had still been a semi-barbarian people. As Homer draws them the heroes who fought before Troy had been ignorant of reading and writing.

Nevertheless, Michael Ventris did not merely make assertions; he came forward with more and more proofs. The script is still far from deciphered as completely as Egyptian hieroglyphics. But the road is now open. Although we know that many of the clay tablets hold virtually nothing but accounts, army rolls and lists of tribute, what Ernst Sittig wrote of Ventris's work shortly before the

```
ti-ri-po-de  ai-ke-u  ke-re-si-jo  we-ke     ⋈ ‖
2 tripods;   Aigeus the Cretan(?) brings them

ti-ri-po  e-me  po-de  o-wo-we     ⋈ |
```

Englishman's death in 1954 is as true as ever: "This much is clear today: Europe – which has received its name from the maiden Europa whom Zeus in the form of a white bull abducted and carried to the island of Crete where she became the mother of King Minos – Europe must look again to that mysterious island for more clues to its cultural history."

Incidentally, the disc is an excellent case in point of the way common sense, coupled with logic, can penetrate into the mysteries of an ancient inscription.

Evans attempted to determine where the script began. After prolonged consideration he decided that it must start from the centre of the disc. This assumption was wrong. Rather, one may notice that all the signs have their feet or bases toward the outer rim, their heads toward the centre. It would be absurd for the reader to place himself in the centre of the disc, whence all the figured hieroglyphs would be seen standing on their heads.

Thus simple detective work, without any specialist's knowledge, can lead to initial insights into such problems.

Since restoration and reconstruction

have often been discussed in this chapter, let us close with an example of timely and happy salvage. In Baalbec, Syria, stand the ruins of the mighty Temple of Heliopolis, built in the first and second centuries A. D. The so-called Temple of Bacchus is probably the best preserved example of a monumental Roman temple. Above (the picture dates from before 1860), we can see how dangerously

the ten-foot thick marble keystone of the lintel had dropped down – in fact it was miraculously hanging on with a bearing surface of about two square inches against its left abutment. In 1900 and 1901 the German Archaeological Institute took measures to save the ruin, since the cornice was meanwhile threatening to collapse. The expedition's architect, Bruno Schulz, built a provisional wall on which to stand four large screw jacks borrowed from a railway (upper left). In one and a half days of work he raised the block to its original position. Upper right: view from within the temple of the restored gate.

And now our scene changes. Stimulated by the Renaissance and humanism, men of the seventeenth and eighteenth centuries had reached back into the pasts of Hellas and Rome, where the roots of Western civilization are to be found. The beginning of the nineteenth century saw an expedition start out for a country that was known but not yet understood, toward which men of Western Europe felt neither intellectual nor emotional kinship. It was a land whose monuments, mute and monstrous, seemed only alien or frightening – as mysterious as the face of the gigantic image, half animal, half man, which rose out of the yellow sands of the desert: the Egyptian Sphinx.

84

II

Book II

NAPOLEON

VIVANT DENON

CHAMPOLLION

ROBERT HAY

WILLIAM LANE

BELZONI

MARIETTE

EMIL BRUGSCH

GASTON MASPERO

FLINDERS PETRIE

LORD CARNARVON

ZAKARIA GONEIM

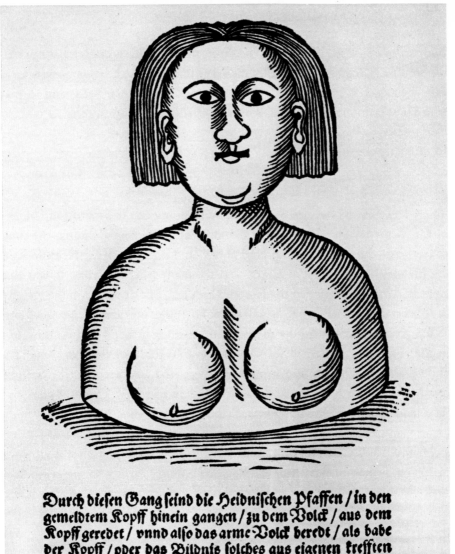

Durch diesen Gang seind die Heidnischen Pfaffen / in den
gemeldtem Kopff hinein gangen / zu dem Volck / aus dem
Kopff geredet / vnnd also das arme Volck beredt / als habe
der Kopff / oder das Bildnis solches aus eigenen krefften
gethan.

The Sphinx

December 13, 1565: "The following day we were early awake and several of
us sought out the place where the great *Pyramides* stand. When we came close
to these, we found firstly a large head, hewn out of a stone, towering on high,
as is to be seen in this figure ... This statue is quite hollow inwardly, so that

87

one can go and come to it under the earth, from far off, through a narrow passage which is lined with stone. By means of this passage the pagan priests went into the aforesaid head and spoke to the people out of the head, and so prevailed upon the poor folk that the head or the statue were doing so with its own tongue …"

In this early depiction of the Sphinx (the text and woodcut are from the diary of a German traveller, Johannes Helffrich, published in 1579), Greek myth is mingled with bad observation.

The Greek Sphinx was *female*, descended from one of the most dread families of Greek mythology. She was the daughter of the serpent Echidna, the sister of Cerberus, the three-headed hound of hell, and sister also of the Nemean lion, the dragon Ladon, the Chimaera, and the many-headed Hydra. It was this Sphinx which propounded the famous "riddle". She appeared in the vicinity of Thebes and mangled the passers-by who could not answer her question: What goes on four feet in the morning, on two feet at noon and on three feet in the evening? It remained for Oedipus to find the answer: man, who as a child creeps on all fours and in old age uses a stick. Whereupon the Sphinx cast herself from a precipice and Oedipus became ruler of Thebes.

The most famous Egyptian sphinx, that of Gizeh, is *male;* it has a lion's body and a man's head. The Sphinx of Gizeh never posed riddles or issued oracles, as Helffrich believed. Nevertheless, it remains to this day the most mysterious of Egyptian monuments. Indeed, the word sphinx stands as the symbol of mystery, although sphinx-like figures of both sexes are common enough in the Orient, in Christian Europe (where in the seventeenth and eighteenth centuries they did duty as baroque garden ornaments), and even in the high civilizations of Central America.

"Toward three-thirty we reach the place in the desert
where the three pyramids tower up. I can wait no longer and give my horse its
head. It races forward at a full gallop ... A wild ride. Involuntarily, I cry out;
we ascend to the Sphinx at a tempestuous pace. It grows, grows, and mounts
up out of the earth like a dog getting to its feet ... Sand, pyramids and Sphinx
appear grey, bathed in a powerful pink light. The sky is deep blue; eagles
circle above ... We stop before the Sphinx; it looks terribly at us ... I am
afraid of becoming giddy and try to suppress my excitement ...

"Its eyes seem still full of life. The left side is white from the droppings of birds.
It sits precisely facing the rising sun; its head is grey; the ears are very large and
protruding, like those of a Negro. Its neck is weather-beaten and has become
thinner; in front of its breast is a great hole in the sand ..."

These are the impressions of the great French novelist Flaubert, recorded in his travel diary on December 7, 1849.

Curiously enough, the draftsman Denon came to the same conclusion. Denon accompanied Napoleon on his Egyptian adventure in 1798 and brought back to France the first drawings of the wonders along the Nile – including the drawing reproduced on page 89. The head-dress is pure invention. Denon could plead that he was supplying what might have been there originally. For the Sphinx had indeed suffered a great deal of damage. During the Islamic period, about A. D. 1400, an iconoclastic sheik destroyed as much of it as he could. Later a Mameluke cannon ball tore a deep gash in the skull. And through all the millennia flying desert sand ground away at the limestone of the neck. Parts of the ornamentation of the brow, and the symbolic beard, fell off. But the picture does at least bear witness to a unique undertaking. While a French army corps set about conquering Egypt militarily, men attached to the same corps were bustling about with plumb line and drawing crayon, engaged in scientific research. Their results, summed up in one of the most monumental publications ever produced (*Description de l'Egypte*, 1809–26) begot another image of the Sphinx.

Only the Sphinx's head

was known to the first travellers. This drawing, from the *Description*, renders the head-dress better, and suggests the *"grand caractère"* and the *"certaine grâce"* the French travellers saw.

The lion's body had been drifted over by

from a hunt and in his weariness sank down "within the shadow of the great god".

"Look at me", a voice spoke in his dream, "and behold me. My son Thut-mosis, I am your father, the god Harachte-Chepere-Re-Atum. I will give you the kingship ... The earth in all her length and breadth will belong to you ... The wealth of Egypt and the great tributes of all lands will be paid to you. For a long period of years my face has been directed toward you, and my heart likewise. *I am sore oppressed by the sand of the desert* on which I stand. Promise me that you will fulfill my desire. For I know that you are my son and my saviour ...''

In the first year of his reign Thutmosis had the sand dug away. But the desert was stronger – stronger, too, than the pro-tective wall erected in Roman times, probably during the reign of Septimus Severus (A. D. 146–211), a Roman emperor who died in Britain. In mo-dern times the monument was once again completely exposed by Caviglia in 1818. But by 1886 the general director of Egyptian antiquities, Gaston Maspero, had to resume the struggle against the desert sands. In 1925–6 Baraize excavated once more – and this time repairs were effected, props placed where needed, to stave off further crumbling.

the blown desert sands in the remote past. But it was not left so. A tablet erected by priests between the paws of the Sphinx relates a dream of Thutmosis IV (1450–1405 B. C.) before he became pharaoh, which troubled him when he returned

Hewn out of a single tremendous rock,

sixty-six feet tall, the Sphinx raises its head above the desert floor. In the whole history of man's art there is nothing more amazing than this human countenance facing eternity – at the foot of the most rational monuments of architecture ever created, the stone geometry of the pyramids. Our photograph, taken during Baraize's 1925–6 expedition, shows the Sphinx from the south-east. The head and forepart of the body are chiselled out of living rock, the body and paws completed by the addition of brick. From claws to tail it measures $242^{1}/_{2}$ feet. The mouth is 7 feet 8 inches; the length of the nose can be estimated proportionally at 5 feet 8 inches; the length of the ears is 4 feet 5 inches.

There are many sphinxes in Egypt; in fact there are whole avenues of sphinxes. During the Middle Kingdom especially (between 2100 and 1700 B.C.) some fine sculptural work was done. We may perhaps consider the Sphinx of Queen Hatshepsut as the last one on which true artistry was lavished. Most sphinxes were portraits of kings. But was the Sphinx of Gizeh also such a portrait? Archaeological evidence and written testimony indicate that it was created at the time of Pharaoh Chephren, that is about 2650 B.C. But does it represent Chephren himself? There is some reason to believe that it was intended as the portrait of the sun god himself, Re-Harachte. Or is it simultaneously god and king? Is it possibly only the watcher over the pyramid tombs? Or nothing but a gigantic whim on the part of the builders of the pyramids who decided to do something with a rock that happened by chance to be suggestively shaped?

We know a great deal about the land of the Nile, about its history, religion, art and social order. It seems peculiarly appropriate that the largest work of sculpture left to us by antiquity, this stone figure with the mysterious look, should remain forever a riddle.

93

"Once the Parisians see me three or four times",

said twenty-eight-year-old General Bonaparte after his victorious campaign in Italy, "not a soul will turn his head to look at me. They want to see *deeds*."

The general went to Egypt to accomplish these deeds. In May 1798 he put to sea with 38,000 men aboard his fleet, including 175 scholars. In the shadow of the pyramids a victorious battle was fought, but the campaign was a failure.

It is paradoxical that naked force was midwife to the birth of a new science. New Egypt, barely won, was lost again at once; but Old Egypt was truly conquered. More scholars followed the soldiers, and they brought home the booty of new knowledge.

The most diligent interpreter of all the ancient novelties was Baron Dominique Vivant Denon, adventurer, diplomat, fine artist – a mixture of Casanova and Cagliostro filtered through the French Revolution. He was fifty-one years of age when, after Napoleon's landing, he accompanied General Desaix to Upper Egypt in wild pursuit of the Mamelukes. While the youth of France fought, he made drawings. And in his book, *Voyage dans la Haute et la Basse Egypte*, published in 1802 in Paris, he gave to an amazed Europe its first pictorial account of the wonderful age-old world along the Nile.

The picture above contains his likeness. In the romantic setting of a medieval vaulted tomb, a bivouac during the campaign, General Belliard is having prisoners brought before him. Around him are his staff officers. In the left foreground, seated on the edge of the rug, near the general, is Denon himself. Today it is apparent to us how wrongly he saw many things (cf. the Sphinx drawing on page 89). But future archaeology profited enormously by his work. Moreover, his labours provided essential documentation for the great *Description de l'Egypte* which was completed by a special commission long after Napoleon's European conquests had eclipsed the Egyptian adventure.

This one work catapulted

a hitherto little-known world into the minds of Europeans. The preliminary labours were performed by the Egyptian Institute at Cairo. There, everything the Institute could lay hands on was collected. The collection waxed enormously, for in Egypt things that elsewhere had to be toilsomely sounded for lay right on the surface. Moreover, collecting was easy behind Napoleonic bayonets. When, under the treaty of capitulation, France had to surrender her collections to England, it turned out that the commission had acted with forethought. Plaster casts had been made of all the pieces, especially of that noteworthy stone covered with three types of script which two decades later was to provide the key to the decipherment of Egyptian hieroglyphs.

François Jomard began publication of the *Description de l'Egypte* in 1809. Here are three examples of the numerous illustrations that adorned the work. Above, a panorama of the Temple of Amon (then described as the "Palace at Karnak"). The artist, in conformity with the custom of the times, did not forget

to place himself in the picture. Above is
the principal gate of the Temple of Luxor.
This print shows the obelisks which a few
years later were sent by Sultan Mohammed
Ali to France as a gift to Louis Philippe,
and which now stand in the Place de la
Concorde in Paris. In the bottom left hand
corner of the lower illustration is the artist
again; here he is standing in front of the
remains of the statue of Ramses III which
guards the entrance to the great colonnade
at Karnak.

Two decades later a British expedition
brought similarly handsome pictorial matter
back to Europe. Attached to this expedition
were three artists whose work practically
compels discussion of the archaeological
merits of drawing and photography.

A hitherto unrecorded disaster in the history of Egyptian archaeology,

such was the Robert Hay Expedition. For fifteen years, between 1820 and 1839, this Scottish landowner's son (1799–1863) scoured Egypt, taking measurements, making drawings, and writing. The fantastic fruit of his labours – more than one hundred volumes full of sketches, finished drawings, architectural plans, descriptions, travel notes and diary entries – has never been published. It reposes at present in the manuscript collection of the British Museum.

The work of Edward William Lane (1802–1876), Hay's most diligent assistant, suffered the same fate. Lane went to Egypt in 1825 seeking to cure his tuberculosis. With the aid of the camera lucida (see page 119) he made such strikingly successful perspective drawings that only modern photography has surpassed his precision. And we must remember that for archaeologists precision ranks – necessarily so – ahead of artistic value. However, in the case of Lane – who incidentally could boast of being related to the Gainsborough family – quality accompanied accuracy. His projected book, *An Exhaustive Description of Egypt*, was never completed because he was unable to find a technique for reproducing his drawings which satisfied his artistic demands. One single picture of his was lithographed (see page 117). The drawings on page 97 as well as the plates on pages 118, 119, 121 are published here for the first time. Page 97 shows the cornice and vault of the temple at Abydos of Sethos I (1317–1301 B. C.), which was then still buried under sand. Below is a view of the interior of the cliff temple of Ramses II (1301–1234 B. C.) at Abu Simbel. Staring silently into the darkness of the temple carved into rock are the gigantic statues of the god Osiris, lord of the hereafter and judge of all the dead. These statues, shown buried to their knees in sand, have since Lane's time been dug out.

It is instructive to recall

how weirdly astray scholars and artists would go in their conception of ancient monuments when they had only literary sources to rely on, and direct inspection was barred to them. The dominance of philology in the study of antiquity – the result of a long tradition of textual criticism and the relatively late beginnings of serious excavation – has frequently led to grotesque absurdities. Eminent scholars, insisting on the authority of their texts, have denied what everyone could see plainly with his own eyes. But the converse has also been true: diggers with the spade have produced "results" which have had to be checked and rectified by the tedious toil of decipherers and philologists. Nowadays there can be little doubt that the diggers and the philologists are both servants of the selfsame master: the historian.

Left is "The wonderful stone statue of Memnon" as Bernard Picart conceived it and pictured it in 1754 in his *Neueröffneter Musentempel* (Newly Opened Temple of the Muses). "His statue . . . was of a black stone, from a mount in Ethiopia. So soon as the sun's rays touched it in the early morn, it was as if it came to life and gave forth a sweet and mellifluent twanging."

This musical sound was heard by the Roman Emperor Hadrian three times one morning in A. D. 130, and the event was immortalized by his court poetess Balbilla. Emperor Septimus Severus (A. D. 193–211) also heard the song of the statue. After the torso was repaired, the romantic phenomenon ceased, and we no longer know what could have caused it.

The name Colossus of Memnon for the gigantic statue at Thebes was conferred by the Greeks of the Ptolemaic period, who took one of the giants for the son of Eos, goddess of the dawn. For there are *two* colossal seated figures – only the northern one gave forth a musical tone. In reality they are statues of Pharaoh Amenophis III (1412–1376 B. C.).

The print on the right shows one of the colossi drawn by Frederick Cather-wood, of whom more later. The picture overleaf is by Bonomi, another member of the Hay Expedition, along with Lane and Catherwood.

Joseph Bonomi: The four statues of Ramses the Great

in front of the cliff temple at Abu Simbel. Such painstaking draftsmanship has gone out of fashion nowadays, inspired as it is neither by the artist's mood, nor desire for expression, but by the object itself. For science, this is regrettable (whether it is fortunate or unfortunate for art is too delicate a question for us to become involved in here); since photography, an invention hailed jubilantly by archaeologists, has proved in the course of time *not* to be always the ideal substitute for skilled descriptive drawing. Sir Mortimer Wheeler, one of the excavators of the Indus culture, makes use of the foreword to a book on the technique of photographing archaeological subjects (written by his friend M. B. Cookson, with whom he wandered for two decades conducting research and taking photographs "from Dorset to Delhi") to state explicitly: "The basic trouble is, of course, that the camera is an awful liar." And Ernst Buschor has pointed out: "Drawings of architecture . . . are quite different from plans drawn before a building is erected. They are always abstractions, phantoms of a physical structure which has extension in space. Photographs go to the other extreme; they exaggerate the manner in which the structure merges with light and air, and in any case distort the harmony, alter the colour, blur the proportions, and introduce optico-pictorial elements."

Nowadays, in fact, there has developed – especially in France and Italy – a method of photographing antiquities which produces pictures of great technical and aesthetic refinement. Often these surpass the original; they always change it. But these qualifications apart, we must keep our sense of proportion, especially in regard to the use of photography in field archaeology. The camera has by now become a priceless and irreplaceable aid, for it can yield excellent results even in the hands of a man unable to produce the crudest drawing.

How did the Egyptians transport these mighty colossi?

The great monuments have long prompted this question. By and by we shall let the Egyptians speak for themselves on the subject. But our picture is one hint of how it may have been done in antiquity. May have been done – because the drawing above, made by the man who directed the operation, was done quite "recently", only 140-odd years ago.

This section of a statue of Ramses II was not only moved a short way along the Nile; it was also transported from Thebes to the British Museum in London.

Oddly enough, the man who organized this feat in 1816 thereafter gave up being what he had hitherto been: a professional strong man!

G. BELZONI.

This "strong man"

proved to be the first colourful personality in the story of Egyptian archaeology.
Giovanni Battista Belzoni (1778–1823) was born in Padua. He intended to
become a monk in Rome, fled from the advancing French, and turned up in
Holland in 1800, in England in 1803. An imposing six feet seven, he found
a scarcely less imposing spouse to share the better with him, and a great deal of
the worse, for they lived in dire poverty. But their situation improved after they

were hired by Astley's circus to appear in feats of strength. Belzoni played the parts of Hercules and Apollo, and later, during a tour of Spain and Portugal, of Samson. From the start of his circus career he mixed variety with his strong-man acts. He demonstrated tricks with water, which he later developed so cleverly that the idea came to him to offer Mohammed Ali, Sultan of Egypt, a hydraulic pump for irrigating the gardens of Subra on the Nile.

Salt, the British consul-general in Cairo, smoothed the path for him. But the strong man seems to have had little success, for he was stranded in Cairo and forced to subsist as a dancer. His acquaintanceship with Salt, however, ulti-mately proved fruitful in another way. Through the consul, he obtained a commission to transport attractive Egyptian antiquities for the British Museum. And the strong man performed his mightiest feat of strength: moving the torso of the colossal statue of Ramses all the way to London.

Thereafter, he could not shake off the fascination of Egypt. He was not a genuine scientist; rather, he was a hunter of antiquities, and he collected them with a passion that brooked no obstacles. In 1820 his book appeared in London: *Narrative of the Operations . . . within the Pyramids, Temples, Tombs and Ex-cavations in Egypt and Nubia*. This was the first sizable account of Egyptian antiquities in Egypt. It contained many drawings by Belzoni himself.

In 1823 the urge took him to seek the sources of the Nile. He attempted to push forward from the African west coast to legendary Timbuctoo – and died miser-ably near the little village of Gwato in the African bush.

Belzoni's accomplishments were sizable. He was the discoverer of the grave of Sethos I, to this day referred to in guidebooks as "Belzoni's Tomb". And he was the first European to set foot inside the second-largest burial monument in the world, the Pyramid of Chephren at Gizeh. His successes were founded on his ruthlessness, and on the magic his tremendous physical strength exercised over the natives; he would take as many as four fellahin in his arms and toss them twenty-five feet into the sand, so it was said. Belzoni was a pioneer of archaeology, but at the same time the foremost representative of the earliest phase of the science: plundering rather than scholarly excavation.

But before we turn to the "Valley of the Kings", the pyramids and tomb robbing, let us pay tribute to the man who as early as 1821, without stirring from his desk, solved one of the greatest riddles of Egypt: the hieroglyphs.

must have heard the word Egypt for the first time at the age of seven, from his brother who had hoped in vain to go there with Napoleon. At eleven he told the former secretary of the Egyptian Institute, Fourier, that he was determined to decipher the hieroglyphs some day. At seventeen, instead of the usual vale‚ dictory, he read to the assembled faculty and students of Grenoble Academy the introduction to a book he was writing, *L'Egypte sous les Pharaons*. Shortly thereafter he saw at Fourier's a copy of the Rosetta Stone, which was to seal his destiny.

Champollion (1790–1832), who by the time he was eighteen had studied more than a dozen languages, was the scholar *par excellence*. Only the tumult and high passions of the Napoleonic Age tempted him to leave his study on occasion and march in the streets with banner in hand. At nineteen he was already a professor at Grenoble. After the Hundred Days he was branded a traitor, more by chance than for good reason. He put exile to good use. In 1822 he published an essay, *Lettre à M. Dacier relative à l'alphabet des hiéroglyphes phonétiques*. It contained the key to the decipherment of the hieroglyphs.

This painting by Leon Cogniet misses the great drive and highly‚keyed character of the man. It shows nothing of the anxiety, the frequent despair, which we encounter in his letters: the fear that he will not finish. After the consummation of his most important labours, he received many honours. In 1827 he was placed in charge of the newly founded Egyptian section of the Louvre; in 1829 the first Chair of Egyptology in Europe was founded for him at the Collège de France in Paris. (The second was created seventeen years later for Lepsius in Berlin.) And from July 1828 to December 1829 he was privileged to see the country to which he had devoted so much study: he led an expedition to Egypt.

Champollion died three years later, in 1832. Today he is justly considered the "classic" decipherer. He owes this reputation to his genius and industry, of course, but also to the lucky find of an unknown Napoleonic soldier: the Rosetta Stone.

came to light in the course of labours by a troop of engineers near the Nile city of Rosetta in 1799. It is a slab of black basalt, about the size of a table top, but almost eleven inches thick. By lucky chance some officers were on hand when it was dug up. Observing the three long texts in three different scripts, they suspected its value and had it sent to Cairo. After changing owners several times, it arrived in good condition in the British Museum. But before this happened two specialists, Citizens Marcel and Galland, were sent over from Paris on orders from the French general staff to make brush-proofs of the stone. Several of these proofs reached Paris.

Even at that early date the three basic forms of Egyptian script had been detected, if not always too clearly. In early times the Egyptians used actual picture-writing. Out of these hieroglyphs there developed, on the new writing materials of papyrus and clay, a simplified script, the hieratic. After the Twenty-fifth Dynasty this was further abbreviated and simplified into a cursive script, the demotic.

The Rosetta Stone contained not only fourteen lines of hieroglyphic and thirty-two lines of demotic text, but in addition fifty-five lines in Greek script and language. The Greek could be read and translated; and even before the stone left Cairo, scholars had determined that it was a document of the year 196 B. C. in which the priesthood of Memphis paid tribute to King Ptolemy V. There was every reason to assume that the content of all three texts was the same, hence that by comparison with the Greek it should be possible to decipher the hieroglyphic text picture by picture.

This supposition was based upon a misapprehension some fourteen hundred years old. It stemmed from the book *Hieroglyphica* by Horapollon, an Egyptian of the fourth century A. D. (by which time hieroglyphic script was already dead). This book described the hieroglyphics as pure picture-writing; hence, ever since the seventeenth century scholars had struggled to interpret *symbols*. Their results were fantastic, and often grotesque.

A decisive step forward seemed to have been taken when the Swedish diplomat and philologist Åkerblad identified in the demotic version of the Rosetta Stone all the proper names found in the Greek version, and in addition the words for

temple and Greeks. Then Thomas Young, physicist, physician and amateur philologist, recognized the names of kings in the clusters of hieroglyphics inside oval frames. These cartouches, as they are called, can be seen in the sixth, twelfth and fourteenth lines of hieroglyphs in our illustration. Finally he detected the names Berenice and Cleopatra in a bilingual stone excavated at Philae in 1815.

But although Young took the bold step of assuming that some of the signs were phonetic rather than symbolic he shrank back, like all other scholars, from the logical conclusion that hieroglyphic script was essentially phonetic and, indeed, the forerunner of our own alphabet as it was later reshaped by the Phoenicians, enriched with vowels by the Greeks, and handed down to us by the Latins. Champollion was the first to adopt this rash hypothesis. And he proved his revolutionary theory on the basis of the royal names. In the names Ptolemy and Cleopatra he established the correlation between individual hieroglyphic signs and single Greek letters. Thus the decipherment began.

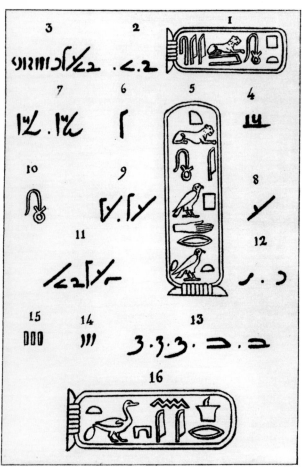

The principle of this first decipherment appears incredibly simple. But we have described only the first step. The next was correlation of the ancient hieroglyphs with the hieratic and demotic scripts. It was then discovered that the three basic scripts had not only undergone consider-able wear in the course of three thousand years of evolution, but that each had de-veloped characters of its own – de-pending on whether the script was used for religious or official texts, personal or govermental messages. Finally it turned out that the phonetic signs coincided with symbolic signs (a pictured face could mean both "face" and the preposition "on"), that there were word signs and meaning signs. The vast amount of written matter which now began pour-ing into Europe, especially in the form of papyri, contributed more to confusion than to clarification. No one knew any longer where to start.

Signes Hiéroglyphiques		Valeur selon M. Young	Valeur selon mon Alphabet
1.		BIR	B
2.		E	R
3.	★	I	I . È . AI
4.	★	N	N
5.		*inutile*	K
6.		KE . KEN	S
7.		MA	M
8.		OLE	L
9.	★	P	P
10.		*inutile.*	Ô . OU
11.		OS . OSCH	S
12.	★	T	T
13.		OU	KH
14.	★	F	F . V.
15.		ENE	T

It is testimony to Champollion's genius that he did not stop at the first step. In fact he succeeded, shortly before his early death, in demonstrating all of Young's errors and writing the outlines of an Egyptian grammar.

On the left page is the decisive plate from his *Précis du système hiéroglyphique des anciens Égyptiens*, published in 1824. The three cartouches show: No. 1, Ptolemy; No. 5, Cleopatra; No. 16, Berenice. The square (extreme upper right of the Ptolemy cartouche) is the sign for P; No. 4 gives the hieratic equivalent. The segment of a circle under the square is T; No. 6 shows the same in demotic. There is scarcely more telling testimony of enormous evolution of Egyptian script than the hieroglyphic symbol for lion and hieratic sign No. 7 – both signify L.

In the same book Champollion set a reading of his own side by side with one of Young's (above). A generation later there was no doubt that the real decipherer of the hieroglyphs had been Champollion.

"Nowadays we no longer decipher texts,

we read them", the Egyptologist Alexander Scharff remarked in 1939. Here is an example of hieroglyphics, probably the most impressive monumental script in the ancient world, carved on an obelisk ("*obeliskos*" means "roasting spit" in Greek!). The stone is one of those innumerable giant slabs which for cen‑ turies were hewn out of the rose granite of Aswan, always in one piece 100 or more feet high, then set upright as towering guards before the temples of the pharaohs. Our picture shows a detail of the eastern obelisk before the entrance to the Temple of Luxor. The row of three cartouches near the top contains two forms (left and right cartouches are identical) of the many names and titles of the king who erected the obelisk, Ramses II. Above the names, three times repeated, are the words: "Ruler of Upper and Lower Egypt", and below: "Son of Re".

Here is the Pyramid of Chephren,

the middle pyramid of the three great monuments at Gizeh, in an infra-red photograph. Pyramids are tombs, tremendous bastions erected above a small chamber containing the sarcophagus of a pharaoh. They are meant to protect the royal remains which must be preserved if the *ka*, the personification of the life-force and man's sole support and succour in the hereafter, is not to abandon the body.

In Egypt's very earliest days, the dead were cremated. The ashes were interred in mastabas, vaults at the terminus of long shafts. Gradually these came to be marked above ground as well, and ultimately they became monuments. The step pyramid of King Zoser at Sakkara (Third Dynasty, about 2650 B.C.) is the first monumental structure; there one can still trace the development of the pyramid from six mastabas heaped one upon the other. The first pyramid proper was that of Snofru (about 2600 B. C.), known as the Pyramid of Medum. It was never completed, and so afforded scholars an insight into the technical process of pyramid-building.

The kings of the Fourth Dynasty (2600–2480 B. C.), Cheops, Chephren and Mycerinus, built for themselves the three gigantic pyramids at Gizeh, which are surrounded by the numerous small pyramids for their wives, and by the tombs of high dignitaries. Until the middle of the second millennium the kings continued raising these monuments, the mightiest expressions of man's power and fear. Hundreds of thousands of men slaved to provide protection for the remains of a few mortals.

Ever since Greek antiquity the pyramids, especially that of Cheops, have been counted among the seven wonders of the world. Extensive reports, especially those of Herodotus, tell us more about them than about any other structures of the third millennium B. C. Still, in the course of time they proved to hold no fewer riddles for the probing eye of the scientist than the Sphinx. The Great Pyramid in particular has given rise to the wildest speculations.

The man at the foot of the ladder,

portfolio under his arm,

is Le Père, the architect of Napoleon's expedition. He is watching his assistant Contelle climb into a hole just beneath the ceiling of this gloomy entrance into the Great Pyramid of Cheops. (This drawing and the one on the right, showing another view of the same chamber, are taken from the fifth volume of the *Description de l'Egypte*). On the same spot some 235 years earlier, stood a man who later wrote of the pyramids: "Of this edifice some say that it was built to be the tomb of the Pharaoh who drowned in the Red Sea, wherefore said grave remained empty." Although this particular statement is open to question, the author's descriptions are sharp and clear. We continue to quote from Johann Helffrich's journal of 1579: "We climbed with great difficulty a high corridor which lay straight before us, because this corridor was both wide and extremely high. On the sides the wall is set back at about half a man's height, with holes each a good pace distant from the next; to these we had to hold on and climb up as best we could."

A "musty atmosphere" greeted them, he wrote, and they became "so full of this same unhealthy air that the following night we fell into such weariness and weakness that, within two days, we could stir neither arm nor leg." The air is not so bad today, but guidebooks still warn against the close, hot air.

Among the mosaics of St. Mark's in Venice

are two representations of pyramids, done around A. D. 1250. They form part of the pictorial narrative of the Joseph story in the ceiling vault of the porch. On the left stands Joseph, who has sent his brothers to fetch sheaves of corn from the pyramids (at the time of the mosaics thought to have been granaries).

The woodcut was done later. It comes from Helffrich's diary. Remarkably enough his pyramids appear much the same as those represented three hundred year earlier in the Venice mosaic, although in 1565 he had actually crawled into the interior of the Cheops Pyramid at Gizeh.

Thereafter, depictions of the pyramids appeared more and more frequently, often in the strangest contexts. In this preoccupation we can feel the burning curiosity of Western man to make contact with his past. To do so he will subject himself to infinite mental toil and physical hardships, using any means, even brute force.

In 1646 John Greaves, a professor of astronomy,

published a fascinating book called *Pyramidographia*. Like all his predecessors, he held that the Pyramid of Chephren, unlike that of Cheops, was a solid structure devoid of entrance or burial vault. On March 2, 1818, Belzoni disproved this by smashing the stone in one section of the former pyramid (he determined the spot for his attempt by comparative measurements of the Pyramid of Cheops) and so breaking in. Such methods were not unusual at the time. In 1837 Colonel Richard Howard-Vyse, the successful British excavator, forced his way into the pyramids with *gunpowder*, and bored deep holes into the Sphinx to see whether it was hollow.

Belzoni actually found the entrance. He must have felt the pride which so many archaeologists after his time have acknowledged: the elation of being the first to enter a pharaoh's tomb since interment. But his experience was like that of so many of his fellows: he found that others had after all preceded him. His great disappointment was the absence of a sarcophagus. He found a funeral vault half closed by a heavy lid, but without a mummy or those precious accompanying gifts which he had hoped for. He found only a few bones, and an inscription in Arabic.

Who had been here before him? And by what route had they made their way into the burial vault? Today we know that all the tombs of Egypt, not only the pyramids, have been the prey of robbers since earliest times, and that the enormous ingenuity employed by the ancient Egyptian architects to seal invisibly the tombs of the kings was almost always surpassed by the cunning of the thieves.

In his drawings on page 115 Belzoni represented himself three times. Upper right he is standing before the hole he had hacked into the pyramid. Below he is leading his workers toward the burial chamber, and then on the left he is seen entering the chamber itself.

The Pharaoh's burial chamber

This is the top chamber in the Great Pyramid at Gizeh. It measures 34 feet 6 inches in length by 17 feet in breadth and 19 feet in height. The red granite sarcophagus is so magnificently polished that Helffrich, when he saw it in 1565 thought it had been made of poured metal. No one knows whether it ever contained a mummy; robbers may have been at work here, too, thousands of years ago. The drawing is another by E. W. Lane.

Always in Arab dress,

Edward William Lane travelled up the Nile in 1826–7. Here is a self-portrait, showing him seated in the cabin of his river boat. The clean perspective lines resulting from the employment of the camera lucida are evident here. Lane was unusually adept with this instrument; he used it to excellent effect in the following aerial view.

No one knows how

the camera lucida was used by Lane to obtain this picture. The camera lucida was a device much favoured by architectural draftsmen of the period. It is still used by beginners in art schools. In principle the instrument is extremely simple. By means of a rotatable glass prism the artist can cast a reduced image of the object upon a sheet of paper. One drawback is that the projected image is extremely dim.

Lane's remarkable "air view" shows the Pyramid of Chephren from above the north-east corner of the Great Pyramid. His accuracy is evident here, but is still more emphatically shown in the next picture.

object of never-ending admiration, symbol of the power and the *hubris* of man, subject of infinite interpretations and misinterpretations: the Great Pyramid of Gizeh, built around 2600 B. C. by Khufu, whom the Greeks called Cheops. (Lithograph from a camera lucida drawing by Lane.)

More than 3.2 million cubic yards of stone were piled up in the Cheops Pyramid. Its height was some 467 feet, the average length of the base-lines 736 feet. According to Herodotus, 100,000 men laboured twenty years to build it. Calculations indicate, however, that no more than 36,000 men could ever have worked on the pyramid at one time, without hampering each other's movements. Since – in military language – the logistics of an operation requires more personnel than the fighting troops, Herodotus's figure may be close. This seems all the more likely since we know today that the ramps over which the stones were moved required even more material than the actual pyramid.

Herodotus also gives some figures on costs: for example the payment to the workers in the form of radishes, onions and garlics. It has recently been calcu-lated that to build such a pyramid today, with the methods of the ancient builders, would cost well over 34,000,000 pounds; applying the methods of our technical age, the cost could be reduced to under 3,500,000 pounds. It was early recognized that the Great Pyramid had been built on certain astronomical principles. But the fact that it continues to be regarded, even today, as a species of oracle, is due chiefly to a man whose character was a queer compound of strict science and wild mysticism.

Charles Piazzi Smyth (born the son of a British admiral in 1809 in Naples) was highly regarded as a professor of astronomy at Edinburgh – until he put forward his interpretation of the Great Pyramid. He was not the first to read the most fantastic propositions into the measurements of altitude and sides and the angles of rooms and corridors in the pyramid; but his reputation as an astronomer lent a respectability to dubious conclusions, and this in part accounts for their tenacious persistency. Egyptologists pointed out that the premises on which he built his assertions were extremely shaky; mathematicians condemned his method of manipulating measurements if they did not suit his calculations. None of this could discredit his system. The pyramid became

known as a "Bible in stone", furnishing not only the most precise astronomical and mathematical data (e.g., the numerical value of pi or the exact distance from the earth to the sun), but also all history to the present day.

Even as late as 1949 an article appeared in a German newspaper containing the following paragraph: "In this connection we must mention the discoveries of Dr. Noetling of Stuttgart who has found that by simple mathematical ope-rations with the given dimensions of the Great Pyramid the radius, circum-ference, volume and specific gravity of the earth, the periods of the planets, the length of their orbits, the exact duration of male and female periods, the time of the climacteric in both sexes . . . can easily be derived."

". . . By simple mathematical operations with the given dimensions" – that is the bad beginning and the still more lamentable end of this method. In truth the preposterous nature of the idea can be bared only by satire; an Englishman proposed to apply the same method to London's Crystal Palace. Employing a suitable unit of measure and a moderate degree of patience, he said, he could easily show that the dimensions yielded the distance to Timbuctoo or the average weight of an adult goldfish.

Oddly enough, this very nonsense sent Egyptward the man who would be the most successful and stimulating Egyptologist of the century: Petrie.

The bearded gentleman at the bus window

is Sir William Flinders Petrie, photographed as he was taking leave of his American hosts in Syria during his last expedition in 1935. For seven weeks this man of eighty-two and his wife (the figure in the doorway) worked, ate and slept in the bus while his assistant, I. C. Ellis (second from right) shared a small tent with the driver. The other three are Petrie's youthful hosts of the Megiddo Expedition, whose comfortable, solid houses were equipped with rugs, club chairs and gramophones.

In his old age Petrie lived and travelled exactly as he had done in his youth. His first trip to Egypt was inspired by his father, a chemist and engineer who fell under the spell of the theories of Charles Piazzi Smyth. Petrie senior saw Smyth's work as a triumphant reconciliation of enlightened science with Christianity. Desirous of finding support for Smyth's ideas, he planned a trip to Gizeh, accompanied by his sons. He was going to use superior modern instruments to measure the pyramids and obtain better results – that is to say, results closer to those required by Smyth's theories.

As it turned out, young Petrie travelled alone. He had earlier developed a passion for surveying, had worked in Stonehenge, and at the age of twenty-two published his first book, *Inductive Metrology*. During the years 1880 to 1882 he spent nine months in Gizeh, measuring, calculating, probing, and at last publishing the best mathematical data on the Great Pyramid that had ever

been obtained. Only extremely minor revisions of these have since been made. However, his data also revealed the sheer silliness of Piazzi Smyth's theses. That was clear enough to Petrie but out of respect for his father he never belaboured the question.

This was his manner of life:

"Excellent accomodation was to be had in a rock-hewn tomb ... formerly used by Mr. Wayman Dixon, C. E. His door and shutters I strengthened, and fitting up shelves and a hammock bedstead, I found the place as convenient as anything that could be wished. The tombs were sheltered ... and preserved an admirably uniform temperature ... The usual course of a day's work was much as follows: ... Lighting my petroleum stove, the kettle boiled while I had my bath; then breakfast time was a reception hour, and as I sat with the tomb door open, men and children used to look in; ... often a friend would stop for a chat ... After this, starting out about nine o'clock; ... if triangulating, it was Ali's business to hold an umbrella, so as to shade the theodolite from the sun all day – the observer took his chance; ... I always had to get on as well as I could during Ali's dinner hour. At dusk I collected the things ... Then, when all was safely housed in my tomb, Ali was dismissed to his home, and about six or seven o'clock I lit my stove, and sat down to reduce observations. Dinner then began when the kettle boiled, cooking and feeding going on together.

Brown ship-biscuit, tinned soups, tomatoes (excellent in Egypt), tapioca and
chocolate, were found practically the most convenient and sustaining articles ...
Then, after washing up the dishes, I sat down again to reducing observations,
writing, etc. till about midnight. Ali's slave Muhammed, the negro, and his
nephew, little Muhammed, used to come up about nine o'clock and settle in
the next tomb, to sleep as guards, safely locked in ... During the excavations I
turned out earlier – about sunrise; ... when working inside the Great Pyramid,
I always began in the evening, after the travellers were clean away, and went on
till midnight, with Ali nodding, or even till eight o'clock in the morning; thus
occasionally working twenty-four hours at a stretch ... The tomb I left
furnished, as I inhabited it; ... it will, I hope, be useful to anyone wishing to
carry out researches there ..."

This excerpt from Petrie's book, *The Pyramids and Temples of Gizeh*, displays a
modesty which has become all too rare. Petrie's accurarcy and his introduction
of new methods proved to be of enormous importance for Egyptology and
archaeology. He showed no inclination to specialize. He provided the best
descriptions of Egyptian monumental structures, but was also the first to
recognize the value of small works of art and ceramics, of "vases and shards",
("the true alphabet of archaeologists in every country") for chronology. He was
interested in modern as well as ancient and even prehistoric Egypt, and wrote
on the science and art, the religious and social life of the country. In 1893 he
was appointed to a professorship and published *Ten Years' Digging in Egypt*,
which proved widely popular and brought him fame outside specialist circles.

He died on July 28, 1942, *en route* to Jerusalem – aged almost ninety. The
picture shows him around 1880 in front of his quarters at Gizeh.

Pyramid of Medum

Final Stage

Second Stage

Entrance

First Stage

Tomb-Chamber

The graves of the Kings

These seemingly simple diagrams of the
three big pyramids are actually the distillation of about a century of measurement
and research. Flinders Petrie's work would,
in its essentials, have been impossible without the preliminary labours of the pioneers; the proper evaluation of his and
others' researches awaited the publication
of a survey such as *The Pyramids of Egypt*,
by I. E. S. Edwards, on illustrations from
which these drawings are based.

Of the many pioneers who are listed in the
table at the end of this book, two merit
special attention. Richard Lepsius's expedition of 1842–6 for the first time yielded
material scientifically arranged. Auguste
Mariette, on the other hand, was something
more than a successful excavator. Not only
was he the founder of the Egyptian Museum,
now located in Cairo, but he was also the
person responsible for protecting Egypt
against further plundering excavations.

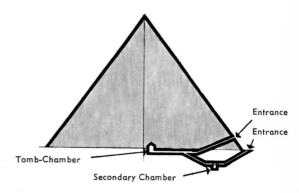

Pyramid of Chephren

Entrance

Entrance

Tomb-Chamber

Secondary Chamber

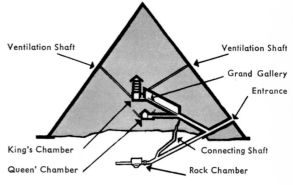

Pyramid of Cheops

Ventilation Shaft

Ventilation Shaft

Grand Gallery

Entrance

King's Chamber

Queen' Chamber

Connecting Shaft

Rock Chamber

The pyramids at Abusir, as drawn by Ludwig Borchardt,

are a fascinating object lesson to those who look to archaeology to bring buried
civilizations back to life, not only back to the surface. This was reconstruction
with the crayon, but it was the result of four years scientific labour.

What Borchardt saw during his preliminary investigation in 1901 was a
grouping of stone piles in the desert sands, the central one about eighty feet
high. There followed a series of excavations from 1902 to 1904 in which he
was able to define the outline of a tremendous burial ground. He inferred the
architecture and the positions of the temples in front of the pyramids, their
connection with temples in the valley by vast, lofty ramps, originally roads for
the transportation of building materials, and later routes for processions. He
was able to date the pyramids. They were erected by kings of the Fifth Dynasty,
about twenty-five centuries B.C., by Nefer-er-ke-Re, Ne-user-Re and Sahu-Re.
A contemporary archaeologist would consider that he had done enough in
finding and mentally reconstructing so vast a complex. But at about the turn of
the century there was as much emphasis on finds in the form of concrete objects as in the form of knowledge. An expensive expedition had to bring home

trophies. And so railway track supplied by the Prussian Ministry of War was laid down upon the ancient soil, and soon gigantic granite pillars and colossal lions were rolling away from the temple area – on their way to Cairo and Berlin. It took two weeks to move each pillar nine miles, because the track had to be pulled up behind each rolling flat-waggon and laid down again piece by piece in front.

No modern archaeologist is seriously out for trophies because, as we have said, the scientist nowadays is more interested in knowledge than in booty. But even if he wanted to, he could not take anything away without breaking the law. (In rare cases he might obtain a special export license.) Egypt is now independent, is aware of the value of her antiques, and has passed extremely strict laws to protect them. It was a matter of tradition for the Egyptian Antiquities Institute, founded by Auguste Mariette, to be administered by Frenchmen. Mariette, in fact, secured the first protective legislation. In 1952, however, the last French director of the Institute, Abbé Drioton, resigned his post. His successor was an Egyptian, Mustapha Amer.

where the sarcophagus lay, and once again I stopped to admire the beauty of the simple alabaster box, the sides of which reflected the brilliant light of the electric lamps which we had installed within the chamber . . .

"I thought of other archaeologists who had stood on the brink of great discoveries: Carter when he opened the sealed antechamber of the Tomb of Tutankhamun; Reisner when he found the deeply hid burial *cache* of Queen Hetephras . . .

"At last all was ready, and I gave the order to begin the operation. Two of my workmen began to haul on the rope, while others applied crowbars to the crack between the lower part of the panel and the sarcophagus. The men heaved with all their might; there was a scraping of metal on stone. Nothing happened, the panel was wedged tightly in position. The men heaved again, but for a long time the heavy panel resisted all our efforts to move it.

"Then at last it began to move, a mere inch or so. Wedges were inserted in the aperture, and I carefully examined the panel to make sure that no damage had been done. I was right in my assumption that there were vertical ribs running down each side of the panel, sliding in grooves. I gave the order to continue. In all six men were at work on raising the panel, but such was its weight about 500 lb.), and the tightness with which it was sealed with a mixture of gypsum plaster and glue that nearly two hours had passed before at last it slowly began to go up. I went down on to my knees and looked inside.

"The sarcophagus was empty."

This is the account of the climax of an expedition, by the Egyptian archaeologist Zakaria Goneim. On June 27, 1954, Goneim, hitherto virtually unknown outside his country, had made his way into a newly discovered, never completed step pyramid near Sakkara. He cherished the hope, as did the whole world of archaeology after reading his first reports, that the untouched mummy of a king of the Third Dynasty would be found inside it.

Goneim, a member of the youngest generation of Egyptian archaeologists, had studied in Cairo with Percy Newberry and Hermann Junker. In 1951 he began digging at Sakkara, near the Pyramid of King Zoser. In November 1953 he found a corner of a hitherto unknown pyramid built by a hitherto unknown

king, later identified from an inscription as King Sekhem-khet. When, in 1954, a burial vault with an obviously undamaged sarcophagus was found, there was every reason for excitement to run high among archaeologists. For a royal mummy not plundered by grave robbers is a great rarity.

A theory accounting for the empty sarcophagus is that a genuine interment was never planned. Possibly a sham sarcophagus had been placed in the vault meant not for the king but for his *ka*; the unusual sliding-door arrangement of the sarcophagus lends support to this idea.

Reporters and photographers had flocked to the scene, hoping for sensations. As far as they were concerned the empty sarcophagus was a huge disappoint-ment. It was not so for the Egyptologists. The data Goneim obtained from the layout of the unfinished pyramid will provide specialists with material for study for a long time to come.

It was on his deathbed

that Mariette learned of his greatest reverse. The theory which he had so vehemently advocated, that all the pyramids are mute – that is, that inscriptions would never be found in them – was proved wrong. In 1881, the thirty-six-year-old French archaeologist Gaston Maspero (1846–1916) discovered in the pyramids of Sakkara no less than 4,000 lines of text in the most ancient hiero-glyphs. These inscriptions threw invaluable light on funeral rites, veneration of the dead, and Egyptian beliefs concerning the hereafter.

The photograph shows the entrance to the Pyramid of Unis, the last ruler of the Fifth Dynasty. This pyramid had been reduced to ruins in ancient times. Here Maspero found the first long inscription, carved into the limestone and painted blue. The photograph was taken in 1881 by Emil Brugsch, brother of the then celebrated Egyptologist Heinrich Brugsch (1827–1894), a diplomat who worked for both the Egyptian and the Prussian foreign services. Heinrich Brugsch was the author of a seven-volume hieroglyphic-demotic dictionary.

In 1891 he had returned to Europe with one of the greatest collections of papyri ever amassed: some 3,000 rolls.

His younger brother Emil is credited with one of the most sensational disco-veries ever to be made in Egypt. He made it not at the head of a great expedition, but all alone with an Arab thief in a landscape of craggy wastelands.

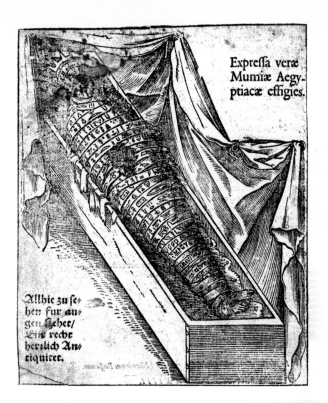

Expreſſa veræ
Mumiæ Aegy-
ptiacæ effigies.

Allhie zu ſe-
hen fur au-
gen ſichet/
Ein rechte
herzlich An-
ciquicet.

"Mumia is that which is found in the graves of embalmed people"

This definition appeared in 1557 in an edition of the principal medical treatise of the period *Hortus Sanitatis*. Our picture dates from 1574; it is taken from the last page of a book whose Latin title translates as follows: "Affidavits by the most noted doctors, historians and philosophers on the most mysterious and precious exotic curatives, and especially on the *mumia*, as well as on everything connected with it and the manner in which it was formerly used in Judea, Egypt, Arabia and quite generally elsewhere." The Latin in the upper right-hand corner of the woodcut declares that this is the "image of a real Egyptian mummy". The German in the lower left-hand corner speaks of the mummy's "right magnificent antiquity". The book claims that this mummy was booty taken at the Battle of Lepanto, the heathens having used it as a talisman.

From the point of view of archaeological history, it is interesting to see that the artist strove for an exact representation. A curious detail: if we examine the script on the mummy's bindings from top to bottom, we see how the artist gradually turned the hieroglyphs into Hebrew letters – which were undoubt-edly more familiar to him.

"Mumiya", an Arabic word,

actually means raw pitch which in early times was thought to have medicinal properties. This was one of the substances used for embalming Egyptian mummies – after a good deal of trial and error. And from tombs the pitch found its way into Europe's pharmacies, where it remained down to the nineteenth century. Gradually the distinction between mummy and *mumiya* was lost, and potions made of pulverized bodies of Egyptian rulers were actually prescribed to rich patients as expensive medicines.

Our picture is taken from the *Histoire générale des drogues*, a book published in 1694 by a Parisian merchant and apothecary named Pierre Pomet. He hoped, by his horrendous depiction of the eviscerated corpse in the foreground, to convert readers away from using pulverized mummy as a panacea. Pomet expressed his own repugnance to the practice by inserting the word *gabbaras* between the pair of mummies on the left; this word may be the ancestor of the English "garbage".

Despoiling of mummies

is one of the oldest forms of Egyptian grave-robbing. Sir J. Gardner Wilkinson published this sketch in his *Manners and Customs of the Ancient Egyptians*, 1837–41. He describes the picture as: "Interior of a mummy pit or sepulchral chamber, at Thebes, with a Fellahs woman searching for papyri and ornaments."

The Dancing Mummy

The Sphinx is identified with the element of mystery, the pyramids with monstrous magnificence. But for hundreds of years mummies have been associated with the uncanny. Cheap novels, inferior plays and bad films are forever making use of mummies to stir horror. A party given by the French amateur archaeologist Emile Etienne Guimet at the beginning of the twentieth century also drew upon this theme for theatrical effect. A real Egyptian sarcophagus was borne into Guimet's drawing

133

"As much as possi

room. While subtle and dramatic lighting played upon the scene, a mummy rose up out of the sarcophagus. She represented Thaïs, the courtesan whom the hermit Serapion converted to Christianity. Dressed in swathings perfectly imitating those of a real mummy, she performed a macabre dance.

This might have been only a foolish prank if the host, M. Guimet, had not actually been a scholarly collector who founded the excellent museum which bears his name. Moreover, the man who supplied him with the mummies which inspired the dance was likewise a serious scientist, Gayet, a specialist in Coptic art.

Nevertheless, in their collecting, these two gentlemen from the very start merged science with the most frivolous sort of romanticism. For example, the expedition which went to work in Antinoë from 1900–4 was entirely inspired by the hugely successful novel of one of the greatest novelists of the period, namely *Thaïs* by Anatole France, which had been published in 1890 and created an extraordinary stir. In this novel France had exercised poetic license to cast the well-known story of Thaïs and her hermit into a new form. Gayet came home with two mummies, and in order to gratify his patron and backer Guimet, presented them as the preserved bodies of Thaïs and Serapion. What was more, he was able to fabricate enough reasons for this claim to have the scientific world accept it for a time.

On page 133 is the dancer in the costume of Thaïs, performing the "mummy's dance".

the brain is extracted through the nostrils with an iron hook,

and what the hook cannot reach is rinsed out with drugs; next the flank is laid open with a flint knife and the whole contents of the abdomen removed; the cavity is then thoroughly cleansed and washed out, first with palm wine and again with an infusion of pounded spices. After that it is filled with pure bruised myrrh, cassia, and every other aromatic substance with the exception of frankincense, and sewn up again, after which the body is placed in natrum, covered entirely over, for seventy days – never longer. When this period, which must not be exceeded, is over, the body is washed and then wrapped from head to foot in linen cut into strips and smeared on the under side with gum, which is commonly used by the Egyptians instead of glue. In this condition the body is given back to the family, who have a wooden case made, shaped like the human figure, into which it is put. The case is then sealed up, and stored in a sepulchral chamber, upright against a wall." (Quotation from A. de Selincourt's translation of *The Histories* of Herodotus, by courtesy of Penguin Books Ltd.)

This method of mummification is described as "the most perfect process" by Herodotus, who travelled through Egypt in about 450 B.C. Modern study bears out his description. To supplement such written accounts, archaeologists have learned much about the process from Egyptian tomb reliefs such as the one shown above, included in the fourth volume of Champollion's *Monuments de l'Egypte et de la Nubie* in 1847. Both the technique of bandaging and the painting of the face mask can be seen here.

The religious rationale for mummification has not been fully clarified. Most likely the Egyptians believed that the soul, after escaping from the body at death, would return to it again. But how could it find a body that had fallen into dust? Thus they began their struggle against the dissolution which to almost all other peoples seemed the inexorable fate of man. If we consider time on a human scale, they won their battle, for mummies of astonishing completeness have been preserved down to our day.

Mummification certainly had begun by the time of the pyramid builders. The masks which later were made of precious materials – in the case of Tutankhamen, of pure gold – were in the beginning simple plaster casts. The more complicated technique described by Herodotus did not develop until the Middle Kingdom. From the Twenty-first Dynasty on, the embalmers began their remarkable imitations of life. They forstalled the shrinking of the skin; they filled the cavities of the body; they added artificial eyes.

Much has been said and written about the "riddle of mummification", by which is meant not only the grotesqueness of the whole procedure, but also the apparently lost chemical technique. Recent research has shown that excessive use of chemicals frequently destroyed instead of preserving, and that the success of so much mummification was due rather to a peculiarity of the Egyptian soil and climate than to the skill of the embalmers. One of the best examples of this fact was found in the wild rocky valley of Der-el-Bahri . . .

More than sixty dead warriors, buried in a mass grave,

were found in 1926 by a New York Metropolitan Museum expedition under the direction of H. E. Winlock. The site, Der-el-Bahri, is near the Nile, opposite Karnak and Luxor. The men must have fallen in a heroic battle – for Pharaoh Neb-hebet-Re, who had led them to fight in Lower Egypt, had their bodies transported from the battlefield all the way back to the vicinity of the capital, in order to honour them by common burial. In fact, a start was made on embalming them, although at this time embalming was usually the prerogative of aristocrats. But interest in the heroes must have faded swiftly, for the embalming was begun only for some, and then very casually. Nevertheless, the bodies of all these soldiers, who fell under a rain of arrows around 2000 B. C., were found in a miraculous state of preservation!

Not chemicals, but the unique dryness and sterility of Egyptian soil, together

with the constant heat, had produced mummification. Forged mummies are further proof of this. At the end of the nineteenth century, when mummies were in great demand, many such frauds were offered to collectors. In many cases it could be conclusively proved that the bodies were recently dead, nameless corpses mummified by the desert sands alone. The counterfeiters had merely outfitted them with a few amulets and scraps of genuine bandaging to strengthen the claim that these were real mummies from the days of the pharaohs.

The high point of the excavations near the precipitous cliff at Dar-el-Bahri, however, was not the discovery of the "unknown soldiers" of the Eleventh Dynasty. Some time earlier, under exciting circumstances, a mass grave of kings had been investigated. The shaft which housed so many kings is marked by a white arrow in our picture, taken during the excavations of 1932.

See Tutankhamen Ps. 50 & 53.

of the village of Kurna is shown here with Gaston Maspero (lolling figure with parasol), Director of the Egyptian Museum in Cairo, and his assistant Emil Brugsch. They are looking into the shaft entrance to the cliff tomb of Der-el-Bahri, the most amazing burial vault in the world.

Thutmosis I (1545–1515 B.C.) of the Eighteenth Dynasty made a break with tradition. Instead of erecting an impressive monument over his tomb, the pharaoh had it cut into the living rock in a secret place. The pyramid architects, despite all their skill in covering their traces, had not prevented the discovery of the entrances to pyramid tombs. Tomb-robbers had invariably broken into the sealed bastions, found the sarcophagi, got at the mummies, and robbed them of all their precious adornments. But the cliff tombs proved to be no safer. Even Thutmosis was not left in peace. The tomb-robbers, abetted by corrupt guards and high officials, ravaged so many royal graves that the priests attempted to save the mummies of their kings by moving them secretly, in the dead of night, to other burial chambers.

Thenceforth grisly scenes of "wandering mummies" might be witnessed all over Egypt. Mummies that had been cut open, battered and robbed were often re-embalmed by the priests and toted from tomb to tomb – for centuries.

Not much was known about this in 1881, when one of Gaston Maspero's assistants drifted about the bazaars of Luxor in the attempt to track down the source of a swelling black-market in antiquities. The result of his detective work was the arrest of Abd-el-Rasul, who was soon exposed as the current chief of a dynasty of robbers from the village of Kurna which had made a business of tomb-robbery almost continuously since the thirteenth century.

On July 5, 1881, another of Maspero's assistants, Emil Brugsch, stood near the base of the cliff at Der-el-Bahri, in front of an uninviting hole in the ground, to which he had been led by the confessed criminal Abd-el-Rasul. When he had himself lowered thirty-five feet into the burial chamber, he saw scattered everywhere innumerable utensils, numerous sarcophagi half opened and only partially plundered by Abd-el-Rasul and his clan – and mummies! Some forty mummies had been hidden there, including the greatest kings of ancient Egypt: Ramses the Great, Sethos I, Amenophis I, Thutmosis III.

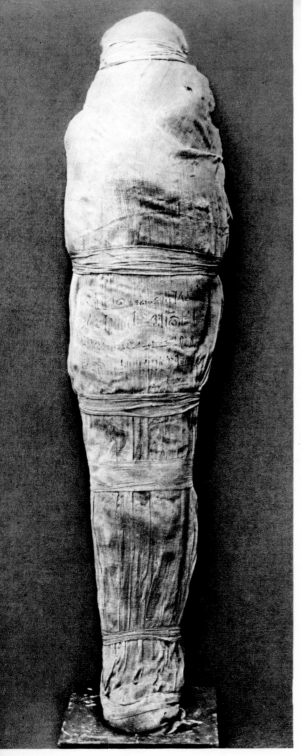

The mummy of Ramses the Great.

This and the following photographs were taken by Emil Brugsch. They are from a group he personally sent to the British Museum, which had them bound and preserved in a volume along with his accompanying letter. These *incunabula* of early archaeological photography have great documentary value. For the condition of the mummies today, after removal of their bandages, has greatly deteriorated since Brugsch first found them.

Ramses II (1301–1234 B.C.), pharaoh of the Nineteenth Dynasty, reigned sixty-seven years and probably reached an age of almost one hundred years. Script can be seen between the second and the third horizontal bandage. The inscription gives an account of the fate of the dead king's body. When its own tomb appeared to be endangered, it was carried to that of King Sethos I, and after further wanderings was finally transferred to its last resting place in the collective tomb where Brugsch discovered it after more than 3,000 years.

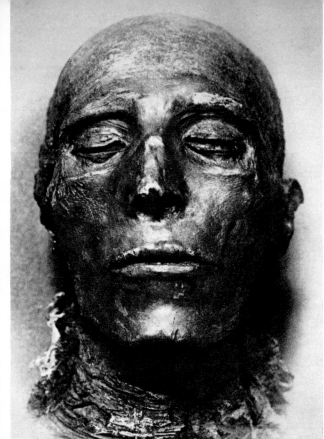

The most uncanny sight

may well have been the mummy of Sethos I (Nineteenth Dynasty, 1320–1301 B. C.), father of Ramses the Great. Its bandages were unwound by Maspero on June 9, 1886. "About the time of Amenophis III", says the Egyptologist K. Lange, "the art of embalming for preserving the cadaver must have reached the height of its development. For the bodies . . . have preserved so much of their original appearance that we must aver we find many persons still living who look more decayed!" This mummy, too, was opened, ravaged and restored. Its first refuge, with Ramses II's mummy, was the tomb of Princess Inhapi. Then both were put with Amenophis I, before entering the common grave.

141

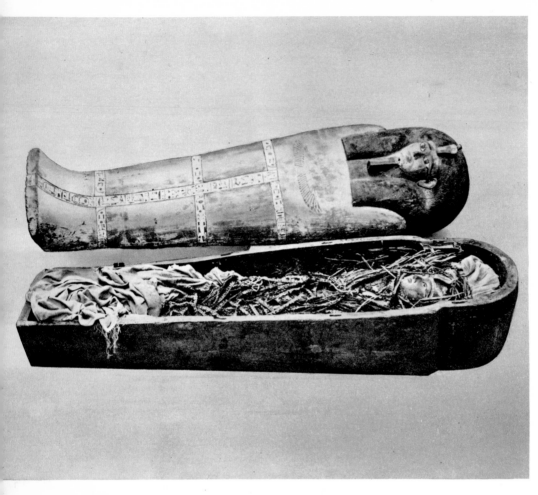

Heaped with flowers –

this was how the mummy of Amenophis I (Eighteenth Dynasty, 1559–1539 B. C.) was found. These flowers were identified as skillfully as the body which they wreathed. They consisted of a type of delphinium, *Acacia nilotica*, *Sesbania aegyptiaca* (a breeding ground for caterpillars), and *Carthamus tinctorious* (safflower). A wasp which had been among the flowers by chance proved to be likewise "mummified".

Although this mummy had been twice plundered in ancient times, its condition was so good that Maspero refrained from unbandaging it, in order not to destroy it.

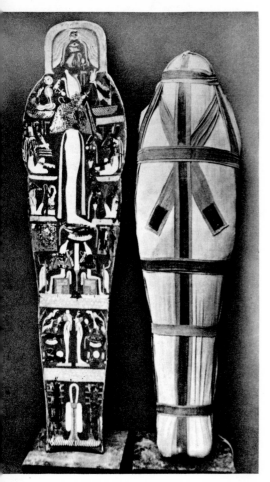

The queen's wig

and the box that went with it (top right), were considered as vital as the lavish meal placed with her in her tomb to equip her for the long journey (bottom right). Her *ka* could take its choice of a leg of lamb, a leg of gazelle, two geese, and a calf's head – all almost as carefully mummified as the corpse itself. Brugsch identified this mummy as pretty little Queen Isimkhobiu, wife of a king of the Twenty-first Dynasty. The mummy is slightly over 5 feet 1 inch tall. It was very carefully swathed, and the interior of the third coffin was richly painted with representations of the dead queen's fine reception by the gods Osiris, Isis and Nephthys. Left: the innermost coffin and the mummy.

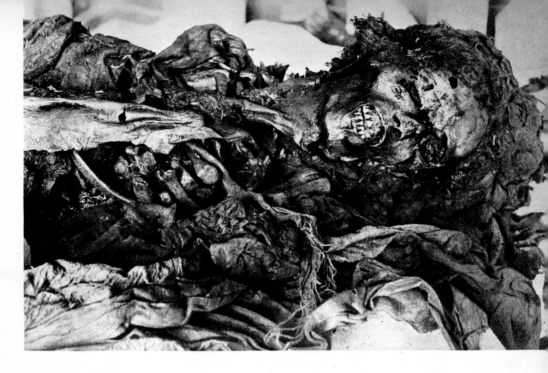

The death agony

is still imprinted upon the pharaoh's shrivelled features. He was Tau-a-quen III, a king of the Seventeenth Dynasty of which we know little. Hence it was a boon to the scholars to encounter a mummy whose state led to certain definite conclusions – which may someday be verified by other means, thus filling in some blanks in the historical crossword puzzle.

Dr. Grafton Elliot Smith (1871–1937), the first physician to examine mummies with all the resources of medical knowledge, determined that the king had suffered five severe wounds from spears and battle axes. He had been struck repeatedly on the head. The variety of the weapons suggests that the attack was carried out by several persons. Moreover, he seems to have been embalmed very hastily, in a more or less temporary fashion, immediately after his death. It seems likely, therefore, that he fell on the battlefield.

Such Sherlock-Holmesian conclusions are dangerous, of course. In fact Elliot Smith considers that the first or second wounds may well have been fatal, and therefore suggests that the king may have been assassinated.

Scholarship cannot move ahead without hypotheses. We must attend the day when a new find transforms one or the other hypothesis into historical fact.

V Egyptian Death-Ship

VI Pharaoh Tutankhamen

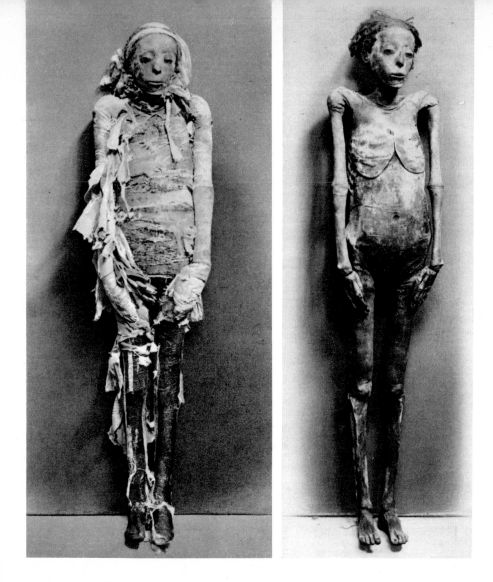

Opinions differ on the best-preserved Egyptian mummy

in so far as anatomists and archaeologists judge the matter from different points of view. Dr. Smith, the anatomist, nominated Princess Nsitanebashru (above) as the best preserved mummy he had ever examined – and he had examined many. At one time in 1903 Maspero sent forty-four mummies to him. Like all pioneers, Smith was resourceful. Placing the mummy of Thutmosis III on the seat beside him, he drove in a hired carriage to a sanatorium near Cairo which

owned the sole X-ray apparatus in Egypt. He was probably the first person who ever looked inside a mummy without destroying it.

Under the withered, leathery skin we can still imagine the living Princess Nsitanebashru. Her brown hair was once waved, and her manicured finger-nails and toe-nails testify to her careful grooming. The scepticism of those full, arched eyelids and high forehead, the arrogance of that hooked nose, the extraordinary protruding lips, almost apish in quality, suggest that this was a woman of deep licentiousness ... But enough of such speculations, which scientists justly abhor. These are matters for the historian and the poet. That history and poetry at their finest must be identical, cannot be said too often.

146

**Some of the earliest
painted portraits,**

that is to say, the first attempts to depict individuality with the brush –
were found on the small plaques
which, during Egypt's Roman
period, supplanted masks as face-
covers for the mummies. Our reproductions also show the high
elaboration given to the mummy
bindings at the beginning of the
Christian era. The Greek boy (left)
who was found at Hawara in Fa-
yum seems to have been treated with
the utmost care. But by this time
mummification had already become an empty form. Its religious
content had been lost. Consequently, the aim ceased to be
preservation of the body itself, but
representation of that body's outer
appearance during life. An even
better example of this is the mummy
of a boy shown on the right. It is also
of the Roman period. The shroud
is painted; the dead boy holds a
bunch of flowers in his hand. This
is no longer mummification, but
trickery – an illusion produced by
a skillful painter. This picture has
not been published before.

This is the mummy of Wah,

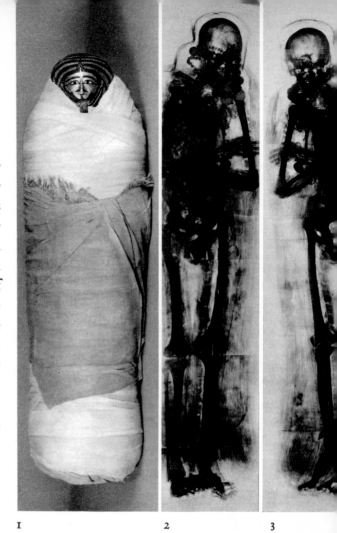

one of the estate stewards of Chan-cellor Meket-Re (Eleventh Dy-nasty, about 2000 B. C.). It was discovered in 1920 by H. E. Win-lock, the head of the New York Metropolitan Museum's Egyptian expedition, in the western part of Thebes, at the foot of the chan-cellor's tomb. The position of the body and the inscription identi-fying Wah as a steward led the diggers to the conclusion that there would be no precious orna-ments hidden with him. Thus the mummy arrived, still wrapped, at the museum, where it stood for fifteen years. In 1936, however, Elliot Smith's example was fol-lowed: the mummy of Wah was X-rayed. The first X-ray photograph yielded a sensational surprise.

1. Wah's mummy as it was found, wrapped in an enormous linen cerecloth which bore traces of having once been dyed red.

2 and 3. The X-rays reveal that the body of this "poor, simple steward" was bedecked with orna-ments. Photograph No. 2 shows strings of beads at the level of the ear, others between arm and chest. No. 3 indicates the presence of a heavy necklace.

4. In 1940 scholars began the unwinding process. Removal of the cerecloth revealed more fully the mummy's plaster mask.

5. After removal of many bandages and much padding, the first layer of the chemical preparations appeared: a conglomeration of resinous substances which had turned quite black.

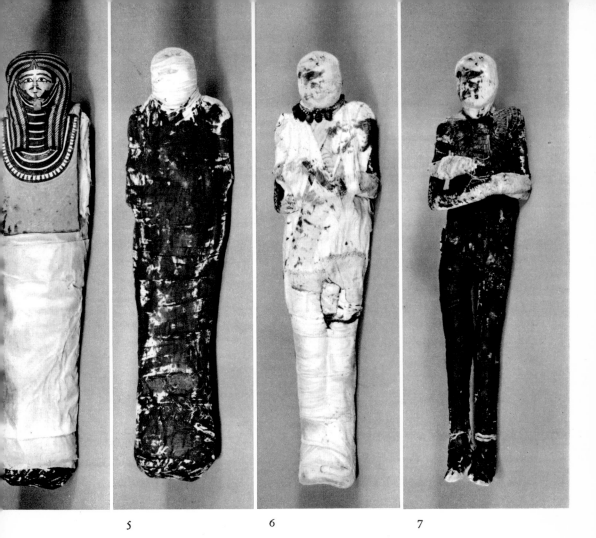

5   6   7

6. Along with this layer of hardened gum, another dozen bandages were removed, exposing the first ornaments at the mummy's neck. A total of 450 square yards of linen was unwound!

7. The bandaged body itself appears. The rich ceramic necklace was only slightly dislodged in the course of some 4,000 years. Further examination of this steward who had been buried at his master's feet yielded silver and gold ornaments, four large reproductions of the sacred scarab, two made of massive silver, one of lapis lazuli and one of blue faience, and sets of beads of various precious materials.

Mummified animals,

that is to say, mummified gods. Innumer-able animals were worshipped as divini-ties in Egypt: bulls, falcons, cats, croco-diles, among others. Whole cemeteries of sacred animals have been found – the most famous of these being, probably, the cemetery of the Apis bulls, which Mariette discovered. Animal cults were usually local; they took on greater im-portance only in the later period of Egyptian history, under the Ptolemies. Hence they should not be considered typical of the religious life of Egypt at its peak. Even the Apis bulls, which were mummified and entombed with in-credible pomp, did not reach the pin-nacle of their glorification until the Eighteenth Dynasty.

Above, crocodiles, one wrapped and one unwrapped. Right, a cat mummy from Abydos, and a mummified falcon, the embodiment of the god Horus.

Today women archaeologists

are honoured members of the profession. (Our picture shows such a lady examining a late-period mummy.) In the last century they were still a great rarity. Young Sophia Schliemann, who helped her husband so actively at Troy, was considered a phenomenon. Lady Flinders Petrie, who also accompanied her husband, became something of a myth in the Arab countries. Today women lead expeditions of their own. The American archaeologist Hetty Goldman dug in Anatolia. At Karatepe a young Turkish woman, Halet Çambel, was in sole command of a crew of thirty Turkish labourers for an entire season. Since 1953 Theresa Goell has been directing an American expedition that has been excavating the outdoor temple tomb of Antiochus I of Commagene (ruled about 69–34 B. C.) on the summit of Nemrud Dagh, in south-east Turkey, some 6,500 feet above sea level. A dozen other examples might be listed.

Jefferson Caffery, former American ambassador in Cairo and inveterate visitor of Egyptian excavation sites, has made some interesting comments on this question. Caffery had grown quite accustomed to the habit of the Egyptian workmen of welcoming every stranger with a friendly song. But one day, when he appeared on the site accompanied by two ladies, he was somewhat startled to be saluted with this (in A. D. 1955):

"You beautiful, you sweet creation. Your hair is like the golden rays of the sun. Your eyes outshine the stars, your mouths are like Solomon's ring, and your teeth are more beautiful than the best of pearls ... When you walked in as though angels were carrying you, your silken clothes waved in the breeze, and you looked like the daughter of the moon. Your ear-rings and bracelets of gold, your necklaces of precious stones, are beyond compare, and you rustle your beautiful ornaments as does the horse of a rich prince!"

Caffery observes dryly: "As I recall, the ladies wore simple clothing and little jewelry. But tradition is stronger than fact, and they graciously accepted the compliments."

We mention this incident in order to compare these tributes with a love-song of the time of Thutmosis IV, more than 3,350 years ago. The reader may make his own surmises as to the relationship between these two texts:

"With high throat and shining breast, she has hair of real lapis lazuli; her arms surpass those of the goddess of love, her fingers are like the cups of the lotus. With solid loins and narrow waist, she – whose thighs dispute each other's beauty, who walks with noble carriage when she steps upon the earth – she steals my heart with her greeting. She makes all men turn their heads to look at her ... When she stepped out of the house, it was as if we saw the one and only One ..."

VII A Dead Man's Prayer

VIII Entrance to the Tomb of an Egyptian Queen

Almost a thousand years after

the last mummifications in the old religious tradition, a mummy like the one above was embalmed – in about A. D. 400–500. The eye-sockets were sealed by the age-old technique, and the same resinous substances were employed to preserve the body. We show the face of the so-called Thaïs (see page 134) which was discovered in 1900, placed first in the Musée Guimet, and then transferred, as of purely anthropological interest, to the Musée de l'Homme in Paris.

No less than forty pharaohs' tombs

in the Valley of Kings were already known to the Greeks. This valley was the original resting place of all those kings whom Brugsch found in the mass grave at Der-el-Bahri. The first modern account of the valley was given by an English traveller named Richard Pococke, in 1743. He, too, spoke of bands of robbers who made the valley a dangerous place for strangers.

Above is the vestibule to the headquarters set up by the Robert Hay expedition

(see page 97). The tomb is probably that of Ramses II. The pencil drawing of
the interior, by E. W. Lane, shows the archaeologists relaxing in picturesque Oriental style in the antechamber of the tomb. The three men in fezzes
are Lane, James Burton (Haliburton), and either Bonomi or Catherwood.

Then came Belzoni's discoveries, and those of many other diggers – plundering
parties, for the most part, such as accorded with the nineteenth century's
collecting mania. Layard (see page 235 ff.) candidly stated that his aim was "to
obtain the largest possible number of well-preserved objects of art at the least
possible outlay of time and money."

Nowadays the Valley of Kings is a tourist mecca. It harbours more than sixty
tombs. In one of these, open now to sightseers, a find was made with direct
bearing on the foremost archaeological sensation of the twentieth century.

"Pick something special to show to a VIP" –

that was the word passed down to Edward Ayrton, head of the Theodore
Davis Expedition digging in 1908 in the Valley of Kings. Luckily, Ayrton
had just dug up a number of large storage jars. The first of these – position of
find marked by the arrow in our photograph – had contained a charming face
mask. But when he opened the others under the eyes of Sir Eldon Gorst, the
distinguished guest, he found nothing but "trifles" – some carefully wrapped
chemicals, a few cloths, simple utensils, and several wreaths of once fresh
flowers. The consul general thanked him for an excellent dinner and gave no
further thought to the finds he had been shown, thereby ignoring one of the
most dramatic clues in the history of modern archaeology. For these "trifles"
had served, about 3,250 years earlier, for the embalming of Tutankhamen, the
king who for reasons not yet determined was buried in greater splendour than

156

any ruler, before or after him. Ayrton put the finds aside, although they bore the seal of Tutankhamen and therefore should have alerted him to the presence of a royal tomb in the vicinity. Eventually they reached the Metropolitan Museum in New York, where they were also ignored. No account of them was published until 1941, fifteen years after Tutankhamen's tomb had been opened (the site of which Sir Eldon had passed unaware), the whole world standing agog. H. E. Winlock, constrained, because of the war, to "dig" in the museum rather than in Egypt, finally reported on them. In this manner a connection was established between this "routine" find and the greatest discovery in archaeology.

The age of discovery in the Valley of Kings was past.

That was the general opinion among professionals in 1914, when Lord Carnarvon took over the Davis expedition's excavation franchise and engaged the British archaeologist Howard Carter to conduct new excavations for him. War conditions prevented their beginning until 1917. In 1919 and 1920 they unwittingly dug in the immediate vicinity of Tutankhamen's tomb. But they ceased work there and dug at another spot, in a lateral valley – dug for two winters without success. Pledging themselves to devote only one more winter to the Valley of Kings, they went back to where they had begun several years before. In November 1922 they plunged their spades into the ground again – and found the entrance to the tomb of Tutankhamen.

Thereafter the excavation was a tense drama of rising hopes alternating with crushing disappointments. The rubble-strewn passage lying behind the entrance, led Carter to believe that here at last was the realization of the dream of all Egyptologists: an unviolated royal grave, a mummy that had never been pillaged. But then he recognized that seals of various periods had been applied to the door; hence others had been here before him. Presently he reached a narrow tunnel that robbers had made long before. But when Carter broke through the second sealed door and flashed a lamp into the dark chamber beyond, he was so shaken by the sight before him that for a while he was unable to speak. The chamber contained whole piles of precious objects, all thrown higgledy-piggledy. Robbers had certainly been here, but for reasons unknown they had obviously plundered very little or not at all.

Right: view of the antechamber. Carter replaced the sealed door with a strong iron grill.

The contents of this antechamber

provided such extraordinarily vivid information on an epoch of Egyptian life that any single piece would have delighted an archaeologist who had spent a whole winter's digging to find it. But here lay hundreds of objects, from simple utensils to the most luxurious ornaments. In the left foreground we see parts of the young king's war-chariot. It later posed a difficult problem in restoration, since the harness leathers had dissolved into a slimy mass. Here stood (on the right) couches such as had never been found before: gilded, inlaid with ivory, fashioned into fantastic sacred animals. The rear was an elongated, rhinoceros-headed lion, the front some form of cattle in panther skin. In addition there were chairs, tables and storage chests. In the strange cases beneath the couch were ducks and other foods. The most artistically surprising, resplendent and

at the same time most precious piece in this motley assortment was the king's throne, with Tutankhamen and his wife depicted on the back rest.

It is easy to understand why the discoverer of such treasures went wild with excitement when he found a sealed door in this antechamber, and a hole in the wall behind one of the couches. The hole proved to be the entrance to a small annex. When it had been widened, Carter crawled in and raised his flash-light. The cone of light played upon a new wealth of treasures, strewn indis-criminately about the room. Here the robbers – this seemed the obvious explanation – had been surprised, and forced to flee without their booty.

Confronting a third sealed door, which appeared untouched, the archaeologists looked at one another with a single wild surmise: Was the king's mummy laid to rest behind this door?

28

Lord Carnarvon (left) and Carter (right)

at two-fifteen on the afternoon of February 17, 1923, about to open the third sealed door. George Edward Stanhope Molyneux Herbert, Fifth Earl of Carnarvon (1866–1923), sportsman, yachts-man, immensely rich collector of art, and Howard Carter (1873–1939), a student of Petrie's who had been excavating since 1899, formed a good team. Lord Carnarvon's controlled enthusiasm paired well with Carter's cool scientific precision. Consequently, the excavation of the tomb was conducted with unprecedented care.

The stones were pried apart with an air of solemn ceremony. Some twenty persons attended. Carter, working with pedantic deliberation, made an opening in the wall large enough to permit the introduction of a flashlight. While the on-lookers waited in breathless silence, he peered through the hole. He saw what seemed to be a wall of solid gold. It was, as it turned out, the front of a tremendous gilded shrine. This shrine contained a second gilded shrine, with an un-broken seal covering the bolts! Although the archaeologists stood before the most precious golden treasure to come down from antiquity, that small unbroken seal was of more staggering significance to them. It meant that the innermost shrine must contain an undamaged mummy!

Inside the second shrine stood a third, inside the third a fourth – all sheathed with gold. In the fourth shrine stood a yellow quartzite sarcopha-gus, about 8 feet 10 inches long and 4 feet 10 inches high. Would it contain the mummy?

Who was this king

who had literally been enshrined in gold?
Here is the first bust of Tutankhamen, which was found at the entrance to the tomb at the very beginning of the excavation. The head is of painted wood. In accordance with tradition, the neck rises out of a lotus blossom, like the young Sun God rising out of the waters.
It is almost incredible, but this king, who was buried with such unprecedented pomp, was remarkable solely for having died and been buried – as Carter himself commented. He reigned around 1350 B. C., was the son-in-law of Amenophis IV, otherwise known as the "heretic king" Ikhnaton, and probably his son, too. He was married very young and died, according to anatomical evidence, at the age of eighteen. Probably we shall never learn why this particular royal youth should have received so magnificent a burial. How utterly fantastic that burial was, the archaeologists did not discover until the sarcophagus was opened. By then the project had become such a sensation that the world's newspapers carried every latest development in banner headlines.

The ropes and pulleys groaned

as the thirteen hundred pound granite lid

of the sarcophagus rose into the air. Layers of linen cloths appeared. But when these were removed, the dazzled onlookers beheld a golden face encrusted with gems: the pharaoh's image.

All sorts of circumstances cropped up to hamper continuous progress. It was not until 1925–6, by which time Carnarvon was dead, that Carter proceeded to open these sarcophagi. For there was not one sarcophagus; inside the first rested a second (as often an image of the king as Osiris), and inside the second a third. This third displayed another golden face, surrounded by a collar of pearls and flowers which still retained something of their erstwhile colours and could be botanically identified.

The third coffin, shown here, was of solid gold, woven through with flower wreaths of pearls! And inside this precious coffin rested the body of the pharaoh, untouched by the robbers, exposed to the light of day for the first time in 3,270 years. Alas, it was badly eaten by the excess of oils and resins the embalmers had used.

bequeathed us by the artists of the New Kingdom. Three of four golden statuettes are shown here; Neith, Isis and Selquet. They stood in the small annex, watching over the heart and internal organs of Tutankhamen.

It was a great pity that the pharaoh's mummy should have been in so poor a state. But this was a small disappointment when set against the amazing plenitude of other finds, whose artistic and scientific value is altogether inestimable, and whose purely material value has to this day not been fully calculated. The value in gold of the innermost coffin alone has been reckoned at around 64,000 pounds.

The principal finds, such as the chairs and the chariot, have been reproduced innumerable times. For that reason, in the following illustration we show some of the minor finds, of which hundreds upon hundreds were discovered in the tomb and on the king's mummy.

The king wore seven bracelets on his right forearm,

six on the left. Above: appearance of the bracelets at the time they were found; right: the bracelets after cleaning. They are of gold, semi-precious stones and glass beads. Eight of the thirteen are amulets; the Eye of Horus occurs on five bracelets; the scarab – betokening the protection of Isis and Re – on three.
The photograph also conveys something of the grossly decayed condition of the mummy, which made the cleaning an extraordinarily tedious and difficult process; parts disintegrated when barely touched by a sable-hair brush. Nevertheless, the position of the arms crossed over the chest is quite plain. On the

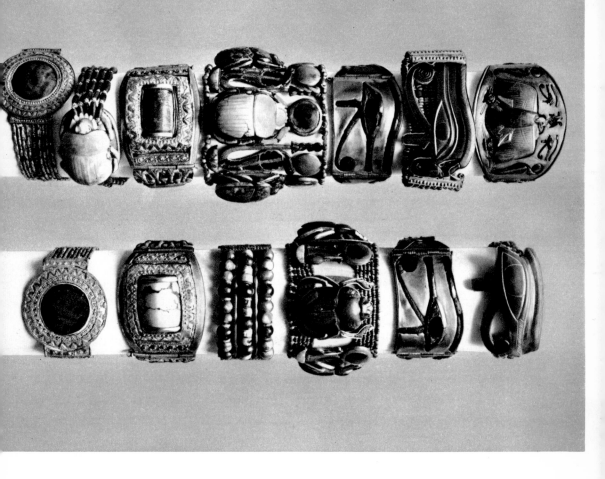

little finger of the right hand (upper left hand corner of photo) can be seen one of the golden sheaths which protected the fingers and toes. The round "shield" is the border of the gold mask covering the king's head and shoulders. Tutankhamen's grave was a treasure trove in every sense. Archaeologists could now see and handle a multitude of objects whose existence had hitherto been only deduced from texts and paintings.

On the following pages we leave behind the ornateness of a pharaoh's life and death and catch a glimpse of the existence of the average Egyptian.

offer an answer to the ever recurring question of how the Egyptians could have transported enormously heavy stone objects. It records the transportation of a twenty-two foot high alabaster statue of Prince Thuti-hotep (Middle Kingdom). Extensive study has taught us that reliefs of this type are for the most part amazingly precise in their data. Thus we are justified in assuming that the size of the crew shown in this picture was not determined arbitrarily. The artist has included 172 figures, which must correspond approximately to the facts.

The statue is lashed with ropes to a wooden skid. Cushions protect the delicate alabaster, wherever the ropes might damage it. Four other ropes serve as tow lines; eighty-eight labourers draw on these lines. The operation is directed by the overseer, who is stationed on the statue's knees, beating the rhythm of "pull and slack" with his hands. An assistant overseer amplifies the sound of the clapping hands by striking wooden mallets together. In the prow of the skid a worker stands pouring water on the roadway, to diminish friction. Three water-carriers are supplying him. Three workers stand ready to thrust a notched beam under the skid when a rough piece of ground is reached. Behind them stand three overseers, accompanied by twelve assistants. Sixty soldiers in six groups, armed with clubs and lashes, escort the party. In other words, the number of actual workmen, counting the overseer on the knees of the statue and his assistants, is $88 + 6 + 3 = 97$. This proportion is surprisingly in accord with Petrie's estimates of the numbers employed in building the pyramids. He estimated that eight workers would have sufficed to move one of the largest blocks in the Great Pyramid – a weight of more than two and a half tons – into any desired position.

According to Herodotus, the cutting and setting of the blocks required about twenty years. Petrie estimated that there are 2,300,000 blocks in the pyramid, but this is a rather arbitrary guess, because no one knows how big the rock core of the pyramid is. From this he concluded that during the annual spell of forced labour from late July to early November – the time of the Nile flood, when the farmers were not otherwise occupied – some 120,000 blocks were transported. From the size of the workmen's barracks, traces of which he found, he estimated that from 3,600 to 4,000 men were quartered in them. If we

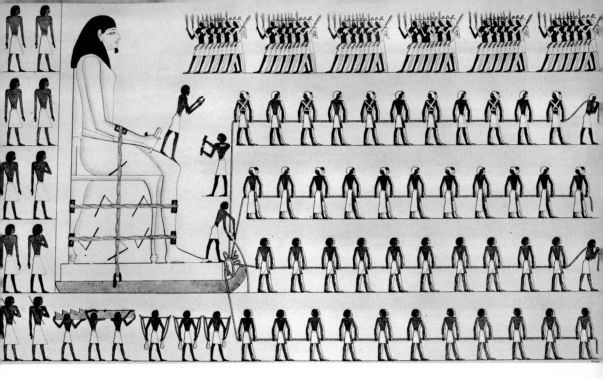

assume that these were professional stonemasons who laboured the year round, then it is possible that with the means at their disposal a team of four men could prepare ten blocks a month. Therefore 4,000 men could handle during a year's work the 120,000 blocks transported in the summer and autumn. Work on the pyramids was organized in military fashion. The largest unit was of 800 to 1,000 men. Each of these units immortalized itself by chiselling its name into the stone. We know, for example, that the company called "The white crown of Khufu is mighty" worked on the Great Pyramid. One of the Third Pyramid companies was named "Men-kau-Re is drunk."

Every company was divided into four "watches" whose nautical designations such as "Stern Watch" and "Bow Watch" suggest that they were derived from the Nile boatmen. Each watch consisted of 200 to 250 men. These watches, finally, were subdivided into groups of from ten to fifty men known by animal names such as "Antelope Group" or "Ibis Group".

If we consider, then, the vast hordes of workers employed, it becomes clear that the ancient Egyptians by no means performed superhuman feats.

Note: Readers may be impelled to check the count of figures in the illustration. I therefore assure those who attempt to make their own reckoning that (excluding the statue) there really are 172 figures depicted: 79 face left and 93 face right.

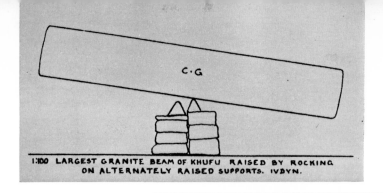

1:100 LARGEST GRANITE BEAM OF KHUFU RAISED BY ROCKING
ON ALTERNATELY RAISED SUPPORTS. IVDYN.

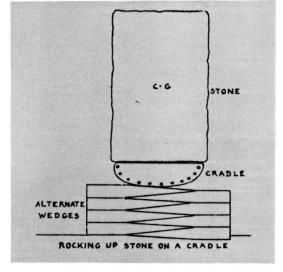

ROCKING UP STONE ON A CRADLE

**What implements and
techniques did the
pyramid builders have?**

Today we know that they were familiar with the lever, the roller and the inclined plane. They had pickaxes and copper chisels, plumb-lines and carpenters' squares. They knew the trick of driving wooden pegs into chiselled holes, then pouring water continually upon the pegs until the swelling of the wood cracked the rock away from its cliff. Whether they knew the use of block and tackle remains a moot question.

These diagrams from Petrie's *Egyptian Architecture* show the extremely simple devices by which the Egyptians could move the greatest weights. In the upper diagram we see how even granite beams twenty feet long can be raised with comparatively little effort by supports applied close to the centre of gravity (C. G.). The lower diagram shows another method, better suited to upright blocks. The stone is mounted on a rocker base, and as it is swung from side to side wedge-shaped supports are slipped under it alternately from each side. Once it starts swinging it is easily kept in motion by its own momentum.

172

Stonemasons at work

with wooden mallets and copper chisels. This drawing is a copy of portions of wall-paintings in the grave at Thebes of Rekhmara, last chancellor of Thut-mosis II. The paintings were done some time after 1445 B. C. By way of explaining the sometimes staggering feats of the Egyptian builders, we should point out another factor which has been overlooked until quite recently. This is the workman's psychological relationship to the work demanded of him. Present-day sociologists have rediscovered, rather than discovered, not only that such a relationship exists, but that it can be accounted a distinct and calculable factor in production on a large scale. Today, in the age of social welfare, strikes and union contracts, apparently inhuman tasks which ancient civilizations required of the labourer may well seem unfair. But the moment we see this relationship between the workman and the work in its historical context, we are forced to realize that feats which today seem so prodigious were in those days accepted as a matter of course. The great monuments were not always the product of forced labour. The ancient Egyptian worker would not have thought in terms of "exploitation". He might have objected to his hours and to the conditions of his work, but he would not have protested against the physical feats he was expected to per-form.

In this connection Goneim in *The Buried Pyramid* (see page 128) tells a story that demonstrates how the workman's attitude, combined with those technical tricks which are fostered by necessity, can result in astonishing feats. Speaking of his Egyptian workers, Goneim writes: "They work among the monuments which their ancestors built, and it would seem that some of the ancient skills have descended to them; for instance, an extraordinary facility in moving heavy objects with little mechanical assistance. An English friend told me how he watched with some amazement and trepidation the moving of a granite colossus in the Cairo Museum, a statue weighing perhaps a hundred tons. 'A few wiry little chaps in *gallabliyehs*', he said, 'gathered around the statue with iron levers and a few baulks of timber. There was an awful lot of shouting and heaving, the thing began to rock and catastrophe seemed im-minent. I felt like shutting my eyes and stuffing my fingers in my ears, but in a short time the colossus was shifted several yards and ended up in its new position quite unharmed.'"

Very likely European or American workers would have re-fused to touch the pillar without heavy equipment. Indeed, they probably would have asserted in good faith that such a monster could not possibly be moved without the aid of modern machinery.

Not toys but images of life itself –

so the Egyptians of the Middle Kingdom looked upon the little houses and
ships, peopled with men and animals, which they deposited in their tombs
along with the dead. Indeed, these clay and wood models were supposed,
according to the Egyptian faith, to transform themselves ultimately into genuine
workrooms and work people who would serve the dead man as he had been
served in his lifetime. The Egyptians' stress on accurate representation has
afforded archaeologists knowledge of their most intimate domestic institutions,
their crafts and their commercial life. The clay figurines in the wooden box
enact work in a granary during the Middle Kingdom.

Almost equally informative are the little ships of the dead,

which were often found in pairs. One was to carry the dead man through the heavens, one through the underworld. The upper model shows the shipment of a mummy, accompanied by a priest, protected by the goddesses Isis and Nephthys; it comes from a Middle Kingdom grave in Thebes and dates from about 2000 B. C. The vessel below is a rich man's yacht; it too comes from Thebes, from the tomb of Meket-Re, a chancellor of the Eleventh Dynasty.

The soil of a country which has harboured three millennia of rich civilizations is inexhaustible. On May 26, 1954, a death-ship was discovered in the course of road work close to the Great Pyramid – that is, in a spot where not a square inch of the land had not been explored and probed countless times. Kamal El-Malakh, director of all excavation work at Gizeh, discovered it, and it was dug out by the archaeologist Zaki Nour. No small model, this was a beautifully formed ship, 120 feet long, built for a Fourth Dynasty pharaoh. The wooden parts are well preserved, the ropes, with which the pharaoh was to be tied down for his long journey, were still intact. Above: a drawn reconstruction.

An archaeological find is meaningless in itself.

Its significance is all in the interpretation. Modern archaeologists can take pride in knowing more about ancient Egypt – the life of the masses as well as of the elite, the thought and beliefs of the average man as well as those of the educated minority – than did the Greeks who were two thousand years closer to them in time.

In addition to paintings and narrative reliefs, scholars find a wealth of information in the innumerable papyri that have been recovered. All the great museums in the world now possess specimens of these. The reproductions on pages 178–9 show "pages" from the so-called *Egyptian Book of the Dead*, whose original title, *Per-em-hru* has been translated into English as *The Book of Coming Forth by Day*.

Both the script and the illustrations are executed with great neatness and care. And the sheets are so well preserved (the manuscript reached the British Museum in 1888) that it may be considered one of the finest examples of Egyptian papyri. The entire papyrus contains 190 chapters, which deal in detail with the Egyptian cult of the dead. Three chapters are shown here. In one square we see the jackal-headed god Anubis, the heavenly embalmer, performing his office. To the left of him kneels the goddess Isis, sister and wife of Osiris and mother of Horus. To the Egyptians she was the kindly goddess of love and motherhood. During the imperial age of Rome she was ascribed demonic powers and her cult, which had in the meanwhile acquired many strange and unsavory rites, had to be suppressed by force in A. D. 560. Opposite Isis kneels Nephthys, her sister and the sister of Osiris, who bore to Osiris the god Anubis.

Egypt was opened up for archaeology in 1798 with the Napoleonic expedition. At that very time travellers were visiting a neighbouring country and bringing back accounts of strange ruins. The land between the Euphrates and the Tigris was not explored by archaeologists until long after the Egyptian monuments were widely known. Yet this was the land which figured more in the Bible than any other, and where was reared an edifice which has remained a symbol to this day: the Tower of Babel.

III

Book III

PIETRO DELLA VALLE

THOMAS HERBERT

JEAN CHARDIN

ENGELBERT KÄMPFER

DE BRUIN

CARSTEN NIEBUHR

GEORG FRIEDRICH GROTEFEND

CLAUDIUS J. RICH

ROBERT KER PORTER

HENRY C. RAWLINSON

FRANCIS CHESNEY

PAUL EMILE BOTTA

AUSTEN H. LAYARD

HORMUZD RASSAM

ROBERT KOLDEWEY

LEONARD WOOLLEY

The Tower of Babel,

of which we read in Genesis xi, 4: "And they said, Go to, let us build us a city and a tower, whose top may reach unto heaven; and let us make us a name..." But then "the Lord came down..." and He confused their tongues and "scattered them abroad from thence upon the face of the whole earth..." Babel, which originally meant "gateway of God", became the synonym of confusion.

Herodotus, the Greek historian, and Ctesias, the personal physician of Artaxerxes II, King of the Persians in about 450 B.C., have described the building. It has exerted endless fascination over men's minds, has remained for poets and painters the symbol of human arrogance. As Pieter Breughel the elder (1525–1569) renders it, it is a structure of sinister complexity and mystery, while in the

French miniature of 1423 (from the *Duke of Bedford's Book of Hours*), it is an exalted pleasure pavilion. In reality what the Babylonians built was not a tower, but a pyramid-like brick structure 288 feet square and 288 feet high, with seven terraces, crowned by a temple which Marduk, the great god of Babylon, was said to favour with his presence. The Babylonian ziggurats, as these step pyramids were called, were not tombs like the Egyptian pyramids; they were temples built for the nation, and as such were not allowed to fall into neglect. Only a few fragments have been found of the "tower" mentioned in the Bible, for it was destroyed several times. Nabupolassar and Nebuchad-nezzar rebuilt it in about 600 B.C., and made it greater than ever, "grounding its base securely upon the breast of the underworld". Xerxes the Persian (485–464 B.C.) destroyed it once again. Alexander the Great, on his way to India, paused in admiration before the ruins; he set first 10,000 men and then his entire army to work cleaning up the rubble. Empires rose and fell; sand drifted over the Babylonian remains, until nothing was left but the legend of this building whose pinnacles had strained upwards to the skies. Twenty-two centuries had to pass before someone came to dig and discover what had truly existed.

Robert Koldewey's excavations of Babylon will be discussed later in this book. For Koldewey, though the excavator of the Tower of Babel, was not the actual rediscoverer of its site.

Coment on edifia la tour de babiloine. et le langage fut mue en .lx. ij. Langueges. et les anges la despartirent.

until well into the nineteenth century, to follow the ancient pilgrims' route through Venice, Cairo, Sinai, Palestine and along the borders of Mesopotamia as far as the Tigris and Euphrates – those waters of Babylon by which the Jews once wept when they remembered Zion. But again and again bold individuals found their way to the spot, impelled by – by what? "What is the purpose of this toiling in a distant, inhospitable, dangerous land?" asked Friedrich Delitzsch (1850–1922), the great German Assyriologist and philologist, in his famous lecture *Babel und Bibel*. "What is the reason for this expensive churning up of rubble that has lain undisturbed for many thousands of years, for this digging down as deep as the ground water, with no hope of gold or silver? . . . What is the basis of this ever-mounting, world-wide interest in the excavations in Babylonia-Assyria?" His climax was one calculated to fire the minds of our fathers and grandfathers: "To both questions there is one answer: . . . *the Bible!*"

The first travellers to bring back fresh accounts from the lands which figure so gloriously and terribly in the Bible were adventurers, some rich and some poor, some learned scholars and some ignorant curiosity-seekers. The reports of these discoverers, most of them men of the seventeenth century, conjure up an exotic and forbidding scene:

"It may still be seen . . . but is so decayed and in ruin that it is of no height at all, and the ground is everywhere for about half a mile so full of vermin that no one dare go near . . . Among these vermin are especially small beasts which in the Persian are called . . . *Eglo*, and are very poisonous; they are larger than lizards and have three heads . . ." Such is the account given in 1582 by Leonhard Rauwolff, a physician and botanist of Augsburg, ten years after he had visited the place.

In similar vein, George Mainwaring writes in 1598 of "the Tower that Nimrud built . . . It standeth in a wilderness, and so many wild beasts be about it that a man cannot come near to it by two miles or more; but it may be seen plainly".

However: "I made a complete circuit of these ruins," reports the first traveller of the seventeenth century, in which men of the West began to feel an ardour

186

for digging up their past. "I climbed to the highest point, walked all over the crags and made a detailed examination." The traveller who wrote this was Pietro della Valle (1586–1652).

This picture was first published in 1679 by Athanasius Kircher in his learned work, *Turris Babel*, and purports to be based on the observations of "Petro a valle" (see scroll at the top of the picture). The Pietro whose authority was thus appealed to was an Italian nobleman who, rejected by a lady whom he had wooed passionately for years, set off on a pilgrimage to the Holy Land. From there he rode off into the desert and fell even more passionately in love.

Der Zierde Babylons sohier wird vorgestellt
Ist ihres gleichen nicht zu finden in der Welt:
Sie hat eins Mannes Herts und spricht den
Lastern Hohn
Darumb gebuhrt ihr auch der Tugend Ehren
Kron.

Pietro had difficulty in curing her of wearing a nose-ring.

Sitti Maani was a bewitching Nestorian Christian girl from Baghdad.
In 1616 Pietro married her. She became for Pietro the same inspiration that the lovely Greek girl Sophia became for Schlie, mann centuries later: not only a wife, but an assistant, a brave and indefatigable companion on journeys that soon became legendary. This ideal partner, ship lasted only five years; then Maani died from a fever re, sulting from a miscarriage. Pietro brought her body back to Rome for burial.

All in all, Pietro della Valle spent some twelve years travel, ling in the East, venturing as far as India and Goa. In 1626 he returned permanently to Europe. A first volume of his account of his travels, *Viaggi di Pietro della Valle il Pellegrino*, was published in 1650; two further volumes appeared six years after his death, in 1658. They had a profound effect upon the mentality of Europe.

Pietro was the first European traveller in the East with a scientific point of view and the first to describe the ruins of that legendary metropolis of the Persians: Persepolis. His books are more valuable for their descriptive than their pictorial material, for he used for illustration copies of drawings by other eye, witnesses. A period of twenty, four years intervened between the end of his travels and the publication of his first book. Meanwhile others had followed his footsteps to Persepolis, and had not waited so long to publish their view of it.

188

The first "view" of Persepolis

"From this room is a stately prospect of all the Plaines thirty miles about it. The ascent to this is cut out of marble Rockes, the staires (reserving their durance and beauty to this day) are ninetie five, and so broad that a dozen Horsemen may ride up abreast together ... The breadth of the Gate is sixe of my paces, the height of each side or Gate (engraven with a mightie Elephant on one side, a Rhynoceros on the other) thirty foot high, very rarely cut out of the marble, fixt and durable for ever."

Instead of attempting to convey this overall grandeur, the artist concentrated on reproducing all the details furnished by the traveller's text – details altogether false because they were seen in classical and Biblical terms. Thus a rearing

189

Pegasus appears amid the ruins of Persepolis and elephant and rhinoceros are presented as tidy little sculptures, not as reliefs. The traveller was Thomas Herbert, who found the artist's work so unsatisfactory that for the third edition of his book he had the drawings done anew by Wenzel Hollar, the famous landscape artist. Hollar gave a sense of the splendour and spaciousness of the ruins, but his work, too, left much to be desired.

Thomas Herbert (1606–1682) set out on his first journey to the East in 1626, a penniless boy of twenty attached to the retinue of two profit-hungry diplomats, Sir Robert Sherley and Sir Dodmore Cotton, whose sad end is described with notable brevity in the *Dictionary of National Biography:* "They then visited Mount Taurus and Casbin, where Cotton and Sherley died." Herbert coolly and simply concludes his report: "at Kazvin ... where we left our two ambassadors in their grave, the Shah sent each of us two long mantles or coats of gold brocade, as a sign of his favour." Three years later he returned home via Ceylon, and served Charles I as chamberlain. He remained so unflinchingly loyal to the king until, and beyond, Charles's execution that Charles II knighted him.

Persepolis was the capital

of one of the mightiest empires of antiquity. Cyrus (559–529 B. C.), Cambyses (529–522 B. C.) and Darius I (522–486 B. C.), starting from the existing king‐doms of the Medes, the Lydians, the Chaldeans and Egyptians, absorbed Iranian principates extending as far as the Indus, took over the politically chaotic coastal countries of Asia Minor and forged all this into a great Persian empire that extended from Cyrenaica in Africa into Europe as far as the Danube. For two centuries that empire governed the destinies of the ancient world.

The City of the Persians (*Parsa* in Old Persian) was the metropolis of this immense empire. Darius I founded Persepolis as a fortress on an enormous artificial terrace. The site is colossal; only the latest excavations, undertaken for the Oriental Institute of the University of Chicago between 1930 and 1940 by Ernst Herzfeld (1879–1948) and Erich F. Schmidt (born 1897), have revealed the tremendous wealth of buildings. The royal palace contained vast treasure and countless works of art – one of the early travellers speaks of more than 2,000 reliefs. It was set on fire by Alexander the Great after the Battle of

Gaugamela (331 B. C.), in which he overwhelmingly defeated Darius III. Ancient writers relate that the razing of the palace was an act conceived in drunkenness and arrogance.

Our picture shows the first view of these ruins which was actually drawn on the spot – the artist being a young French merchant, André Daulier des Landes, who accompanied the explorer Jean-Baptiste Tavernier from 1664 to 1666. He drew these ruins in 1665 and published his work eight years later.

It would be wearying to list examples of the many copies of this one drawing; the seventeenth century was not scrupulous about artistic or intellectual property. But it is amusing to observe the peregrinations of the small rider in the foreground from copy to copy. Almost every copyist included him, but each placed him in another spot.

After these last examples some reader may ask why we should reproduce pictures so obviously faulty by the light of present knowledge. There are three reasons. First, these drawings abound in quaint details which have a charm of their own. Second, matching these early "views" with later, scientifically inspired pictures of the same scene offers dramatic proof of the progress of scientific archaeology. We can actually *see* how the first tentative sketches necessarily proceeded from wholly inadequate accounts, and with what painful slowness scientific reports developed out of fabulous narratives. And the third reason is the respect due to the men themselves, who were driven to far places by an insurmountable craving for knowledge, and who almost always risked their lives to bring home these first tidings; they pioneered the path to the sources of our civilization.

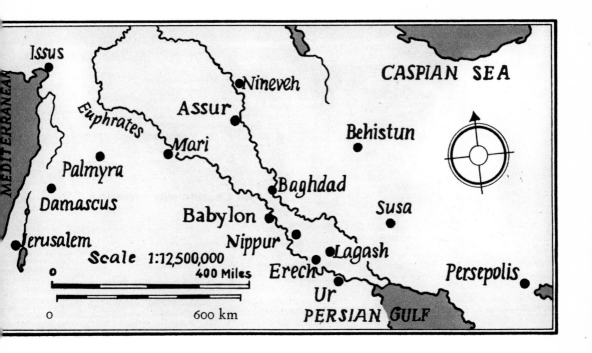

Blood-soaked soil.

The simple-hearted historical maps of the past place the Garden of Eden in Mesopotamia. The map above is modern. Whether or not it was here that Adam toiled and Eve span, and mankind had its cradle, it was very likely the cradle of human civilization. Here emerged the earliest scripts, the earliest architecture, and the earliest sciences. Here the Sumerians and their successors, the Babylonians and Assyrians, founded the first states. Egyptians and Persians invaded them; rarely did peace prevail in these lands which nevertheless gave birth to the religion of peace and good will. Here the road travelled by Abraham still winds across the plain, and here the teaching of Mohammed took hold and spread. Here was the world of the "Arabian Nights", the world of Harun-al-Rashid. Here Greeks, Romans and Arabs ruled; and through this gateway passed all the trade and bustling commerce between Orient and Occident. Buffer land, occupied land, border land – Mesopotamia has always been in upheaval, down to the present day.

Jean Chardin was a jeweller.

Born in Paris (1643–1713), he went to Baghdad in 1666. Thence, as Sultan Soliman III's gem expert, he was sent to India, and returned to Paris in about 1670. On his first journey, perhaps, he had been nothing but a man seeking worldly success by adventurous routes. But on his second he manifested a lively interest in the history, languages and monuments of Persia. As it happened, in 1666, *Philosophical Transactions*, the journal of the Royal Society, then the most important body of scholars in the world, had queried: "Whether, there beeing already good Descriptions in *Words* of the Excellent Pictures and Basse Relieves, that are about *Persepolis* at *Chilminar*, yet none very particular; some may not be found sufficiently skill'd in those parts, that might be engaged to make a Draught of the Place, and the Stories there pictured and carved?"

When Chardin arrived in England in 1681, after much voyaging, he was knighted, appointed court jeweller, and elected a Fellow of the Royal Society. He had provided an answer to the Royal Society's challenging question.

This was the reception given a distinguished European traveller

in about 1666 by one of the lesser Persian potentates. The viceroy of Tiflis, Kanavas Khan, held this feast in honour of Jean Chardin. The scene is the princely banquet hall, 110 feet long and 40 feet wide. Chardin is seated in the foreground on the left, accompanied by Capuchin monks. The Khan is presiding at the other end of the huge pavilion. Before the feast he had received several presents from Chardin: a watch, a rock crystal mirror framed in silver, an enamelled gold box for his opium pills ("most Persians take these pills several times a day") as well as a handsome set of surgical instruments.

Many archaeologists' reports testify to the importance, and the often disconcerting features of Oriental hospitality to this day. The field archaeologist must be not only a scholar, but a diplomat and man of the world as well. He must hold his own with cabinet ministers as well as with bands of rioting workmen. Frequently the success or failure of an expedition is decided at a banquet!

One hundred and two
pounds
and a few shillings

posthumously bought not only this picture but also the complete manuscript left by Engelbert Kämpfer (1651–1716), a German physician who had returned from his travels in Persia with an amazingly accurate sketchbook. The purchaser was Sir Hans Sloane, avid English collector whose bequest formed the beginning of the British Museum.

Of all the early visitors to Persia, Kämpfer was the first to anticipate the spirit of the coming century. He was the first to speak of the artistic value of the discoveries, and again the first to mourn the senseless destruction of antiquities. Speaking of the portals to the throne room of Xerxes in Persepolis, he wrote: "These gates are decorated with most elegantly sculptured reliefs, and offer a most outstanding example from which to understand the excellence the arts had attained in those ancient times." And he adds: "One must deplore the criminal act of the tyrant who caused the main portions of these images to be defaced, as well as the ravages wrought by the centuries passing over them, in the course of which most of the lintels and part of the door-jambs were broken, apart from those carried off . . . for private use by those living nearby."

The strange world of the East

was extraordinarily difficult for men with Western eyes to render. That fact emerges clearly from the reproductions on this and the next page. Above is the very first representation of the human-headed winged bull which guarded Xerxes' gates at Persepolis. It seems almost incredible that this unfortunate and stilted engraving was made by a professional draftsman who had been at the site; but so it was. It was by Chardin's draftsman, Guillaume Joseph Grélot, who had accompanied Chardin and who worked from Chardin's sketches.

Contrast such crude work with the drawing by Cornelis de Bruin (1652–1726/7) on the next page. De Bruin, we may well say, had the first critical mind among the early travellers. He reproduced the lineaments of the original with almost photographic faithfulness. Moreover, he left blank those portions of the sculpture which were broken, instead of filling in with fanciful details of his own. Now we take for granted such striving for exactitude; in de Bruin's time it was eccentric for someone to wish to depict what he actually saw.

De Bruin consciously stressed his critical approach and took issue with the copying, "restoring" and pure plagiarisms current at the time in his pamphlet, *Remarks of Cornelis de Bruin on the Plates of the Ancient Palace of Persepolis*

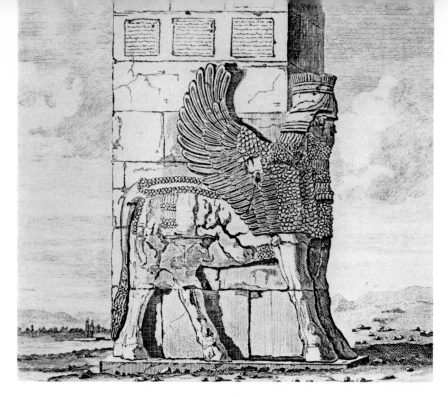

Published by Sir John Chardin and Mr. Kempfer, "in which their faults and lacks are clearly shown", and in his *Travels over Muscovy, through Persia and India*, where he commented: "I can affirm, too, that I have drawn with my own Hand, and immediately from the Life, all the Plates, now presented to the Public, without having recourse to any ancient Authors who have described *Persepolis* and its Antiquities, and without adding or diminishing one Particular . . . I might say much the same of *Persia*, and the august Ruins of the Ancient Palace of *Persepolis*, of which several travellers have published Descriptions, without due Examination of what they saw. For which reason their accounts have more the air of Romance than of any Reality, or complete Knowledge of those fine Antiquities . . . not to be obtained without pains."

With Cornelis de Bruin we come to a new phase in the advance of archaeology. For not only did he bring back the first reliable descriptions of the world of the Orient; he also brought back not the first, but the first *legible* cuneiform texts in as accurate a transcription as could be had at the time. Studying one of these transcriptions, the German school-teacher Grotefend hit on the solution for deciphering cuneiform script. A fantastically bold hypothesis, it was the first step in the West's penetration of the thought of the ancient East.

annoch nicht begreiffen kan.

Es mögen nun dieses gleich blosse Buchstaben / oder gantze Wörter gewest seyn / so habe ich fünff derselben/ die ich in dieser Schrifft
am öfftersten gesehen/ und gefandt/so gut/als
mir müglich gewest / abgeschrieben. Weil
es aber gantze Zeilen gewest / so kunte ich nicht
wissen / ob man diese Buchstaben / nach der
Orientalischen Völcker Gebrauch / von der
rechten / zur Lincken / oder aber / auf unsere
Weise / von der lincken zur rechten Hand
schreiben müsse. Die fünff Buchstaben nun/
die ich auffgezeichnet / waren folgende.

Der zweyte Buchstabe aber / welcher in Unbekandte
vier Strichen bestunde/ worunter drey gerad/ Schrifft.
und unten zugespitzt / der vierte aber über-
zwerch darüber gesetzt war / gab mir ein An-
zeichen / daß sie / auf unsere Weise / von der
lincken zur rechten Hand geschrieben werden
können; alldieweiln das Obertheil an diesen
Strichen / wie an allen andern Buchstaben
zu sehen / breit ist / und wann sie gerad sind/
M 4   allzeit

From right to left or from left to right?

These are the first five signs in cuneiform script that reached Eu-
rope. They were transcribed in a letter from Pietro della Valle to his friend Schipano in Naples, and later appeared as the sole illustration in the first printed edition of these letters.

The substance of Pietro's letter, dated Shiraz, October 21, 1621, is most interesting. His first question was the very one any decipherer must pose when confronted by an unknown script: In what direction are the figures to be read? A
clay tablet presents many possibilities – not only right to left and up and down;
a widespread mode of writing, used for example by the Hittites, was the fashion
later called *bustrophedon*, which means "as the ox turns in plowing",
namely ⇥ , so that the first line is read from right to left, the second
from left to right, the third like the first, and so on.

Remarkably enough, Pietro immediately deduced correctly from the position
of the wedges that the script was written "in our manner, from left to right",
as he puts it on the page reproduced here.

His transcription is not accurate. And he could not guess that by chance he
had selected a group of signs which, as we know today, forms part of the
Achaemenidean title "king of kings" – the very inscription which some 180
years later allowed a German school-teacher to decipher cuneiform script.

This is how cuneiform script struck the first Europeans to set eyes on it. Some called it "nail script", but a good many persons, among them serious scholars, denied that it was a script at all. Unlike the Egyptian hieroglyphics, cuneiform script had already been forgotten in classical times. Herodotus barely mentions it as *Assyria grammata*. Yet cuneiform script had been diffused far wider than hieroglyphics. Along the whole of the eastern Mediterranean coast, in the empire of the Hittites in Anatolia, in the land of Urartu in the Armenian mountains, in south-western Iran and as far as the land of Elam, many languages adopted cuneiform script for their writings. It was a vital script at the time of the Persian Great Kings.

The apparently hastily done transcription reproduced here is in fact an amazing prize. This first long example of a cuneiform text comes from Engelbert Kämpfer's sketchbook. After his long journey through Russia, after crossing the Caspian Sea and after months of vain attendance at the shah's court in Isfahan – the shah refused to help him, claiming that the astrological signs were unfavourable to the venture – Kämpfer reached Persepolis in 1685. Events did not permit him to remain longer than three days amid this vast congeries of ruins. During those days he laboured feverishly, forgetting to eat, drink or sleep, making innumerable notes and sketches. Later he was fully conscious of the value of what he brought home. His pride rings out in his aside: "My un-inspired engraver has not succeeded in rendering the beauty of this lettering, for he has not given it the proper spacing which makes the characters stand out distinctly. I mean by this, that my own copy of the inscription which served as model to the engraver, is far more accurate." But then he admits, still over-whelmed in memory as he recalls his toil: "In truth the copying of this single tablet made such a unthinkably lengthy job, particularly as the place is so high up which makes the sun most obnoxious, that I was forced to give up the idea of copying the others ..."

A man who had not only a keen eye, but an astounding organizing ability, brought home the next cuneiform texts. He was a Dane whose books Napoleon always had by him during the Egyptian campaign.

and returned home alone.

Carsten Niebuhr (1733–1815) was a geographer who by no means confined his interests to his specialty alone. Accompanied by von Haven, a philologist, Forskål, a natural scientist, Cramer, a physician, and Baurenfeind, an artist, he set out on an expedition in January 1761. Although they sailed on a Danish man-of-war, it took them almost two years to reach their destination, Yemen. In the course of the following year all the members of the expedition except Niebuhr died. His account of this in his *Reisebeschreibung nach Arabien und andern umliegenden Ländern* (Description of Travels to Arabia and Neighbouring Lands), published in Copenhagen in 1774–8, is certainly singular:

"The scholars ... might surely have expected to bring back much important information on Arabia, if we had remained as long in this country as we intended, and if all had returned. However, we did not arrive in Yemen until the end of December 1762. Mr. von Haven died very soon, on the 25th of May, at Mokha, and Mr. Forskål on July 11th at Yeri, another town in Yemen. After the sudden loss of these two companions, the rest of us decided to go to Bombay aboard the last of the ships that were sailing this year from Mokha to India. On this voyage Mr. Baurenfeind died at sea, near the island of Socotra, on August 29th, and Mr. Cramer on February 10th, 1764, at Bombay. Although death has almost entirely wiped out our company, I do not think that this should deter others from making journeys to Arabia ..."

This curt catalogue of successive deaths brings to mind the children's jingle, "Ten little Indians": "Then there was one". Niebuhr was a cold man but he was possessed of extraordinary intelligence and a gift for observation. It may well have been his youth which brought him safely through the unspeakable hardships of this hazardous expedition, and enabled him to return with such a bag of scientific trophies.

The plate from Niebuhr's book, reproduced here, shows reliefs from Persepolis and six lines of cuneiform signs. Without these, Grotefend, the Göttingen school-teacher, would probably never have succeeded in his attempt at decipherment. For Niebuhr's transcript was not a mere sample of an inscription. With admirable keenness and instinct for the most fruitful line of departure he

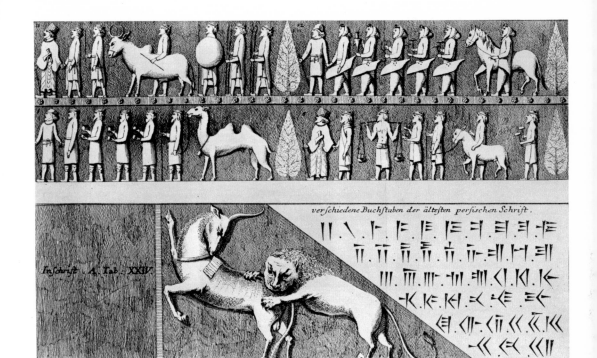

verfchiedene Buchftaben der älteften perfifchen Schrift.

Inschrift. A. Tab. XXIV.

had sorted individual signs out of the numerous inscriptions, and drawn up a list of forty-two characters. (Assyriologists nowadays reckon with thirty-nine basic signs.) Furthermore, solely from the number of signs he correctly deduced that the script must be based on *letters* – that is, it was an early form of alphabet – simply because there were too few signs for syllabic writing. On the other hand, he perceived that there were too many signs for a purely consonantal alphabet; vowels must also be included. And finally – this is the most astonishing feat of all – he recognized that three different systems of writing were represented by the inscriptions at Persepolis. Scholars later named these systems Old Persian I, Elamitic II and Babylonian III. He also made vital observations on ancient geography. While scholars were still assuming that ancient Babylon had been located in the vicinity of present-day Baghdad, Niebuhr stated correctly: "There can be no doubt that Babylon was situated in the neighbourhood of Helle (Hillah)." He established the site of Nineveh with equal accuracy.

To explain the manner by which cuneiform script may be deciphered, we must leap somewhat ahead of the state of knowledge in Niebuhr's day.

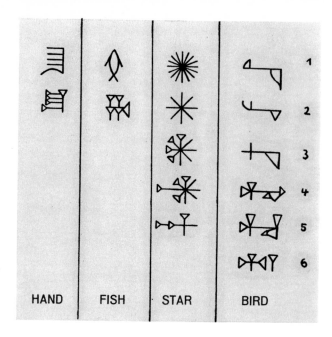

| HAND | FISH | STAR | BIRD |

Cuneiform script developed out of pictures, too.

While this is fairly obvious in the case of Egyptian hieroglyphics, cuneiform writing seems at first glance quite another proposition. But the examples above make the evolution from picture to sign quite plain. The five fingers of the sign for "hand" are intelligible enough, as are "fish" and "star". We may not, however, recognize at once that the uppermost sign on the right represents a bird, flying from left to right, since it is already so highly abstract.

A factor making for radical stylization was the writing materials themselves. Egyptians used ink and papyrus; Babylonians impressed clay tablets with a stylus. The more laborious method entailed simplifying the script.

The publication of Niebuhr's *Reisebeschreibung* in the 1770's sent a wave of excitement through the scientific world. More and more scholars pored over cuneiform script. In 1798 a German Orientalist, Olav Gerhard Tychsen, identified an apparently insignificant but highly important sign. It was an oblique wedge which he recognized as the word-divider. He was thus able to insert some order into the apparently endless lines. He also hazarded, quite correctly, that three different systems had been employed for writing three different languages. Friedrich Münter, a Danish scholar, ventured still further in 1802. For historical reasons he maintained that the Persepolitan inscriptions dated from the Achaemenidian period, the era of the Great Kings of Persia, between 500 and 330 B.C. He also advanced the thesis that the trilingual inscriptions contained the same text in three languages.

These were conjectures which turned out to be marvellously apt. In point of fact, these early investigators were voices crying in a wilderness; wrong theories by and large prevailed. The first real decipherer to approach the inscrutable scratchings found the way to a solution blocked by a host of wild theories. His primary task consisted in sifting the few correct hypotheses out of the many that were utterly misleading. He succeeded.

In 1802 Georg Friedrich Grotefend made a wager.

While walking with his friend Fiorillo, secretary of the Royal Library at Göttingen, Grotefend (1775–1853) wagered that he would decipher the cuneiform scripts from Persepolis, if Fiorillo would supply him with the previously published literature on the subject. This daring fellow was twenty-seven, and a mere nobody; he taught at the *gymnasium* in Göttingen and knew scarcely anything about the ancient languages of the Orient. By a stroke of genius this man performed one of the most amazing feats of human intelligence. Not that he became famous thereby; he continued on through life as a schoolmaster without ever again climbing to the chilly heights of intellect which he had scaled at his first youthful attempt.

Unlike Champollion, who had spent over fifteen years in preliminary study of ancient languages before he tackled the decipherment of hieroglyphics,

Grotefend's professional equipment was scanty. The specimens at his disposal were also scanty and he had no way of ascertaining whether these were exact. Above all, he had not one single parallel inscription in a readable language, like the Greek on Champollion's Rosetta Stone. Nevertheless Grotefend deciphered Persepolitan cuneiform script! He set forth his conclusions in three reports. Since the subject was of such high current interest, these were read almost at once before the Academy of Sciences in Göttingen on September 4, October 2 and November 13, 1802. Grotefend himself did not read his papers – how could an obscure young schoolmaster deliver a lecture before that illustrious learned society? But he was honoured by having the above mentioned Professor Tychsen read his reports. Tychsen also published a first account of Grotefend's work in the *Göttinger Gelehrte Anzeigen* on September 18, 1802. It was not until 1815 that Grotefend was given the chance to present a complete account of his decipherment in less transitory form. His summing-up appeared in the appendix to someone else's book, Heeren's *Ideen über die Politik, den Verkehr und den Handel der vornehmsten Völker der alten Welt* (Ideas on the Politics, Communications and Commerce of the Principal Peoples of the Ancient World), at Heeren's own request. Due to a lack of publicity, Grotefend's brilliant contribution fell into oblivion. Decades later Persepolitan cuneiform had to be deciphered anew.

Here is the same text twice,

once in de Bruin's excellent copy (left), and again as re-transcribed by Grote-fend and cast into alphabetical equivalents. Grotefend's method can be presented here only in the most rankly simplified form. For a first step, Grote-fend examined the available texts, including the one reproduced above (In-scription taken from the folds of the clothes of Darius' and Xerxes' portraits. In the heading Grotefend writes Lebrun instead of de Bruin) and reviewed the existing hypotheses. He accepted the thesis that there were three systems of writing, that the content of all three texts was the same, that the inscription dated from the era of the Achaemenides, the Persian kings, and that the single oblique wedge represented a word-divider.

Second step: He decided to begin his solution with Script I, Old Persian, because this was an Indo-European language which might be easiest to crack with the assistance of recent researches in Sanskrit. The character of the script and the site at which it had been found led him to the conclusion that he was dealing with royal inscriptions. Hence Old Persian kings ought to be mentioned by name. He knew some of the Achaemenidian kings from the writings of Herodotus (to this day we are hardly any wiser on the subject than Grotefend).

207

And he set up the premise that the inscriptions began, as such did in New Persian, with a list of generations, thus:

X, Great King, King of Kings, King of A and B, son of Y, Great King, King of Kings ...

Third step: In counting up the groups of signs, he found precisely the repetitions which, according to his hypothesis, must mean *king*. But he also found a new arrangement, namely:

X, King, son of Z,

Y, King, son of X, King.

Here he had worked out, in pure theory for the time being, a distinctive dynastic succession. Father and son had been kings, but the grandfather had not been a king. Now he took the names of known kings and tried to fit them into his scheme. Some were eliminated immediately because the number of letters in their names were too many or too few. After much trial and error, only Darius and Xerxes remained. And they matched, for the father of Darius, Hystaspes, had not been a king.

Fourth step: One great difficulty still remained. Herodotus had given the kings' names only in Greek. But what were the Old Persian forms? There were a great many possibilities. But in choosing among them, Grotefend demonstrated amazing intuition. For although, as we know today, he made many errors, he also found a great many correct correspondences. He interpreted rightly numerous letters, thus laying the basis for his decipherment.

To anticipate: Grotefend deciphered only the Old Persian form of the Persepolitan cuneiform scripts. Decipherment of the Babylonian and Elamite inscriptions – far older forms of cuneiform writing – were matters for professional philologists, as we shall see shortly. "Decipherer and philologist", says Professor Johannes Friedrich, one of the foremost German philologists, "must not be confounded." He pays ample tribute to the genius of the decipherers, but points out that final interpretation and establishment of all the grammatical laws in the deciphered script and language are the business of the pure professional. Grotefend himself, incidentally, had made the same point.

For all that, Grotefend's inspired solution remains immortal. It is one of the incomprehensible whims of history that Champollion won an international reputation while Grotefend was almost ignored.

"It was accidentally

discovered by a director

of the East India Company, that the young cadet was a perfect self-taught master of the Arabic, Persian and other Oriental languages", *The Times* reported in 1804. The "young cadet" was called Claudius James Rich (1787–1821), born in Dijon, France, and taken to Bristol, England, at an early age. He was an authentic child prodigy: while still a boy he acquired a command of Turkish, Persian, Arabic, Hebrew, Syrian and a little Chinese. The East India Company was eager to employ a young man with such linguistic gifts. He was sent to Bombay in 1807, en route passing through Mesopotamia for the first time. In Bombay, though penniless, he won the hand of the eldest daughter of the chief magistrate, Sir James Mackintosh.

Baghdad, where he settled with his wife in 1808, served him as the starting point for many scientific excursions. His first visit to Babylon in December 1811 lasted only ten days; the material and observations he brought back from this little jaunt were sufficient to keep scholars occupied for years. With a tiny crew of ten workmen, he had conducted a regular excavation, and reaped a fine harvest of inscribed stones, clay tablets and seals. In 1817 he made a second trip, accompanied by Carl Bellino, a young artist who acted as his secretary. Bellino happened to be a good friend of the schoolmaster Grotefend, who was thus supplied with new texts to study. Rich's two publications, *Memoir on the Ruins of Babylon* (Vienna, 1812) and *Second Memoir on Babylon* (London, 1818), aroused great excitement, and not only among scholars, as a mention in Byron's *Don Juan* (V, 62) indicates. Rich himself commented modestly that his work was but "the first fruits of imperfect research", adding: "I had expected to find on the site of Babylon more, and less, than I actually did . . . I announce no discovery, I advance no interesting hypothesis".

In 1821 Rich was once more in Shiraz. A cholera epidemic broke out. Rich refused to leave the city; he took a hand in nursing the sick and dying, and organized shipments of medical supplies into the city. On October 4, 1821, he too fell victim, and was dead the following morning aged thirty-four.

His collections were purchased by the British Museum for 1,000 pounds, including 800 Oriental manuscripts and 32 cuneiform tablets. Moreover he left behind voluminous writings from which his widow extracted several books, published under his name but with a heavy admixture of her own ideas.

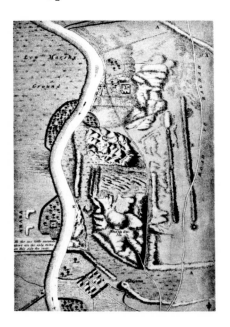

This plan of Babylon exemplifies

the precision of Rich's work. On his first visit to Babylon in 1811 he surveyed the area of ruins on the eastern side of the Euphrates, and had Captain Abraham Lockett, then British military commander at Baghdad, execute the map shown here. Amazingly enough this plan, the frontispiece of his *Memoir on the Ruins of Babylon*, largely coincides with one Robert Koldewey was to make nearly a century later – after he had excavated the ruins.

A painter of battles

gathered new facts about the empires of the Babylonians and Assyrians. Robert Ker Porter (1777–1842), whose once highly admired pictures no one ever looks at nowadays, switched careers, so moved was he by the sublime mono⁄ tones of the Mesopotamian landscape, and by the mute testimony of its scattered monuments. He gave up grandiose painting for painstaking copying. It was through a friend, Alexis von Olenin of St. Petersburg that he came to realize the need for such dispassionate recording. One day in 1817 Olenin showed Porter four drawings by Niebuhr, De Bruin, Morier and Chardin, all of the same carving (see page 212). Comparing the four, Porter's practiced eye at once recognized how strongly subjective differences had influenced the artists in their treatment of the same subject.

Ker Porter must have been a cosmopolitan spirit with a great flair for society. Born in Edinburgh, he was elected a member of the Royal Academy, London, at the age of fourteen, and at twenty⁄three painted his 130⁄foot panorama, *The Storming of Seringapatam*, which created a great sensation. As a matter of fact, this immense canvas is by no means devoid of artistic and technical skill. In 1804 he resided at the court of Czar Alexander I as the official painter of battles. There he fell in love with Maria, daughter of Prince Theodor von Sherbatoff. This was not regarded favourably and he was forced to leave the country. Eccentric King Gustav IV of Sweden knighted him in 1806. By 1811 he had managed to return to Russia, and after the retreat of the Napoleonic army he married his Princess Sherbatoff. His reputation as an artist, his polished manner and his many influential connections brought him a knighthood in England in 1813. By grace of George IV he was thenceforth Sir Robert.

After 1817 he made a journey through the Caucasus to Teheran, Isfahan and

Persepolis. In October 1818 he met Rich in Baghdad. For the next two years he drew and described everything he saw – with sterling accuracy.

On November 18, 1818, Bellino, Rich's secretary, sent a letter from Baghdad to his friend Grotefend in Göttingen, Germany: "On October 13 an Englishman arrived here from Persia. His name is Sir Robert Ker Porter ... His drawings ... surpass everything that anyone in the past has made of these antiquities, in the opinion of Mr. Rich ... Although they differ from those of earlier travellers, I do not doubt that he is concerned chiefly with fidelity to his original ... The drawings which Sir Robert has prepared here of Babylonian cylinder seals and other objects are also uncommonly faithful."

In 1821 Porter published his book, *Travels in Georgia, Persia, Armenia and Ancient Babylonia*. Typhus robbed him of his princess in 1826, and he sought forgetfulness in the New World, assuming the post of British consul in Venezuela. There he painted what has come to be the best-known portrait of Simon Bolivar the liberator of South America. He died of a stroke in 1842 – all in all a remarkable personality, whose biography remains to be written.

Four artists, four different conceptions

Here is the sample Olenin showed to his friend Ker Porter. All four artists had drawn the Naksh-i-Rustam relief, which had earlier been drawn by Kämpfer. It is highly instructive to see the distortions Niebuhr, De Bruin, Morier and Chardin imposed on the selfsame subject. The juxtaposition is itself a nice example of the romantic manner; it is completely in keeping with the spirit of the age, decorated above with two Babylonian inscriptions by two different artists, a cylinder seal, three Greek inscriptions, and finally three different representations of Alexander the Great, from three coins.

IX Goat at the Tree of Life

X Model of a Persian War-Chariot

"The figure drawn up

to explore the interior of the tomb of Darius Hystaspes, is that of Sir Robert Ker Porter himself – a height of sixty feet", wrote his sister Jane. It is amusing to visualize the gentleman‑painter portrayed on page 211 in such a situation – and this in 1818, when there might have been at most a few dozen persons in the world who could understand a man's risking his life for the sake of archaeo‑ logical knowledge.

"The morning was at first stormy,

and threatened a severe fall of rain; but as we approached the object of our journey, the heavy clouds, separating, discovered the Birs frowning over the plain . . . Just as we were within the proper distance, it burst at once upon our sight, in the midst of rolling masses of thick black clouds, partially obscured by that kind of haze whose indistinctness is one great cause of sublimity, whilst a few strong patches of stormy light, thrown upon the desert in the back-ground, serve to give some idea of the immense extent, and dreary solitude, of the wastes in which this venerable ruin stands."

The picture by Ker Porter (the text is by Rich) shows Birs Nimrud, on the Tigris near Mossul, as seen from the west. The diagram Porter presents in the drawing on the right is an inspired piece of deduction, although the height is wrong. Porter reckoned 260 feet; modern archaeologists calculate 140.

"I should suppose the mass we now see to be no more than the base of some

214

loftier superstructure, probably designed for the double use of a temple and an observatory; a style of sacred edifice common with the Chaldaeans and likely to form the principal object in every city and town devoted to the idolatry of Belus and the worship of the stars."

This intuition of the purpose and original form of all Babylonian "towers", the ziggurats, inevitably struck his age as revolutionary. But people were already beginning to ask for more than drawings and narratives. Museums sprang up; originally mere curio-cabinets, they now grew into scientifically classified collections. Their nucleus consisted of sculptures and casts of the Greco-Roman period, but now monuments from the ancient East were in demand. Soon the demand was supplied. A Scottish army officer, defying innumerable difficulties and bad luck, proved the feasibility of transporting such monuments.

"Take your steamship on your back and walk . . .

from the Orontes to the Euphrates."

A Scottish officer disgruntled because he could not participate in the fight against Napoleon, sought a different kind of adventure in the Orient.

Captain (later General) Francis Rawdon Chesney (1789–1872) brooded over the possibility of opening new routes between England and India. After a voyage to Egypt in 1829 he published a report on the possibility of piercing the Isthmus of Suez – a dream that decades later prompted Ferdinand de Lesseps, the builder of the canal, to dub him: "Father of the Suez Canal."

Unable to muster support for the Suez undertaking, Chesney turned his attention to another possible route, and this by chance led him past those ruined cities whose names were soon to be on everyone's lips: Assur, Babylon and Ur. The fantastic route he had in mind was the following: from the Mediterranean near Antioch upstream on the Orontes, then by land to the Euphrates, downstream to the Persian Gulf, and on to India. The wildness of this plan seems obvious. How could ships be transported overland? Moreover, was the Euphrates navigable at all, especially for steam vessels?

In 1830–1 Chesney began investigating the navigability of the Euphrates.

The lithograph reproduced here, from the account of the journey which he later published, shows him, disguised as a Moslem, aboard a raft in the middle of the river. Since he was having difficulties with the Turkish government, he used only two simple instruments for sounding the river and determining the best channel: a pocket compass and a ten-foot pole, which he thrust through a hole in the centre of the raft in order to measure the depth of water. In this way he mapped some 180 miles of river, from Ana to Hit.

Is this not reminiscent of those ancient Egyptian scenes

of a pharaoh's statue being hauled to its final site (see page 171)? The object being moved with so much effort is actually a steam boiler. Chesney had returned to England and spent four years convincing the government that his plan was practicable. Finally the House of Commons made him a grant of twenty thousand pounds. At the shipyard in Laird, Scotland, Chesney built two of the most modern river-steamers designed up to that time. They were iron framed. He then had them shipped in parts to the mouth of the Orontes at Antioch. The overland trip required almost a year. Chesney had a staff of thirteen officers and large numbers of artillery and engineering troops, but only the most primitive equipment. The picture shows the triumphal entry of the last steam boiler into Port Williams on the Euphrates. To the load are harnessed 104 oxen; 52 natives and Chesney's entire company are assisting.

In spite of dire predictions, Chesney and his men successfully reassembled and launched the steamers. The vessels set out on their voyage down the Euphrates. But they travelled under an evil star.

Calamity descended on May 21, 1836.

The two steamers, *Tigris* and *Euphrates*, had passed a number of ruined cities without incident – in his *Narrative of the Euphrates Expedition* (1868) Chesney took careful note of each of them. Suddenly the sky darkened menacingly.

"The weather had been very fine and promising during the forenoon, but a change took place soon after we left Salahyah . . . with the full expectation of reaching Ana that afternoon . . . In the course of a few minutes, dense masses of black clouds, streaked with orange, red, and yellow, appeared coming up from the W.S.W., and approaching us with fearful velocity. To secure the steamers against what promised to be an ordinary strong gale, immediately occupied all our attention, at the very moment that we were arriving at the rocky passage of Is-Geria. Indeed we were already so close to it that there was no sufficient space to round to and bring up: consequently, it became most prudent to steam onwards, the result of which I now give in the words of Mr. Fitzjames: '. . . As soon as the rocks were passed, the *Tigris* made signal to pick up our berth, and she rounded by us to the left bank . . . It was blowing tremendously, and the air so thick with sand that we could scarcely see. On

218

our bow touching the bank, Charlewood and a number of the crew jumped on shore, and by the greatest exertions got an anchor out, which, with the full power of steam, held her till two chain-cables were got out, and secured by means of jumpers driven into the ground; but with all this she dragged, and would have gone down at her anchor had the storm continued – for the waves were then four feet above the bank of the river. When at its height, we saw the poor *Tigris* fall off from the shore and drift past us at a fearful rate, broadside to the wind, and healing over considerably. She soon disappeared in the cloud of sand, but on looking astern, soon after, I saw her in a sinking state, with her bow already under water – in fact going down, and it is believed that, on reaching the bottom, she turned keel upward' . . . Barely 25 minutes had seen the beginning, progress, and termination of this fearful hurricane.''

The *Euphrates* completed her voyage to the mouth of the river.

The adventure bore fruit in two ways: in the first place, the ruins, already known in a general way, were systematically listed, and in the second, the Euphrates was proved to be navigable.

"Arise", the Lord said to Jonah,

"go to Nineveh, that great city and cry against it; for their wickedness is come up before me." Next to Babylon and Sodom, no city of the ancient world has so impressed itself upon the mind of the Christian West as the epitome of urban arrogance and rampant luxury, as a nest of all vice, as has Nineveh. This is, of course, the Bible's doing.

The first European to recognize the site was Carsten Niebuhr (see page 202). In March 1766 he was on the way to Mosul.

"Heading westward for Mosul, we must first ride through Nineveh . . . I did not learn that I was at so notable a spot until I was close to the river. Here I was shown a village on a large hill, which is called Nunia, and a mosque in which the prophet Jonah lies buried . . . Another hill in this vicinity is called Kalla Nunia or the castle of Nineveh. Upon this eminence is a village named Koinsjug (Kuyunjik). At Mosul, where I stayed close by the Tigris, I was also shown the walls of Nineveh, the which I had not noticed in passing through, thinking them a line of hills. Afterwards I sketched a plan of all these points." (1. The mosque with the grave of Jonah. 2. The village of Nunia. 3. The walls of Nineveh. 4. Mount Ain Safra.)

Here, in the nineteenth century, Mesopotamian archaeology was to be born.

XI Persian Drinking-Horn

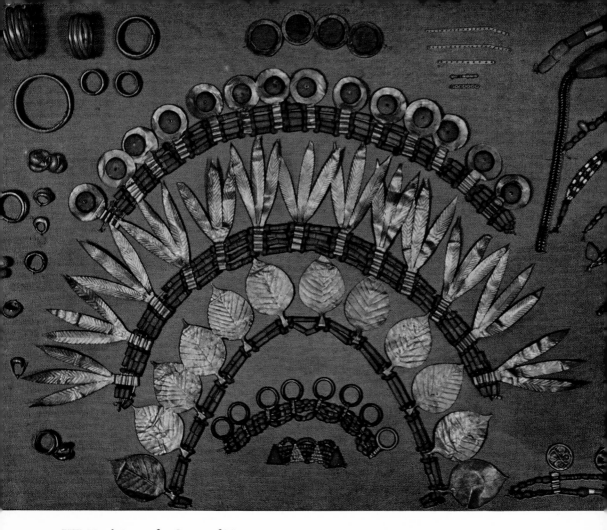

XII Head-Dress of a Queen of Ur

The unearthing of such Assyrian reliefs

suddenly brought Europeans face to face with an advanced civilization whose existence no one had hitherto suspected. For these sculptures dug up in and around ancient Nineveh by a French physician were extraordinarily beautiful, although their beauty had a rigid and alien quality. One could see at first glance that they represented the art of a highly sophisticated people.

The French doctor was Paul Emile Botta (1802–1870). As a young man he had toured the world. Then, after an interlude in the consular service at Alexandria, he was appointed consular agent in Mosul in 1842. Botta could not resist the lure of the sand-drifted mounds. In December 1842 he began to dig at a mound near Kuyunjik which was later to yield astounding treasures – but not to him. He gave up there and tried anew at Khorsabad, ten miles away. And here luck was with him from the start. Like a magician's hat producing rabbits, the earth disgorged reliefs, statues, winged bulls with faces of bearded men. The outlines of a tremendous palace came to light – the Palace of Sargon (about 710 B.C.) of whom the prophet Isaiah speaks.

Botta went on digging like a madman, despite refractory conditions. His government began to send him funds, and when he asked for an assistant "capable of preparing drawings", he was fortunate in being given Eugène Napoléon Flandin (1809–1876). This brilliant draftsman not only made copies; he saved the finds for posterity. For when those wholly unique alabaster figures were brought into the sunlight for the first time after thousands of years, the delicate stone began to crumble. And Botta himself did them further violence. Paris had been begging to see some of the actual sculptures, instead of mere drawings. In order to transport the gigantic blocks of stone, Botta actually had each of them sawed into six pieces! Then the worst disaster of all took place. The first large shipment, loaded onto crude rafts known as *keleks* for floating down the Tigris, were caught in raging rapids. The gods and kings of Assyria, but newly recovered, were lost once more in the depths of the river. But Botta was not a man to give up easily. A new shipment was assembled, the problems of river transport mastered, and in May 1847 Europe saw the art of Assyria exhibited for the first time at the Louvre.

We cannot overlook the fact that Botta's methods in Khorsabad made his excavations mere plundering operations like those of Belzoni in Egypt. Science, nevertheless, was to benefit indirectly from the shabby treatment accorded to this pioneer. For instead of promoting Botta, an ungrateful French government transferred him to a less important post in Syria. Thus the way was cleared for a successor who was to work far more carefully.

In Botta's day,

and for some time afterwards, the techniques of transporting such mighty loads across desert country and on unpredictable rivers were scarcely more advanced than they had been in the first millennium B.C. Victor Place (1822–1875), who succeeded Botta at Khorsabad, handled the task far better. He did not saw the sculptures into pieces, but took the bold step of shipping the colossal statues (one winged bull weighed 32 tons) in one piece, on specially constructed wagons and with the aid of hundreds of natives (see picture on left). But he, too, suffered disaster on the river. Of the hundreds of pieces of sculpture ultimately excavated from the 209 large chambers and the 31 hallways and courtyards of Sargon's palace, 235 were finally shipped off on specially constructed *keleks* (above). But at the mouth of the Tigris and Euphrates the *keleks* were attacked by hostile Arabs; hundreds of irreplaceable works were lost, and only twenty-six reached the Louvre at last on July 1, 1856.

In the meantime, scholars and the public alike were becoming increasingly eager to know something more about these mighty monuments. This meant a reading of the inscriptions. And the same year that Botta began his excavation – 1843 – an Englishman, unaware of Grotefend's labours, deciphered cuneiform script for the second time.

223

Two remarkable examples of Assyrian art

The king hunts: reliefs from the gatehouse of the Palace of Assurbanipal at Nineveh, brought to the British Museum by A. H. Layard. The king, accompanied by his guard, pours sacrificial oil upon the lions he has slain.

The relief on the left shows wild asses attacked by dogs, and beset by hunters' arrows. What range of style these two scenes comprise. The artist has given the figures in the sacrifice scene that hierarchic stiffness which the Assyrians considered the due of such solemn subjects. In the other plaque the artist obviously rejoices in the grace of animals leaping and running so lithely and freely. For all the realistic details, the treatment is not simple realism; one feels the vastness of the plain where the animals dwell, one hears the clamour of the hunters pursuing the frightened beasts. A supreme facility, a mastery of artistic form, is evident here. No wonder these Assyrian reliefs stirred the hearts of those men of the nineteenth century who were seeing them for the first time after twenty-five hundred years. Their beauty and power is still intact.

225

To copy an inscription,

a young British army officer named H. C. Rawlinson had himself lowered from this cliff at Behistun in 1837. Robert Ker Porter, who drew the picture, could detect the lettering only by means of a telescope, and could barely make out the contours of the tremendous relief, whose subject he arbitrarily and wrongly identified as "the ten tribes before Shalmanesar".

The relief is in fact a self-glorifying representation of Darius, King of the Persians (521–485 B.C.), chiselled into a 2,000 foot cliff along the ancient caravan route running from Hamadan to Kermanshah in Persia. To dangle from a rope more than 300 feet above the floor of the valley and work slowly along the 60-foot length of the relief, copying with extreme accuracy completely strange writing – this we can certainly term an extraordinary athletic feat. Yet the scientific feat which resulted was even more impressive.

The carved figures in the photograph on the right (which suggests the vast height of the relief) are completely surrounded by the massive inscriptions.

226

"I had excellent health,

was in the heyday of youth, had tremendous spirits, was distinguished in all athletic amusements ... and had the whole world before me."

So Henry Creswicke Rawlinson (1810–1895) described the period of his lieutenancy in India, when he and his comrades of the First Grenadiers spent their time in "running, jumping, quoits, racquets, billiards, pigeon-shooting, pig-sticking, steeple-chasing, chess and games of skill". But he also occupied himself incidentally with far more serious matters. On the four-month voyage to India, he made the acquaintance of Sir John Malcolm, the governor of Bombay, who was not only a soldier, but an Orientalist and linguist. "It was, without doubt, an enormous advantage to the lad of seventeen to be associated with the 'Historian of Persia', whose tales of his battles with the Mahrattas, and his experiences amongst the Persians, probably fired Rawlinson's youthful imagination, and gave that bent to his tastes which resulted in his subsequent choice of a career", comments a biographer.

When Rawlinson was transferred to Persia in 1835, on a purely military mission, he found his own true work awaiting him at the cliff of Behistun and immediately went far beyond Grotefend's readings. He was fortunate in having the actual texts before his eyes; Grotefend had only transcripts, and by no means good ones. Moreover Rawlinson was a person who could make the most of his opportunities, as is shown by his copy of the Behistun inscription, as well as by his sketch of the whole panorama (below).

Military duties interfered with his work on the inscriptions for eight years, and it was not until 1843–4, when he was appointed British consul-general at Baghdad, that he could concentrate on his studies. In 1846, he published *The Persian Cuneiform Inscriptions at Behistun*, in which were presented *translated* inscriptions that properly won him the epithet: "Father of Assyriology".

Rawlinson later occupied a high place in the Council of India. But he never lost his passion for penetrating the secrets of cuneiform script. Nor was he ever at a loss for problems, since thorny new and old ones awaited solution.

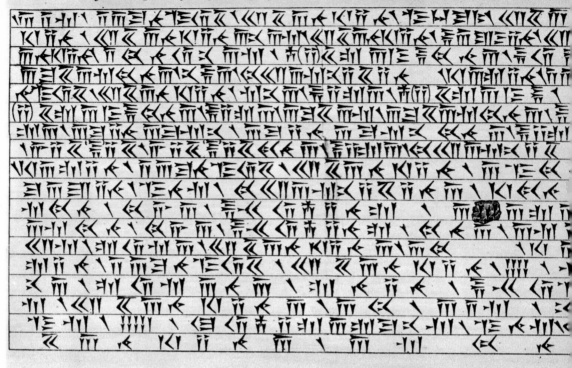

Rawlinson's transliteration and Latin translation (right)

of one of the smaller inscriptions at Behistun (above). We will recall that Grotefend, too, chose to decipher the text which held the greatest number of clues, the
Old Persian text called Class I. But there were also Classes II and III. And
while Rawlinson was fighting indolence and corruption as reorganizer of the
Persian shah's army, and later while he was pursuing a highly dangerous life
as a political agent in Afghanistan and Turkish Arabia – all this without ever
neglecting his hobby, cuneiform script – other scholars were doing their utmost
to crack the still undeciphered scripts. Prominent among them were Burnouf,
Lassen, Hincks, Oppert, Norris, and Löwenstern.

An extremely confusing and difficult situation arose. The following quotation
gives us some idea of the dilemma of the cryptologists. In 1850 Rawlinson
wrote resignedly: "I will frankly confess, indeed, that after having mastered
every Babylonian letter, and every Babylonian word, to which any clue existed

in the trilingual tablets, either by direct evidence or by induction, I have been tempted, on more occasions than one, in striving to apply the key thus obtained to the interpretation of the Assyrian Inscriptions, to abandon the study altogether in utter despair of arriving at any satisfactory result."

Similarly, in the same year the Irish scholar Edward Hincks asserted that in Babylonian cuneiform script there is no sign which stands for a consonant alone; rather, each sign stands for a consonant plus a preceding vowel, or a consonant followed by one.

Rawlinson once again underscored the confusion in 1851, writing: "It can be shown beyond all possibility of dispute, that a very large proportion of the Assyrian signs are Polyphones – that is, they represent more than one sound." "Polyphonic" signifies that the same sign in cuneiform script might be read in several different ways, and given the most various meanings, depending on its context in a word or sentence.

When Rawlinson first advanced this theory of polyphony, there was a loud outcry from the professionals. It was not long, however, before the Royal Asiatic Society of London settled the disputes in a singular manner.

OF THE INSCRIPTION AT BEHISTUN.   XXiii

DETACHED INSCRIPTIONS.

MARKED A.

. Adam . Dár(a)yawush . k'hsháyathiya . wazarka . k'hsháya
  Ego   Darius,   rex   magnus;   rex

thiya . k'hsháyathiyánám . k'hsháyathiya . Pársiya . k'hsh
        regum;   rex   Persidis; rex

áyathiya . dahyunám . Vishtáspahyá . putra
           provinciarum; Hystaspis   filius;

Arshámahyá . napá . Hak'hámanishiya . Thátiya . Dár(a)
Arsamis   nepos; Achæmenensis,   Dicit   Da-

yawush . k'hsháyathiya . maná . pitá . Vishtáspa . V
rius   rex;   mihi   pater   Hystaspes;

ishtáspahyá . pitá . Arsháma . Arshámahyá . pi
Hystaspis   pater   Arsames, Arsamis   pa-

tá . Ariyáram(a)na . Ariyáram(a)nahyá . pitá
ter   Ariaramnes;   Ariaramnis   pater

. Chishpish . Chishpishahyá . pitá . Hak'hámanish
  Teispes;   Teispis   pater   Achæmenes.

. Thátiya . Dár(a)yawush . k'hsháyathiya . awahya
  Dicit   Darius   rex;   eá

rát'iya . wayam . Hak'hámanishyá . thahyá
ratione   nos   Achæmenenses   ap-

mahya . hachá . par'uviyat . amátá
pellamur; ab   antiquo   invicti(?)
                               [oriundi(?)]

amahya . hachá . par'uviyat . hyá . amá
sumus;   ab   antiquo   quæ   nos-

k'ham . tumá . k'hsháyathiyá . áha . Tha
trum   stirpe (erat,) reges   fuere.   Di-

tiya . Dár(a)yawush . k'hsháyathiya . ma
cit   Darius   rex;   mei

ná . tu'máyá . tyiya . par'uwa
     generis (sunt) qui   prius

m . k'hsháyathiyá . áha . adam . na
    reges   fuere;   ego   no-

wam . 9; . dhuvitátaranam . wayam . k'h
nos (sum)   diutissime   nos   re-

sháyathiyá . amahya
ges   sumus.

2

231

XLIII. (vii. 49).

Hincks.   **Oppert.**

Son of grandson of Asar-dayan,
who bore the sceptre of the rising
of the star Taspir (?), who asked
from (or, owed to) the great gods,
the mankind of Bel-Dagon, that
is the work of his hands, and the
formation of his fingers, and who
walked (in the right line) afterwards and formerly:

XLIV. (vii. 55).

Fifth descendant of Ninip-pallu-kin, the king of the commencement, the pupil of Asur, whose
power grew over his land like a
pine (?); who founded the first,
the army of Assyria.

XLV. (vii. 60).

At that time the house of Anu
and *Iv*, the great gods, my lords,
which in former days Samsi-*Iv*,
champion of Assur, son of Ismi-
Dagan, *champion* of Assur, and so
forth, built; for 641 years it went
on decaying. Assur-dayan, king
of Assyria, son of *Ninip-pal-içr*,
king of Assyria, and so forth,
threw down that house and did
not rebuild it. For a period of 60
years its foundations were not
laid.

Then the house of Anu and Ao,
the great gods, my lords, formerly
Shamshi-Ao, sovereign of Assyria,
son of Ismi-dagan, sovereign of
Assyria, built it; 641 years
elapsed in the cycles of time, then
Assur-dayan, king of Assyria, son
of Ninip-pallu-kin, destroyed this
same temple: he did not fear to
deface the names (?); but its
foundations were not attacked.

In 1857 a sealed envelope

was laid upon the desk of the Royal Asiatic Society: the translation of an
inscription of Tiglath Pileser, King of Assyria, by W. H. Fox Talbot. In the
accompanying letter Fox Talbot made the unusual proposal that the text be
submitted also to Rawlinson and Hincks (later the Franco-German scholar

XLIII. (vii. 49).

Rawlinson.

The glorious offspring of Ashur-dapur-Il, who held the sceptre of dominion, and ruled over the the people of Bel; who in all the works of his hand and the deeds of his life placed his reliance on the great Gods, and thus obtained a prosperous and long life (?).

Talbot.

Great grandson of Ashur-daba-lan ...... of the glorious sceptre .... who rested upon the favor of the great gods, the works of his hands and the gifts of his ....

XLIV. (vii. 55).

The beloved child (literally heart of hearts) of Barzan-pala-kura, the king who first organized the country of Assyria, who purged his territories of the wicked as if they had been ...., and established the troops of Assyria in authority.

Fourth descendant of Ninev-bal-ushat, who ....

XLV. (vii. 60).

At this time the temple of Anu and Vul, the great Gods, my lords, which, in former times, Shansi-Vul, high-priest of Ashur, son of Ismi Dagan, high-priest of Ashur, had founded, having lasted for 641 years, it fell into ruin. Ashur-dapur-Il, king of Assyria, son of Barzan-pala-kura, king of Assyria, took down this temple and did not rebuild it. For 60 years the foundations of it were not laid.

The temple of ANU and YEM, the great gods, my lords, which in former days Shemsi-Yem, supreme lord of Assyria, son of Ishmi-Dagon, supreme lord of Assyria likewise, 641 years ago had con-structed, that temple had fallen to decay. And Ashur-dabalan, king of Assyria, son of Ninev-bal-ushat, king of Assyria likewise, destroyed that temple and rebuilt it not. During sixty years its foundations were not ....

Julius Oppert was added) for translation, and that the separate translations should be delivered sealed to the society, to be opened in the presence of a commission. Rawlinson agreed to this at once. Six weeks later the four contes- tants had delivered their versions, and the commission drew up its report.

The report was sensational. Although two of the entries were of shorter length, Hincks and Oppert having had only a brief time at their disposal for the

decipherment, the parallel passages showed an astonishing agreement. Wherever there were significant deviations, the translators had in nearly every case indicated that they were dubious about their versions. In regard to numerals, there was complete agreement.

As a result, the society put out a two-shilling pamphlet entitled: *Inscription of Tiglath Pileser I, King of Assyria, 1150 B. C., as translated by Sir Henry Rawlinson, Fox Talbot Esq., Dr. Hincks, and Dr. Oppert.* This publication was a milestone in the history of philology.

Two pages of this pamphlet are reproduced on pages 232, 233. Left, a photograph of the original inscription.

XLV. (vii. 60)
A most recent scholarly translation of the third passage on page 233

In those days (this happened): the Temple of Anu and Raman,
the great gods, my lords,
which formerly Samsiramanu, the Isakku of Assur,
the son of Ismidagan, the Isakku of Assur,
had built, and which in the course of 641 years had more and more decayed:
Assurdân, King of Assyria,
the son of Ninebpalekur, King of Assyria,
had torn down this temple, but not restored it;
throughout sixty years its foundation stone had not again been laid.

**At twenty-four
a romantic adventurer**

with scarcely a penny in his pocket, at sixty a respected diplomat, wealthy collector of Venetian art, Knight Grand Cross of the Order of the Bath: such was Sir Austen Henry Layard, excavator of the palaces of Nineveh. His was a thoroughly English career, and one which again exemplified the tendency of the adventurer to turn to diplomacy and politics.

Layard was born in Paris in 1817, was reared in Italy, England and Switzerland, and was already fluent in several languages while still a child. Cosmopolitan in temperament, he fretted for six dull years in a London solicitor's office. Meanwhile he nursed his dream of undertaking a journey by land through Asia Minor and the Near East to India and Ceylon. By 1840 he could wait no longer; he set out, and was captivated by Turkey and Persia. The picture above, taken from his memoirs, *Early Adventures in Persia...* (1887),

shows him (standing) and his servant
Salah in the costume of the Lurisans, a
nomadic tribe of the Syrian border region;
Layard lived in their ill-smelling tents
and shared their goat cheeses. In 1842
Layard was back in Constantinople, full
of tales about the mysterious mounds by
the Tigris beneath which ancient Nineveh was said to slumber. In 1845 the British ambassador, Sir Stratford Canning,
gave him sixty pounds for a first excavation. With unprecedented luck, Layard
attacked the Hill of Nimrud and promptly
discovered the palace of Assurnasirpal II,
King of Assyria from 884–859 B. C. It
was full of fabulous art treasures, far
surpassing in beauty those things which
Botta had found shortly before. Layard
took a few months leave from the Middle
East, and repaired to London to see to

the publication of his book, *Nineveh and
its Remains*, which appeared in two
volumes in 1848–9, and was followed
by a volume of illustrations. Unlike
Botta, who had received such shabby
treatment from his government, Layard
returned to Constantinople as an attaché.
and in 1849 he chose to do something
which seemed utterly mad. After recon-
noitering Babylon, he went to Kuyunjik,
and with numerous other potential sites
in plain view started upon the very
mound where Botta had dug for so long
without result. There Layard found the
tremendous palace of Sennacherib (704–
681 B. C.), one of the most powerful
despots of the ancient world. Moreover,
he conquered the problem of transportation down the Tigris. Precious reliefs
and sculptures were shipped in quantity
to London.

In 1852 Layard won a seat in Parliament,
then became twice under-secretary for
foreign affairs, ambassador without
portfolio, political observer in the Crimean
War and in India – and finally retired to
Italy, where he collected Venetian paintings. He died in 1894.

is revealed in his reports, which over and
above their importance for Assyriology
constitute first-rate travel literature. Entering Turkey all afire to begin his excavation, he found the place in uproar – the
wild tribes around Mosul had just
revolted against a despotic governor.
Layard won the friendship of a tribal
sheik, set to work on the desert sands,
and struck treasure. Besides conducting
his own project, he found time to examine
the recent discoveries of other archaeologists. Right, for example, is the great
bas-relief at Bavian, then the newest and
most exciting find. Layard, who appears
here as the tiny figure suspended by a
rope before the rock face, comments:
"These figures, which are about 25 ft.
high, represent Sennacherib worshipping
before a god. They are carved upon the
rock in a valley East of Nineveh. The
excavated chambers are probably tombs
of a later date than the sculpures. On
tablets adjoining this bas-relief are inscriptions, by which it appears that these
monuments were sculptured to record
the opening of some great canal by
Sennacherib, and to celebrate his conquest of Babylonia."

Layard had scarcely begun probing the Palace of Assurnasirpal

when the most sensational event of the entire excavation took place. He was riding early one morning to the camp of his friend, Sheik Abd-er-Rahman when he was overtaken by two Arabs galloping toward him as fast as their steeds would go. " 'Hasten, O Bey', they called in high excitement, 'hasten to the diggers, for they have found Nimrud himself. Wallah, it is wonderful, but it is true! We have seen him with our own eyes. There is no god but God.'" And Layard continues: ". . . and both, joining in this pious exclamation, they galloped off." He turned around and spurred after them. "... the Arabs withdrew the screen they had hastily constructed, and disclosed an enormous human head sculptured in full out of the alabaster of the country ... I saw at once that the head must belong to a winged lion or bull, similar to those of Khorsabad and Persepolis."

This find created a furore among the natives. News of it reached Mosul, and provoked a governmental investigation which paralyzed the work for days. The picture on the left, from Layard's *Nineveh and its Remains*, is more descriptive of the drama of the discovery than words can be.

Some had the bodies of bulls, others of lions.

These monsters, which represented virtues, were called *lamassi* by the Assyrians. They played a role similar to that of the cherubim of the Jews.

Here is one of the guardians of the gate of the Palace of Assurnasirpal II, taken from under the Hill of Nimrud. The inscription between the legs (there are five legs – an idiosyncrasy of Assyrian style, which apparently held it necessary to show four legs even in profile) gives the name of the king, lists his titles, and recounts his victories.

One of Layard's most interesting finds,

from the scientific point of view, the Black Obelisk of Salmanassar III (859–824 B. C.). This obelisk, about six and a half feet high and covered on all four faces with script and reliefs, not only tells us of the king's military expeditions, but gives us vignettes of the clothing and customs of the peoples whom Salmanassar boasts of conquering.

Our sketch on the right is from Layard's *Monuments of Nineveh*. The photograph above singles out the second row of carvings. Kinsmen of Jehu, son of a man named Khumri are shown bringing tribute consisting of bars of metal and vessels of silver and gold. Oddly enough *Khumri* was the Assyrian designation of the Jews, but they are not mentioned in the chronicle on the obelisk.

Two reliefs

which Layard found during his last excavation at the mound of Kuyunjik, the spot Botta had abandoned too soon. Above, a recumbent lioness, outstretched in a magnificent union of power and grace beneath a cypress tree entwined by a grape-vine. On the next page, a lion hunt, also from the Palace of Assur-banipal. The lion is attacking the king, springing directly upon the body-guards' deadly spears.

These reliefs created an enormous sensation when they were first exhibited in the Assyrian Saloon of the British Museum. The mound of Kuyunjik was to yield still another find, one that roused not only excitement and admiration, but also a prolonged discussion. This find, however was not made by Layard himself, but by one of his most talented disciples.

Hormuzd Rassam (1826–1910), a Chaldaean Christian

and Layard's pupil, had been educated at Oxford. In the midst of a brilliant diplomatic career, he was so unfortunate as to incur disfavour with the ruler of Abyssinia, who had him cast into prison in 1866. Freed two years later, he felt the lure of his early interests and went to Nineveh, where he had dug with Layard many years before. He laid bare a new temple, 165 feet long and 100 feet wide. At Balawat, south-east of Nineveh, he found the remains of a gate which had once been the entrance to the Palace of Salmanassar III (859–824 B. C.). The bronze fittings were chased with crude reliefs picturing the king's heroic deeds. These remains not only provided the first proof that

the Assyrians were acquainted with gates and doors, but also showed just how they had made a gate 20 feet high by 15 feet wide function.

The illustration above shows one of the bronze strips covering the door-jamb. In the lower left hand corner is a citadel. The clearly delineated crenelations were one of the chief clues for the reconstruction of such citadels as, for example, the late hittite citadel at Carchemish. A citadel occurs again in the upper right-hand corner, and the disposition of the defenders fully explains the crenelations. The principle of fortification, and of the battering ram set on a cart, remained essentially the same well into Europe's Middle Ages.

which had held the knowledge and literature of Babylonia and Assyria, lay cracked, shattered and half burned, in wild confusion. They made a pile a foot and a half high. These thousands of clay tablets, representing King Assurbanipal's library at Nineveh, were among the last triumphal finds made by Layard and his assistant, Hormuzd Rassam, in the spring of 1850. One fragment, containing part of the Gilgamesh Epic, is shown here.

None of the excavators recognized the value of this find. Consequently, they packed the tablets higgledy-piggledy into baskets, did not bother to wrap them, and sent them by rafts down to Baszra, whence they were taken aboard a British naval vessel bound for England. This careless handling caused more damage to the tablets than did the pillaging of the Medes who had long ago burned Assurbanipal's palace.

The tablets were then "dug up" a second time – in the British Museum. The man who performed this feat was again one of those self-taught geniuses who appear so frequently in the history of archaeology. Among thousands of tablets he succeeded in piecing together some eighty fragments containing a text which, as he deciphered it, proved more and more momentous.

The man was George Smith (1840–1876), a former bank note engraver who by sheer erudition won himself an assistantship in the Egyptian-Assyrian section of the British Museum. What he deciphered was the literary work now called the 'Gilgamesh epic' – probably the first great written epic in the history of the world, composed long before Homer and the Bible. Gilgamesh, two-thirds god and one-third man, was the legendary hero of prehistoric times who overcame Khumbabam, the terrible ruler of the cedar forest. With supreme daring he called Ishtar, the goddess of love, a harlot when she offered herself to him. He killed the heavenly bull. But tragedy struck when his friend Enkidu, with whom he had performed all these exploits, died of an inexplicable disease. Gilgamesh set out in search of eternal life. In this hunt for immortality he

encountered Utrnapishtim "who had found life" – and it became evident to
George Smith that Utrnapishtim was none other than the Biblical Noah. His
heart beat faster: here in cuneiform script was the story of the Flood. But when
he came to the crucial chapter, several tablets were missing. What followed was

as dramatic as the content of the tablets. Smith issued an appeal to the British public with its enthusiasm for Biblical studies. A newspaper, the *Daily Telegraph*, provided him with a grant to go and seek the rest of the tablets. Still more fantastically, Smith found what he was looking for, found the very clay tablets which were missing amidst the enormous heap of rubble at Nineveh. He translated them – and established clearly that the Bible's story of the Deluge derived from a Babylonian source. The Bible could no longer be regarded only as pure revelation; it was also a history into which age-old tales had been woven.

Another archaeologist was to discover the historical basis of the Flood – but not until the twentieth century. Excavations at Nippur later in the nineteenth century might have contributed a good deal of information bearing on this theme. Unfortunately, a number of its most significant results were not published until very recently.

The Gilgamesh epic remained, therefore, the single document confirming the Biblical account. Here is a passage of startling congruences:

What I had loaded thereon, the whole harvest of life,
I caused to embark within the vessel; all my family and my relations.
The beasts of the field, the cattle of the field . . .
I entered the vessel and closed the door . . .
When the young dawn gleamed forth,
From the foundations of heaven a black cloud arose . . .
All that is bright is turned into darkness,
The brother seeth his brother no more . . .
The gods feared the flood . . .
For six days and nights,
Wind and flood marched on, the hurricane subdued the land.
When the seventh day dawned, the hurricane was abated . . .
The flood ceased.
I beheld the sea, its voice was silent,
And all mankind was turned into mud! . . .
Unto Mount Nitsir came the vessel,
Mount Nitsir held the vessel, and let it not budge . . .
When the seventh day came,
I sent forth a dove . . .

246

Rioting, fire and death

marked the end of the first American excavation in Mesopotamia. In 1884 the American Oriental Society decided that the United States should also delve into the ancient Land of the Two Rivers, which had hitherto been the preserve of England and France. The University of Pennsylvania undertook to sponsor the expedition and chose a minister named Peters, a specialist in Biblical history, as director. After a year of careful reconnaissance, Nippur was selected for the site of the excavation. A sizable fund (for those days) was collected, amounting in fact to 70,000 dollars, which was to be spent in the next ten years. Thus the expedition started under favourable circumstances – save for one factor. The Reverend Peters was unfortunately the complete opposite of such cosmopolitan, politic persons as Botta, Rawlinson and Layard. He was a stern, puritanical man with rigid principles who held Orientals in contempt and would not dream of making concessions to their mentality. He proved inept even in the matter of obtaining a *firman*, or permit for digging, from the Turkish government. (Nippur is about 100 miles south-east of Baghdad; until 1918 the entire region was under Turkish rule.) Two years passed in fruitless negotiations, and the expedition, although prepared by 1887, did not arrive in Nippur until January 1889. Disputes began at once. The upright minister came with his contingent of Turkish guards. Supported thus by the central authorities, he saw no need of presenting the sheiks of the surrounding tribes with the customary gifts. He next made a decision totally absurd from the point of view of excavational technique: he placed the expedition's camp on top of the hill he intended to dig, proudly calling it *kal'at America*, American citadel. No sooner had the Arab workmen committed their first small thefts – standard

247

practice in the country – than this professional exemplar of Christian charity issued an order without precedent in archaeological work. He instructed his watchmen to fire at suspicious nocturnal prowlers.

On April 15, 1889, after two months of excavation, a Turkish soldier shot an Arab who attempted to steal a horse. At once the tense situation passed out of control. The Arabs screamed for bloody revenge. Peters was loth to turn over to them the soldier who had obeyed his order, and instead concluded that his party had better go elsewhere. On the morning of April 18, only three days after the fateful shot, when packing was almost complete, the cry of "Fire!" rang through the camp. Sure enough, the huts were all ablaze. The Turkish troops, instead of helping, snatched whatever they could lay hands on. Arabs poured into the camp and looted left and right. Three horses, including the minister's, were burned alive. With a measure of dry insight, the Reverend Peters later observed: "Our first year at Nippur had ended in failure and disaster."

The drawing on the preceding page is modern. Ulrica Lloyd, wife of the archaeologist Seton Lloyd, made it for her husband's book, *Foundations in the Dust*. The spectacle of flaming huts and wildly dashing horsemen is based on written accounts, while the ruins are modelled after older drawings.

Peters learned a lesson from his failure. Returning the following year, he took care to placate the Arab sheiks as well as the Turkish government. By the middle of February he had struck one of the richest stores of cuneiform tablets ever to be found. Almost fifty years passed, however, before these finds were turned to scientific profit. In 1937 and then again in 1943 and 1946 the American Sumerologist Samuel N. Kramer studied them. And he learned that far back in the third millennium B. C. Sumeria had abounded in tales of Gilgamesh and of the man who escaped the Flood on a ship with all sorts of creatures aboard. He also found the conclusion, which hitherto had been missing from the epic. Gilgamesh, the passionate seeker after immortality, does not find eternal life in spite of all the advice of Ut-napishtim (Noah). He must die. But Enlil, the father of the gods, appoints him lord of the underworld. In ruling over what he had feared, he loses his fear – a remarkable conclusion indeed for the oldest epic in world history. But then it springs from an age when priests and poets were in charge of the human psyche, there were no psychiatrists.

"Koldewey took on the most gigantic task

that any excavator ever assumed – to dig up Babylon. No comparable task remains for any one else", writes Oscar Reuther, the German art historian, in his obituary of the man who had excavated Babylon.

Robert Koldewey (1855–1925) was no beginner when he first conceived his plan. After having studied architecture, art history and archaeology at the universities of Berlin, Munich and Vienna, he acquired experience in excavation on the Greek is‑ lands, and in Italy and Syria. At this time Dörpfeld, with his excavation at Olympia and his highly systematic work at the city of Priene, had already begun to point out new paths to archaeologists, to teach them not only to search for interesting objects, but much more to discover contexts, the total picture of a city.

Koldewey set his own goal. A man of lively mind, he seasoned his under‑ takings with humour and imagination. Anything but professorial, he could charm people into believing that apparently impossible tasks were easy – though he himself never lost his keen sense of what was really possible. "If", Reuther comments, "he had actually communicated the plans he had been nursing for years, his patrons, the Administrators of the Berlin Museums and the German Oriental Society, would scarcely have taken him seriously."

By dint of personal magnetism he succeeded in keeping alive the interest of his patrons for almost twenty years. Although he frankly admitted that his excavations would harvest no material treasures, they endowed him over a period of years to the tune of almost 2,000,000 marks (170,000 pounds). Nor does this include the support he received from the German Kaiser, Wilhelm II, who was fond of dabbling in all the arts and sponsored other archaeological projects besides this.

249

Reuther continues: "Koldewey undertook an exploratory trip, accompanied by Eduard Sachau, to the Land of the Two Rivers. Then, early in 1899, he set out with Walter Andrae as his assistant and with Bruno Meissner as the Assyriologist of the expedition ... In March 1899 digging started at Babylon. Eighteen years later Koldewey left the site of his life-work, having remained there until the road to Baghdad, his only exit-route, was being pounded by British heavy artillery. In those two decades, during which he took only the briefest of home leaves, and then only to re-cuperate from the effects of the climate, Koldewey had wrung from the ages the secrets of ancient Babylon and dispelled the darkness which covered the greatest metropolis of antiquity. Gradually the buildings rose out of the rubble and assumed form: Nebuchad-nezzar's gigantic palaces ... the city walls ... the Gate of Ishtar ... the Street of Proces-sions ... the Euphrates bridge ... and the legendary Tower of Babel, whose form Kolde-wey deduced, from the ruins and the descrip-tions of Greeks and Babylonians, with keenest logic and persuasive artistic imagination."

Walter Andrae, his assistant, and himself later to become a famous archaeologist, adds: "For nineteen years in Babylon and for the last eight years of his life in Germany – Kolde-wey lived for Babylon and thought of Baby-lon, I might almost say, day and night."

This painting gives us some idea of the magnitude of Koldewey's work.

It was done by Elisabeth Andrae, his assistant's sister. What a city this must have been almost two and a half millennia ago, when Nebuchadnezzar was king, indulging his passion for building, erecting more and more walls, palaces and bridges, and marking them with his seal for all eternity!

Koldewey worked under fortunate conditions. Cuneiform script had been deciphered. Assurbanipal's library at Nineveh had provided an abundance of information. Items from the Bible, from Herodotus and Ctesias, from Babylonian tablets and the latest excavations, could be collated and interpreted. He was able to prove that neither the Bible nor the Greek authors had distorted the picture in essential points. Age-old Babylon, so often destroyed and rebuilt, had become under Nebuchadnezzar II the greatest city of antiquity. She was complex and cosmopolitan – a true metropolis.

Nebuchadnezzar's Babel rises out of the earth.

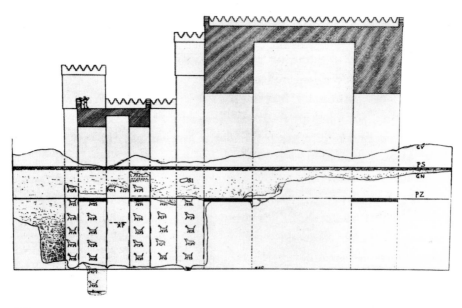

A tower of the Gate of Ishtar is brought to light. Koldewey spent years exposing this structure. At the start he had no idea of the tremendous proportions of the gate – which in fact consisted of two connected gatehouses – or of how deep he would have to dig. Finally he went down eighty feet. As the cross-sectional drawing shows, the original gates had several times been destroyed or had decayed (the long horizontal lines indicate the different levels). Time and again the streets had to be raised, additional layers built upon the towers. The original reliefs were buried under rubble, and new ones were erected on top.

The Gate of Ishtar

in Koldewey's reconstruction. It opened upon the splendid avenue meant for the processions of the great god Marduk. But the street was also a sunken road overlooked by battlements from which death could be hurled upon any invading enemy. The beetling walls were adorned by more than one hundred lions in coloured glazed reliefs. Similar reliefs adorned the gate itself, though here there were bulls rather than lions. There were representations also of that strange mythical beast which may be the animal Daniel tamed in order to prove the power of his God.

The Dragon of Babylon

(above, right) which was sacred to Marduk. This is the *sirrush*, or *sir-russu* in our present reading of the texts. It was a fabulous monster that can scarcely be identified with any living animal, although many persons have speculated about it. The body is scaly, the neck serpentlike, but with a hairy mane; from the horned head a forked tongue darts forth. The fore-feet are like those of a great feline, the hind-feet griffon's claws. This drawing was the first to reach Europe.

The walls of the Gate of Ishtar and the Street of Processions were studded with more than 500 reliefs of animals. Above, left, one of the bulls. The panel with the reliefs is composed of unglazed bricks; the wall above it is of glazed bricks set in geometric designs.

We must visualize all this in colour, mostly in blues and yellows, agleam in the perpetual sunlight, as colour-drenched as the reliefs and winged beasts on the palaces at Nineveh, as vivid as the pillars of Egyptian temples – as marvellously gaudy, indeed, as the entire world of antiquity which we still imagine as impeccably white because we know only the blanched sculptures or plaster casts of our museums. A classical Greek would shudder at the pallor of our plaster casts. How much more repelled would be the Sumerians, the Baby-lonians and the Assyrians, who lived in a world blazing with colour.

254

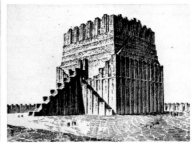

The actual remains of the Tower of Babel.

These are not remains of Nebuchadnezzar's ziggurat, but of the very oldest tower, probably the one of which the Bible tells.

Koldewey dug up a city surrounded by the mightiest citadel wall that has ever been found, guarded by more than 300 watch towers and moats. He found thousands of fragments of reliefs and cuneiform tablets, but his excavation of the remains of the Tower of Babel, and his subsequent reconstruction, are his crowning achievement. The discovery of the stele with Hammurabi's table of laws is incomparably more important to ancient history than the whole Tower of Babel. But to those who are not specialists in ancient history, Babylonian law is rather abstract, whereas the Tower of Babel is an image which has haunted our imaginations from childhood. Reuther says in his obituary on Koldewey: "His Babylonian tower is no structure of fantasy ... How close he came to reality has long since been demonstrated by the ziggurat at Ur, excavated by C. L. Woolley." This is not quite accurate. The remains and the written accounts are somewhat too scanty to allow us to say with certainty how the tower looked.

But Reuther's comment leads us to an archaeologist who was destined to demonstrate the historical accuracy of other testimony in the Bible.

255

"One has to look out for all such little things . . ."

Thus Sir Leonard Woolley (born 1880) begins an explanation of his working methods at the excavation of Ur, the city where Abraham once dwelt. ". . . For the thin powdery white streak which represents the matting that once lined the pit, for the holes in the soil where once were the upright wooden ribs of a wicker coffin, for the rim of a tall clay vase standing in the grave and not crushed flat by the earth's weight; on encountering any such thing the well-trained Arab pick-man will stop his work and report to the foreman the likelihood of a grave; then the pick will give place to the knife for careful work, and the excavator will get out his notebooks and his measures."

With little fear of contradiction, we may call Leonard Woolley the most important excavator of the twentieth century. Educated at Oxford, by the time he was twenty-seven he was digging in Nubia. He worked there from 1907 to 1911. Between 1912 and 1914 he collaborated with T. E. Lawrence (later to become world-famous as "Lawrence of Arabia") in Carchemish, the Hittite citadel. During the First World War he did intelligence staff work in Egypt, and spent two years as a prisoner of war in Turkey. In 1924 he began the excavations at Ur which continued until 1934, and made a name for himself by discovering the oldest royal graves in the world, and the oldest known civilized people, the Sumerians. In 1935, acting on intuition supported by admirable reasoning, he struck first shot into a city buried for thousands of years, the former capital of Yarim Lim, "to whom twenty kings were subject", near Alalakh, present day Atchana in the Turkish Hatay.

The photograph on the left shows him in Ur (right foreground, seated) taking notes on the precise condition of a newly-discovered vase. His wife (left foreground) his faithful companion amidst the agitations and excitements of camp life, is at work on one of the delicate jobs of the archaeologist: scraping away earth with a knife.

Payment of "baksheesh"

is the best procedure for preventing carelessness and theft, according to Woolley. Some excavators still refuse to adopt this procedure, although all experience bears out its wisdom. Here, at the end of a day's work, the foremen line up with the finds their small parties have made. Woolley notes each find and values it at the price a black market dealer might pay for a stolen object. "On an average season the 'baksheesh' bill may amount to 15 per cent of the wages", Woolley writes. The gain to science is altogether out of proportion to the sum. In the first place there is no purloining of the finds, which would then be lost to science. In the second place the system trains the workmen to exercise extreme care during excavation, for baksheesh is paid only for objects which are not broken or damaged by clumsiness during exhumation. "The system", says Woolley, "does create an astonishing amount of good will."

Salvaging cuneiform tablets

was a troublesome problem. Tablets are among the most precious finds, for they can speak directly to us. Most of those found in Ur were unbaked clay tablets which had become soft as cheese from lying for thousands of years in damp soil. They have often become shapeless lumps impregnated with salt, which only the practiced eye would recognize as an inscribed tablet. Any attempt at mechanical cleaning, even with the finest brushes, would obliterate the inscriptions. "At Ur", Woolley relates, "any lumps of clay looking like tablets are lifted from the ground still encased in their covering of earth, and are packed in metal boxes filled with clean sand; after they have been left for a few days to give the clay a chance to dry, the boxes are put into a rough and

ready kiln heated by vaporized crude oil and are baked until the tins are red-hot and the clay is turned into terra cotta. Then the tablets are taken out; their colour may have altered, which matters little, but they are hard and strong; broken bits can be stuck together, the faces can be cleaned by brushing without any risk to the legibility of the characters; no inscription, however fragmentary, can be overlooked, and its preservation is assured."

Woolley and his wife are shown on the opposite page engaged in this delicate work. The two photographs on this page show, left, Woolley's "rough and ready kiln" and, right, actual fragments of tablets before and after they had been cleaned.

The royal graves of Ur,

from which Woolley extracted extraordinary treasures in gold, and the secret of a frightful funeral ritual. The terraces and steps in the excavation site are due to the differing levels of the approximately 1,800 graves which were investigated; hence this irregular pit nearly 30 yards long and 60 wide.

Woolley discovered this royal cemetery in the autumn of 1922. And he took the amazingly strong-minded step of putting off work on it, not surrendering to curiosity, opposing the powerful urge to follow up a discovery so obviously

important. In fact he waited four years, while pursuing other work. In justification of this decision he points out that the diggers were raw and clumsy, and that for the clearing of a cemetery skilled labour is essential; again, his own party was new to the country and had not time to secure proper influence over the men, for whom the temptation of small gold objects was irresistible. But the decisive argument for postponing work on the graves was this: very little indeed was known of Mesopotamian archaeology, so little that the objects from these graves were vaguely dated by such authorities as Woolley could consult to the Neo-Babylonian, or, as more probable, to the Persian period, and though he could form no alternative theory he felt that this was doubtful in the extreme. The more rich the cemetery promised to be, the more necessary it was to leave it alone until external evidence had given a more or less definite chronology.

This decision was certainly wise. There are, alas, all too many examples in the history of archaeology of excavators who took another attitude, so that Woolley deserves the greatest respect for his restraint.

During the season of 1926–7 he dug away at the vast cemetery with a crew of a hundred workmen for two months. During the third season, 1928–9, with his wife as his sole scientific assistant, he employed 140 workmen and uncovered some 450 graves, including the graves of the kings of Ur and the "Death-pit".

as Woolley called this royal grave, told a horrible story. It contained seventy-four skeletons of women, presumably ladies of the court, in front of the king's grave. There were also gold and silver harps, which had probably been used to play music for the uncanny *danse macabre*, and golden statuettes of rams. All the skeletons wore jewelry. Typical finery were gold and silver hair ribbons, the latter of which, however, were barely recognizable as streaks of purplish powder among the broken remnants of skulls. Beside one of the ladies an entire silver ribbon was found, rolled up; it had probably been kept in a pocket – just as today, to carry a ribbon, we would roll it up and tuck the end around the roll to prevent unwinding.

It was plain that something had taken place here unique, so far as our knowledge went, in Mesopotamia: a mass human sacrifice. But how? The skeletons lay close together, sometimes on top of one another. The bones of many were so smashed that crushing under an enormous weight might have seemed a not unlikely cause of death. But most of the skeletons had their arms bent toward the mouths, and beside them lay a cup. Woolley, after painstaking examination of all the details, ventured the following interpretation of the ritual in his *Excavations at Ur* (1954):

"When the door had been blocked with stone and brick and smoothly plastered over, the first phase of the burial ceremony was complete ... Down into the open pit ... there comes a procession of people, the members of the dead ruler's court, soldiers, men-servants and women, the latter in all their finery of brightly-coloured garments and head-dresses of carnelian and lapis lazuli, silver and gold, officers with the insignia of their rank, musicians bearing harps or lyres, and then, driven or backed down the slope, the chariots drawn by oxen or by asses ... and all take up their allotted places at the bottom of the shaft and finally a guard of soldiers forms up at the entrance. Each man and woman brought a little cup of clay or stone or metal, the only equipment needed for the rite that was to follow ... The musicians played up to the last; then each of them drank from their cups a potion which they had brought with them or found prepared for them on the spot ... and then lay down and composed themselves for death."

262

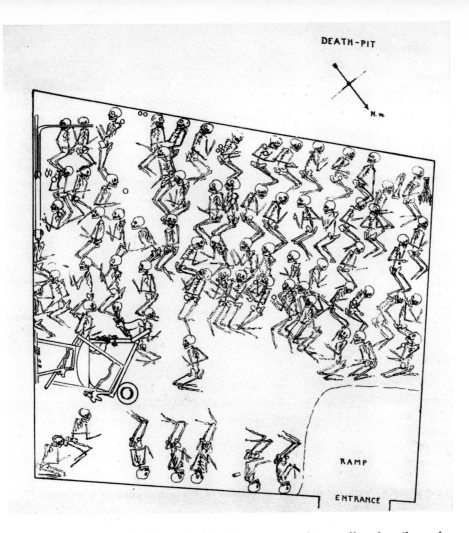

This was not an isolated case, for in the same work Woolley describes other such finds. "The ritual of burial included human sacrifice; the number of victims might vary from a mere half dozen to seventy or eighty" . . . "Against the end wall of the stone chamber lay the bodies of nine women wearing the gala head-dress of lapis and carnelian beads from which hung golden pendants" . . . "A little way inside the entrance to the pit stood a wooden sledge chariot . . . In front of the chariot lay the crushed skeletons of two asses with the bodies of grooms by their heads" . . . "We came to another group of bodies, those of ten women, carefully arranged in two rows . . . At the end of the row lay the remains of a wonderful harp" . . . "across the ruins of the harp lay the bones of the gold-crowned harpist."

263

"Few people, looking at such an object in the glass case of a museum",

comments Leonard Woolley, "realize what it cost to get it there." In freeing
this harp from the surrounding soil and restoring it, Woolley performed a
signal feat, for unlike Carter at the tomb of Tutankhamen he did not have a
whole staff of specialists at his disposal. Nor was he equipped like a contemporary American expedition, which moved into the desert with a first-class
photographic laboratory and a captive balloon, in order to be able to photograph the terrain from the air. Right, above, Woolley with his wife working
on the still-imbedded harps; they are scraping around the relics with a knife
and blowing the soil away with a small bellows. The position of the 4,500-year-
old instruments (made of wood covered with gold and silver, and ornamented
with mosaic) is difficult to make out; behind Woolley's right foot is a silver-
covered harp, which can also be distinguished at the top of the photograph on

the left. Below are others. At first the state of preservation appeared to be good; at any rate, precise measurements could be taken. But moving the object proved to be extraordinarily difficult. The metal sections were nothing but layers of silver chloride; the sheathing on the rods of the frame had been crushed. Only with the aid of a great deal of wax and wax-soaked linen cloths could the instrument be patched together for shipment. Even so, it could never be placed on exhibition. The condition of the golden harp (illustration above left, in foreground) was quite different. The wood of the frame had vanished completely, but the wide mosaic trimming could be lifted with a wax-soaked cloth in one piece and almost undamaged. As for the bull-headed harp, of which a detail is shown on the right, there was enough left of it for Woolley to venture a reconstruction.

The works of art Woolley found in the graves were richly-made and plentiful. Some amazed the discoverer and his colleagues, for no one had suspected that more than 4,500 years ago any people had been so versatile in their creativeness.

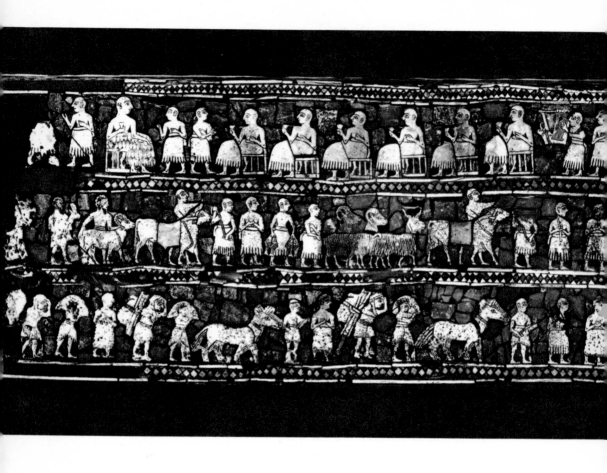

The Mosaic Standard of Ur,

found in one of the royal graves, is a living picture-book of Sumerian life before 3000 B.C. Its purpose has not been definitively established. The figures are fashioned of mother-of-pearl and lapis lazuli embedded in asphalt on a wood base. The scenes are fairly clearly divided into a military and a civilian side, showing the life of a king among his people, and among his soldiers. The civilian side is on the left. Above, we see a banquet; the second complete figure from the left is probably the king; on the right the harpist, followed by a singer; below, two long lines of servants and farmers bringing gifts. Scholars find it useful to know that goats, sheep and cattle were already domestic

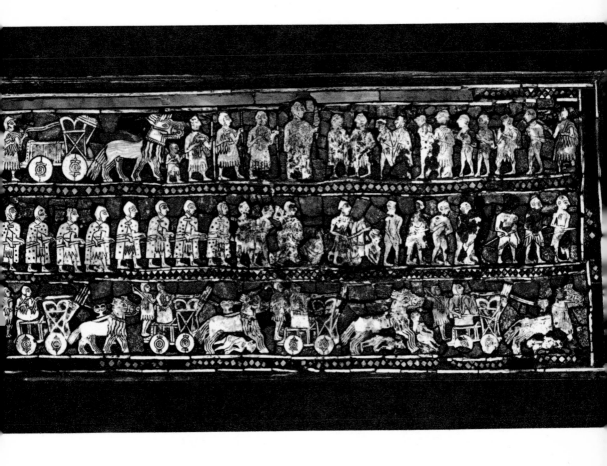

animals at this time, as well as donkeys. The donkey appears on the military side of the standard (right) as a draft animal hitched to wagons. The horse was not employed in this manner until around 2000 B.C. Such carts with soldiers standing on a board at the rear at first led historians to conclude that the ingenious Sumerians had also invented the war-chariot, which later, under the Hittites, developed into a speedy, two-wheeled weapon that, drawn by trained horses, revolutionized warfare in antiquity. But these carts with their four spokeless wheels are heavy transport vehicles; pulled by donkeys, they probably could not even keep pace with rapidly advancing infantry.

A ruler of the mysterious Sumerians,

perhaps Gudea, perhaps his son Ur-Ningursu. The statue cannot be identified with certainty because it was not scientifically excavated by an archaeological expedition; it fell into an art-dealer's hands via the black market in antiquities, and was purchased in the late nineteenth century by the British Museum for 7,500 pounds. The perfection of carving, the artistic coherence in form, are astonishing. The material is green-spotted diorite; the fingernails were once gilded, and the pupils of the eyes painted.

To this day we do not know for certain whence the Sumerians came. Perhaps their original homeland was the Iranian plateau, possibly the valley of the Indus. They were not Semites, but what they were we do not know. They brought with them a manner of writing and a number of basic architectural forms, such as the arch, the pillar and the dome. Moreover, they were acquainted with all the techniques on which the peoples who succeeded them based their own advanced cultures. Their intellectual influence survived long after their city-states had fallen to ruin; their fundamental conceptions of social structure, law and morality outlasted them for thousands of years. They foreshadowed the Mosaic laws before 3000 B.C., and the tale of the Flood, a late retelling of which was found in Nineveh, is Sumerian in origin.

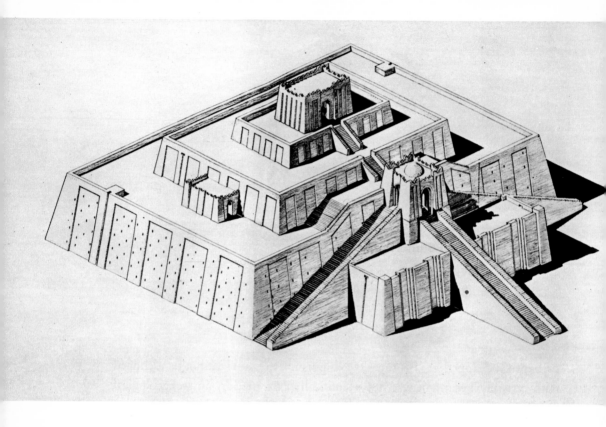

The mighty scale of Sumerian work

is shown by the remnants of their temple tower, the Ziggurat of Ur, which Woolley also excavated; he reconstructed it as it probably appeared under the Third Dynasty. The photograph to the right shows the ruins as they now look. The tiny human figures on the stairway convey something of the enormous size of the building. The structure was begun by Ur-Nammu and his son Shulgi, kings of the Third Dynasty of Ur (about 2100 B. C.). We know the Sumerian kings from king-lists which have been unearthed. The first dynasty is recorded under the title, "List of Larsa No. I". To this a brief explanation was appended. It read as follows: "Now came the Flood. And after the Flood the kings of the mountain peoples assumed dominion."

It fell to Woolley to prove the historical reality of such a flood in the Land of

the Two Rivers. The evidence lay at such a depth that the flood must demon-
strably have taken place shortly after the Sumerians settled the country. What
Woolley found under many layers of cultural remains was a thick layer of clay,
which every geologist could recognize as an alluvial deposit resulting from a
tremendous inundation. Comparison of the king lists, the Gilgamesh epic and
the testimony of the Bible led inexorably to the conclusion that this deposit had
been left by *the* Flood. It is not unreasonable to suppose that this particular
flood, which was obviously of such gigantic proportions, so impressed the
survivors that they immortalized it in myth, which was passed on and passed
on to become that magnificent symbolic story related in the Bible. On the other
hand we know today that the delta of the Tigris and Euphrates was much

smaller 5,000 years ago than it is today. Ur, therefore, was situated close to the Persian Gulf, and there must have been fairly regular floods, which unques-tionably swelled to great disasters more than once. Finally, the layer of mud found by Woolley does not explain the existence of stories of the Flood among the of peoples other continents. But however that may be – there can be no doubt that this Sumerian flood supplied the historical background for the Biblical Deluge.

Most of the great nations of the world have sent specialists to launch excava-tions at Kish, Fara, El-Obeid, Tello, Warka, Nippur, Assur, Mari and Ugarit. Thanks to the labours of archaeologists of many lands, we are able today to write the history – at least in outline – of the oldest known human culture, the culture whose influences were so far-reaching that they still affect our lives and our thoughts.

We turn our attention now to a geographical entity on the other side of the world, and to a group of civilizations which until recently were terribly alien to us. Although they perished not millennia but only a few centuries ago, they left behind them deeper riddles than any we have hitherto encountered.

IV

Book IV

DIEGO DE LANDA

BERNARDINO DE SAHAGÚN

JUANA INÉZ DE LA CRUZ

ALEXANDER VON HUMBOLDT

LORD KINGSBOROUGH

CAPTAIN DUPAIX

COUNT WALDECK

JOHN L. STEPHENS

FREDERICK CATHERWOOD

ABBÉ BRASSEUR

EDWARD H. THOMPSON

EDUARD SELER

ALBERTO RUZ

Archaeology in Middle America* began amid war –

and very nearly ended there. For no "scientific commission" like Napoleon's in Egypt accompanied Hernán Cortés to Mexico. Four hundred men in armour destroyed the highly-civilized Empire of the Aztecs and erected, at the instruction of their priests, the Christian cross upon the teocalli, the heathen temple towers. The Spaniards then methodically extirpated the culture of the

* This term as used by archaeologists includes Central America and Mexico.

275

Indians. Only a few among them saw any worth in the customs and artifacts, the buildings and the accumulated lore of the vanquished.

The drawing on page 275 shows Cortés on November 8, 1519, at his first meeting with Montezuma, the Aztec emperor, in the "floating" capital of Mexico – for the city was at the time a kind of Venice. The woman with Cortés is his mistress and interpreter, Marina (Malinche); standing on a balcony is one of his personal guards; below are tributary gifts: maize, birds, game; seated is the emperor attended by three Aztec generals.

Marina was a slave girl, as cruelly used by her stepmother as a heroine in a Grimm fairy-tale. Her father, a rich cacique of the south, had no sooner died than her stepmother sold her to a chieftain in Tabasco, and seized the inheritance for herself. This had one advantage for Marina: she learned the Maya language, in addition to her Aztec mother tongue, so that after the landing of the Spaniards she was able to help Señor Aguilar, the official interpreter, who knew only Maya. She translated the Aztec into Maya, and Señor Aguilar then put the Maya into Castilian. She must have been both attractive and highly intelligent, for she advanced rapidly, becoming first Cortés's secretary, then his mistress. Later she bore him a child. Marina was a real intermediary; wherever she could, she deftly furthered the interests of her own people, as well as those of her lover.

The Mexicans themselves left a moving record of their downfall. Our picture is taken from the *Lienzo de Tlaxcala*, an impressive hanging painted on cotton cloth, probably of about 1560, depicting in eighty-six separate scenes the part played by the Tlaxcalans in the conquest. The Tlaxcalans, a people with democratic and republican traditions, were the only firm allies of the Spaniards. The textile painting was preserved in the town hall of Tlaxcala. The Emperor Maximilian, the unfortunate Habsburg whom Napoleon III placed upon the Mexican throne, had the painting brought to Mexico City so that a good copy might be prepared. In the confusion following the uprisings and Maximilian's execution by Benito Juárez, the painting disappeared. Fortunately there were earlier copies, including one in colour made by the Mexican archaeologist Alfredo Chavero. The Mexican government published a facsimile of this copy for the Columbus anniversary celebration of 1892.

XIII Aztec Skull overlaid with Mosaic

XIV Ritual Axe from Middle America

Contemporary portraits of Cortés are extremely rare.

"Pitilessly, almost sardonically, he looks out at the world with cruel fire in his eyes; fully to appreciate this image, we must study it for a while", comments A. Suhle in his book on Renaissance medallions. The medallion (top right), although unsigned, has been ascribed to Christoph Weiditz (about 1500–1559) and was probably made in Italy or Spain in 1529.

The tinted pen drawing (lower right) is the only full-length portrait of Cortés that has been preserved. It is taken from Weiditz's travel album. The inscription reads: "Don Ferdinando Cordes year 1529 of his age the 42nd. This man has won all India for Emperor Charles the Fifth" – a statement which errs in two respects; it was Central America Cortés won, not India, and he was forty-four, since his birth in 1485 has been established beyond doubt.

Hernán Cortés was something of a phenomenon in the history of the Western world. There is no parallel for the bloodbath in which he drowned a flourishing civilization. Though we cannot here review his career, we refer the reader to the superb account of him in William Prescott's *Conquest of Mexico*, a book that has lost none of its power in the hundred odd years that have passed since its appearance in 1843.

to arrive in Europe created a sensation by reason of their curiosity and the richness of their materials. Yet these objects made no impact on humanistic scholars who were entirely under the spell of the artifacts of the Greco-Roman period which they were just beginning to investigate.

Montezuma sent a number of presents to Cortés aboard his ship. The gifts which struck the Spaniards as especially precious and desirable were considered bagatelles by the Aztecs. Cortés's men, for example, were dumbfounded by gold and silver discs the size of cart-wheels, whereas the Aztecs placed far more value on their articles of birds' plumage. They had good reason for this.

Right, above, a feather head-dress measuring 5 feet 9 inches at its greatest width, originally among Montezuma's gifts to Cortés in 1519. One of the earliest descriptions of it reads: "A Moorish hat, of long, fine, glistering, greenish and golden feathers, set on top with white, red and azure feathers with golden roses and spangles, with a solid golden beak in front, fitting over the brow." Almost all the long feathers were taken from a bird which sports only two, or at most four tail feathers. When we consider that there are some 500 of these quetzal feathers in the head-dress, the rarity and preciousness of this singular crown is evident.

In 1878 it was taken, badly moth-eaten, from a museum cupboard in Vienna. where it had hung *folded* for decades. It was then restored, but scarcely accurately, the restorer being under the delusion that the head-dress had been a standard. So little attention was paid to authenticity that whole skins of the East Indian halcyon, *halcyon fusca Gray*, were used in place of the blue down feathers of *cotinga maynanna Linné* – the latter being difficult to obtain.

Ultimately, however, the head-dress came under the scrutiny of scholars in the field of American archaeology. In 1887 a book was published on this "magnificent example of Old Mexican feather work". Then, in 1908, for the sixteenth congress of the Americanists, a special study committee was formed, and Franz Heger made the drawing on the opposite page, below. It shows a reconstruction of the complete head-dress. The committee had the head-dress housed in a revolving show-case, so that it could be seen from all sides without handling.

Staggering strangeness –

such was the impression people had of the cultural artifacts of Middle America which found their way to Europe. Certainly this skull encrusted with bits of turquoise embodies an utterly alien quality. The skull probably symbolized Tezcatlipoca ("smoking mirror"), the lord of heaven and earth, inflicter and healer of frightful diseases, among them cancer and syphilis. Such skulls as this probably derive rather from Mixtec than Aztec culture. In any case they represent one of the oldest and most heavily traditional ornamental techniques of Old Mexico. (See also colour plate XIII.)

The first important artist in Europe to appreciate these alien products of Mexican civilization was Albrecht Dürer.

Montezuma's presents were sent from Seville to Valladolid

and then to the Spanish Netherlands. There Dürer saw them. He made a journal entry dated August 27, 1520: "I too have seen the thing which was brought to the king from the new golden land, a sun all of gold ... likewise a moon all of silver ... likewise two chambers full of all sorts of their weapons, armour, cannon, wondrous arms ... These things are all precious, so that they are held to be worth a hundred thousand gulden. And I must say that all my days I have not seen anything that has so rejoiced my heart as these things ... and I have been astonished at the subtle *ingenia* of the men in foreign lands ..." This observation of Dürer's must be understood in its context. Here an artist of the Renaissance was confronted for the first time with exotic art – and was moved by it. The things Dürer saw may have been gold work similar to those later excavated in Oaxaca at Monte Albán – such as the golden breast-plate and mask above, probably the image of a Mixtec god of death.

281

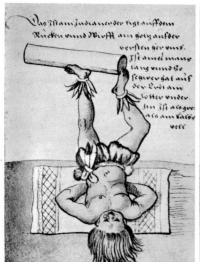

The very earliest European depiction of an Indian

in existence. These tinted pen drawings are not upside down (see the inscrip‐
tions). Rather, the Indian is lying on his back, juggling a log as heavy as a man
with his feet. He was a native whom Cortés brought back to Europe in 1528,
when he returned to justify himself before Emperor Charles V against the accu‐
sations of his enemies. He won not only mercy, but honour, and was granted
the privilege of accompanying the emperor on his subsequent journeys. On one
such occasion Weiditz executed the portrait of him shown on page 277, and
also made these drawings of his captive Indian. Weiditz's superscribed
remarks, in language and spelling quainter and even more idiosyncratic than
the run of sixteenth‐century German, are as follows:
"This is an Indian who lieth on his back tossing a log on his heels. It is
long as a man and as heavy so that he keepeth beneath him a mat as big as a
calf's skin."

282

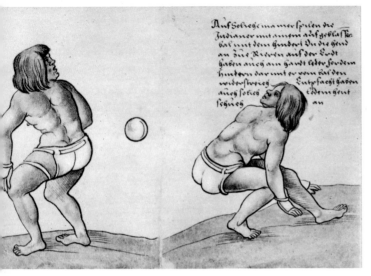

"In such wise the Indians play

with a blown up ball, hitting it with the nether parts and the hands. For moving on the ground they wear a hard leather over the nether parts so that it may receive the impact of the ball, also such leather gloves."

This, too, is a tinted pen drawing from Christoph Weiditz's album. In all probability what we are seeing here is the first rubber ball to be used in a game in Europe. Enormous "ball grounds" were adjuncts of the temple grounds of the Aztecs, and of the Maya before them. In many cultures games and religion were closely connected.

Weiditz's legend on the next picture is quite terse: "In such wise Indian women go. No more than one came out."

At first glance the Indian woman's dress looks as primitive as the proverbial grass skirt of a South Sea islander. In fact the costume is feather work of a high order of artistry, tied by bands exemplifying beautiful dyework and complicated weaving techniques.

These so-called savages had a civilization and a social order in some respects scarcely less advanced than that of the Spaniards. But this could be apprehended only by a man without prejudice – a man with true Christian charity and understanding, who collected and collated where the Spaniards destroyed.

has come down to us. This amazing priest of the time of the conquest was born in Sahagún about 1500 and died in Mexico in 1590. Quite apart from his long and adventurous life, he was remarkable for having developed a method of study for bygone civilizations which was applied to the history of Greece and Rome much after his time, but was not utilized in its own proper sphere, Middle America, until 250 years had passed.

On the right is a sample of his handwriting: the last page of the Spanish version of his great work on the religion, culture and history of Mexico.

In 1529 Bernardino de Sahagún came from Spain to Mexico in a company of nineteen other Franciscans – and there he stayed. For some sixty years he was a teacher, that is to say a missionary; but at the same time – as a scholar engaged in research – he was an attentive listener to the recollections of the upper-class Indians. Immediately after his arrival he began studying the predominant language of the country, Náhuatl. Under highly unfavourable conditions he then systematically recorded everything he could learn about the religion, art, ethics, social order, and military organization of the Aztecs. His book may truly be called an encyclopaedia of Aztec civilization.

The great work was largely completed by 1569. It was written in the Aztec language, for it consisted mostly of verbatim records of narratives by Aztec informants. Then came the grotesque sequel: Sahagún's superiors strongly opposed its publication. They went so far as to seize the manuscript and scatter parts of it among various religious institutions in Spain. At last the president of the Council of India, Juan de Ovando, intervened in Sahagún's favour; he commanded the return of the manuscript to the author, and requested a Spanish translation. Sahagún prepared a translation, and added a lexicon and many illustrations. In order to have his work published at last, he gave his consent to numerous alterations his superiors deemed desirable. Once more the manuscript was sent to Madrid. Nothing happened. Finally one day he was told that it had disappeared. Sahagún died, alone and forgotten, in the monastery of Santa Cruz in Mexico.

Today, both versions have been rediscovered. The Mexican original has been found in Madrid; the fair copy of the illustrated bilingual manuscript is in

XV Maya attacking their Neighbours

XVI Aztec Shield with Feather Mosaic

Florence. The Spanish version was first published in Mexico in 1829, then in London in 1830.

To this day, however, the far more valuable Aztec version, with its uncensored original accounts, has not been completely published. Parts of it were translated into German by the German scholar, Eduard Seler. These parts were published in 1927, almost three and a half centuries after Sahagún's death. Very recently indeed, in 1950 and 1952, another German scholar, Leonhardt Schultze-Jena, has translated additional large sections of the text.

Overleaf are some illustrations from the bilingual manuscript, together with condensed samples of the Aztec original text, as rendered by Seler. These come from the voluminous chapter on making feather ornaments.

"The feather workers who make feather mosaics, whose joy it is to do feather works, begin their labours in the following manner: First they consider how they shall design the pattern. There are first the painters who draw it."

"The feathers are put together with flour-paste; then they are pasted firmly to the agave leaf; the layer is flattened with a bone scraper. What are called shrunken feathers are only ordinary feathers. For they serve as the commencement for the perfection of the feather work. They form the first layer, acting as the bed for the various precious feathers."

"Mixing of the paste is the children's, the apprentices' task; they mix it for the master."

"The feathers are turned hither and thither, examined on all sides; that is, if feathers appear to the eye as too thin in one spot, as too thick in another, as irregular or crushed in any portion, they are thrown away."

286

"There is another procedure ... This is the way fans are made, quetzal fans, arm-bangles, insignia for the back, yellow tunics ... First the frame is tied together ..."

"When the brown and white feathers of the long-tailed coocoo or the yellow feathers of the caquan follow the quetzal feathers, they are all first provided with threads, the threads knotted, and then they are sewed to the frame and the ends threaded through and tied ..."

"What are called yellow feathers are dyed, are dyed yellow. A pigment something like flax dodder is boiled in water, with which alum and saltpetre are mixed."

"And if a very small creature is to be made, say a small lizard ... or a butterfly, the skeleton of the creature is formed of maize stalks or of bits of paper; these are covered with the powder of the dry maize stalk, mixed with paste. Then the figure is scraped . . . and polished. And then it is covered with a layer of cotton, and the pattern laid on in mosaic of feathers. The creature that is to be imitated is used as a model . . ."

287

Mexico was Hispanicized and Christianized.

Sahagún died defeated and no one attempted to carry on his work. Then, in 1615, a book appeared whose illustrations marked a new departure into regions where only the intrepid could tread. It was a new edition of a then widely known handbook of Greco-Roman mythology, by a man named Cartari. The revision was carried out by Lorenzo Pignoria, and contained a revolutionary innova-tion. For the first time Egyptian and Japanese gods were pictured along with the divinities of classical antiquity – and a few of the mis-shapen Mexicans gods as well.

This book, we may say, ushered in comparative religion in an age utterly unripe for such a study. Moreover, Pignoria strove toward an ideal unrecognized by antiquarians until two centuries after him: exactitude; replicas which would retain the true character of the original. He had much to say in his preface concerning the carelessness of engravers and woodcut makers. He himself care-fully checked on the work of his assistants. For his Mexican material he had copies made of drawings in the *Codex Ríos*, a Mexican manuscript also known as *Codex Vaticanus A*, which friends had obtained for him from the Vatican.

We show here an original drawing of the god Omeyocan, from the codex, and the woodcut prepared after it. We who live in an age of photography are at once aware of a host of errors of detail; but for 1615 this woodcut represents an unusually faithful replica. Pignoria's picture is supplemented by the two smaller cuts in ovals of Egyptian divinities. For Pignoria felt that there was a connection between Egyptian and Middle American civilization – a theory of which we shall have more to say.

His descriptions closely follow the original text. Of this picture he said: "Ho-moyoca, the Mexican god, who was the Jupiter of these wretched people."

"These wretched people"

figure on another page of his book (overleaf: left, the original; right, the wood-cut). Here are a number of distortions on the part of the artist for which we must not blame Pignoria, who obviously had a scientific mind. We must re-collect that to point out even the faintest analogy between Christianity and the pagan religions was an act of incredible boldness in an age which burned men at the stake for utterly imaginary heresies. Pignoria was risking his skin when he retailed the prophecy made to the virgin Chimalmam in Tula, namely, that she would conceive without loss of her virginity and give birth to the god Quetzalcoatl. Consequently, his explanation of this picture must be regarded only as a bit of double-talk designed to fend off suspicion: "Thus this emissary was the Gabriel (if we may use the term) of this wretched female; that is, Satan disguised as the angel of light."

This, then, is why the messenger of the god Citlallatonac is shown in this

289

position, rather than directly in downward flight. In order to present this messenger as a diabolic imitation of Gabriel, Pignoria shows him hovering and facing right, consistent with Christian iconography which represents the angel of the Annunciation always approaching from left to right. He also omitted the roses which gave the original its name, Sochiquetzal: "the elevation of the roses into heaven."

We must pass on beyond these attemps to reconcile Christian sensibility with scientific observation of this world of bizarre, alien gods. The Christian world also had to come to terms with another aspect of life among the Aztecs; their frightful human sacrifices, which had no parallel anywhere on earth. Cortés's method of dealing with that aspect was blunt: he closed the sacrificial towers, or planted the cross upon their bloody stones. But the first to attempt to come to terms intellectually with this extraordinary phenomenon was by a woman.

Human sacrifices

Keeping human beings in cages and then slaughtering them for sacrifice was one of the shocking customs of the heathen Aztecs which, the Christian knights claimed, made any harshness against them justified.

The charge was true. The Aztecs did not wage wars primarily to win lands or to extend their power and influence; they waged wars chiefly in order to capture prisoners whom they could sacrifice. These they put to death at the top of their teocalli (step pyramids) by tearing the heart out of the living body and then throwing the bleeding corpse down the steps, as shown above, on the right.

Rios, commenting on the picture on the left, above, says: "In this manner they offer their human sacrifices; those whom we see fallen on the ground are the sacrifices, but the dancers are the same persons who are represented as dead, for they danced and sang before they were sacrificed."

A Christian woman, a nun who was later called the "Tenth Muse of Mexico", daringly endeavoured for the first time to draw up a searching confrontation of Christian and pagan thinking.

was a poet whose intelligence and literary gift matched her courage.

Born in 1651, she took the veil at the age of sixteen. She first entered an austere Carmelite order; then, because of poor health, she transferred to the Sisters of St. Jerome. She was one of the most cultivated persons of her age – an extraordinary thing, indeed, for a woman. In spite of all that was repellent in Aztec civilization she felt, and expressed repeatedly in verse, that the Indians were only erring human beings, and that love, not the sword, was needed to lead them back to the right way. Thus she preached what Sahagún had already practiced. Unlike Sahagún, she was honoured, famous, a radiant example to others. But her death was scarcely less poignant than his. On June 8, 1692, the buildings of the cathedral chapter and the government archives went up in flames. Once again human sacrifices were exacted from the natives: Juana saw with her own eyes the bloody repression of the uprising; she witnessed daily scourgings and executions. Thereupon she gave her bishop all the gifts which the court had lavished upon her, jewelry, gems of all sorts, astronomical and musical instruments, even her library of 4,000 volumes. She asked him to sell everything and distribute the proceeds among the poor. Then she began to practice such terrible mortifications that her confessor had to intercede. Shortly thereafter the plague broke out in the convent. She devoted herself to tending the sick, and was herself carried off by the plague on April 17, 1695.

Here is a selection from the prelude to a religious drama by the "Tenth Muse of Mexico". A personification of Indian idolatry, in open forum, defends his old religion against Fides (Faith). To speak out for paganism was, for the time, scandalous audacity, even though the debate was, ultimately, no more than a literary device.

Idolatry: Not, while my life rages hot,
Shall you, Fides, win success.
Everywhere you preach Christ's tidings,
Opening the ways for Him
By your cunning and your weapons;
Yet though nearly all the nations
Who were once my leal subjects
Have succumbed to your persuasions,
Have received you in their hearts –
Still I say to you again:
Such vast powers are not yours,
That with but a single tug
You can rip up all the roots
Of my deep and ancient customs.
Though I lie half stricken now,
Still I can protect the places
Which you threaten to o'erwhelm,
Where by right of ancient practice
Sacrifices still are taken,
Where men still are being slaughtered.

Fides:

Do you dare resist our plan,
Shameless, execrated creature?
Whence comes this effrontery?

Idolatry:

Vilify me as you please.
Still my task is to protect
Ancient rights, and still I can.
Here I stand for all the manners,
Speak for all the ancient ways
Of these lands and of these peoples,
With the voice and on behalf of,
On behest of all the Indios;
Here I stand and speak this warning:
Though you feel that strength is yours
Since you have converted them
To the banner of your Faith,
Do not seek to use your power
To transform the ancient manner
Of their human sacrifices ...

LE BARON DE HUMBOLDT,
(Frédéric-Henry-Alexandre.)
Associé étranger

"He is off on a singularly beautiful voyage,

and is a lucky and enviable man", wrote the brother of Alexander von Humboldt in a letter to Goethe. On June 5, 1799, Alexander left Europe to travel for five years in the Americas. This German baron (1760–1859) was one of the last universal men, adventurer as well as intellectual, friend of all the great people of his time. The amount of raw material for scholarship he brought back from his first voyage to North and South America was fantastic. For decades afterwards specialists were kept busy publishing the geographical, botanical, zoological, geological, physical, meteorological and sociological results of his travels. The tremendous *Voyage aux régions equinoxiales du Nouveau Continent* began appearing in Paris in 1807; it comprised twenty folio and ten quarto volumes with 1,425 copper plates, and cost untold sums to print. Several publishers had to unite on the project; the king of Prussia provided subsidies; and Humboldt himself spent almost his entire fortune on it – more than 40,000 talers.

For our purposes it is sufficient to note that Humboldt was the first European to study Old Mexican architecture scientifically. He published the first drawings of it, differentiated the styles of various periods, and finally – though with extreme tentativeness – explored the question which is still being discussed today: whether there is any connection between Mexican architecture and the buildings of the Old World in Egypt and Mesopotamia. Are the similarities more than sheer chance?

Humboldt found the parallels most striking in the Pyramid of Cholula.

The gods disapproved of this structure,

which was meant to reach into the clouds, Humboldt reports. He drew his information from native Indians and from the traditions recorded in the *Codex Ríos*. Measuring the height, he found the structure to be 180 feet tall. The sides were between 1,450 and 1,500 feet long; the ground area was twice that of the Pyramid of Cheops. The engraving is after Humboldt's own drawing.

Cholula is one of those places where certain features have survived of the pre-Aztec, pre-Maya civilization, perhaps the oldest of all in Middle America. It is called the Toltec culture – but beyond its name, little is known of it.

Humboldt relates the tale of a great flood that devastated the land. Seven giants saved themselves from the all-engulfing waters. Xelhua, the architect, then built the pyramid. Bricks were baked far away in the province of Tlamanalco. In order to move them to Cholula, Xelhua set up a chain of men who passed them along, from hand to hand, the entire distance. The gods were angry at this plan. They cast fire at the peak of the pyramid, and many workers were killed. Cortés himself was shown a meteorite which, he was told, had fallen upon the top of the pyramid; it was shaped like a toad. The Cholulans had a custom of dancing around the pyramid and singing a song about its building – a song whose first lines were in a language unknown to the singers! ... Who could overlook the analogies with the Biblical Flood and the building of the Tower of Babel?

"The symbolism of the new religion has not entirely dispelled

memory of the old", says Humboldt writing of the small pilgrimage chapel on
the apex of the Pyramid of Cholula. "The people hasten in great crowds from
all directions to celebrate the Feast of Mary on top of this pyramid. An un-
spoken terror, a pious shudder, overcomes the natives at the sight of this monstrous mass of brickwork, covered by eternally fresh grass and shrubbery."

The pyramid of these ancient Mexican Indians has here been made into a
Mount Calvary. Our picture is a hand-painted lithograph from a drawing by
Luciano Castañeda, a member of Captain Dupaix's first expedition in 1805.
Dupaix's role in the history of archaeological discoveries may very well be
compared with that of Robert Hay (see page 97).

But before we come to Dupaix we must mention a man who gave his whole
life and his entire fortune to archaeology, and whose reward was a miserable
death in an Irish debtors' prison.

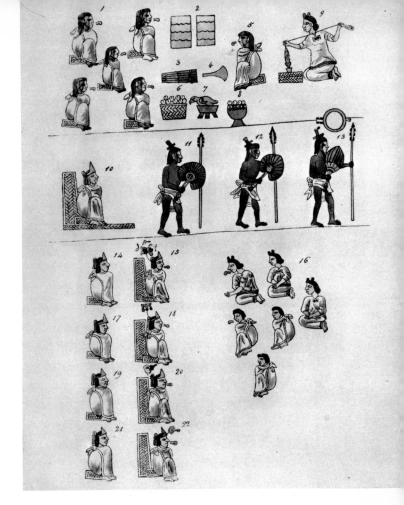

An odd obituary appeared in the "Gentleman's Magazine" for May 1837.

"*Feb. 27.* In the Sheriff's prison at Dublin, of typhus fever, aged 42 (died) the Right Hon. Edward King, Viscount Kingsborough. He was the eldest son of George third and present Earl of Kingston, by Lady Helena Moore..."

Webb's *Companion of Irish Biography* is somewhat more detailed: "His life was devoted to the study of Mexican antiquities. This passion was acquired when a student at Oxford, when the Mexican manuscripts in the Bodleian fired his imagination. His magnificent work, replete with illustrations, was given to the world in 1831, in seven volumes, imperial folio, price 210 pounds. Two additional volumes appeared after his death at a price of 25 pounds 4 shillings. The book cost him upwards of 32,000 pounds and his life; for, oppressed with debt, he was arrested at the suit of a paper manufacturer, and lodged in the debtors' prison, Dublin, where he died of typhus fever ... Had he lived, he would within a year have become Earl of Kingston, with a fortune of 40,000 pounds a year ...''

Kingsborough collected with a passion that almost equalled that of Sir Hans Sloane (see page 196). But he collected not for collecting's sake; he was bent on proving a specific thesis which was in the air at the time. This was that the civilized American Indians had been descendants of the "ten lost tribes of Israel". Part of his huge work was a reprinting of a *History of the North American Indians* by James Adair, every page of which had for a heading: "On the Descent of the American Indians from the Jews."

He had four luxury copies with 1,050 plates printed on parchment, and presented one to the British Museum. But not only did he die ignominiously as a debtor; his name, too, seemed condemned to oblivion. If we look up "Kingsborough, Lord". in the British Museum catalogue we find only a reference to "King, Edward". From this we are immediately referred to "Aglio, Agostino", the artist. Not only the luxury edition, then, but the ordinary edition as well is catalogued under the name of the artist who made the pictures. However, William Prescott, the historian of the conquest of the Aztec Empire, has paid due tribute to Kingsborough:

"The drift of Lord Kingsborough's speculation is to establish the colonization of Mexico by the Israelites. To this the whole battery of his logic and learning is directed. For this hieroglyphics are unriddled, manuscripts compared and monuments delineated ... By this munificent undertaking, which no government, probably, would have, and few individuals could have executed, he has entitled himself to the lasting gratitude of every friend of science."

Today his nine volumes of *Antiquities of Mexico* are recognized as vital source material for students of American archaeology and history. Even modern works depend on it for illustrations.

The preceding page shows one example: a facsimile from the *Codex Mendoza*. At the top are young messengers, the last of them accompanied by his wife. In the middle section we have the Mexican emperor, seated. He has bestowed on some of his messengers the dignity of a *taquilua*, that is, ambassador. In the lower section we have officials and judges on the left, on the right petitioners for justice. We even know the names of the judges: Number 22 is named Tequixquiuahuacatl.

The Feathered Serpent,

one of the incarnations of the god Quetzalcoatl. This relief adorns the pre-Aztec pyramid at Xochicalco ("city of flowers").

Close comparison between the drawing and the photograph shows that the carving has sustained some damage since the day it was discovered. The two men who discovered it along with much other valuable source-material were Captain Guillaume Dupaix and his draftsman Luciano Castañeda.

Oblivion has overtaken

Captain Guillaume Dupaix and Luciano Castañeda; they are not mentioned in standard reference works on Middle American archaeology. This is quite inexplicable, for they conducted three expeditions, in 1805, 1806 and 1807, at the behest of Charles IV of Spain, who gave them a military escort. But amid the turmoil of the Napoleonic era, the results of their efforts were not appreciated. It remained for Kingsborough to unearth Castañeda's drawings and the journal Dupaix kept during the expeditions. His reprint appeared in 1831. Three years later a Monsieur Baradère published in Paris an edition containing essentially the same plates and text, but in Spanish and French instead of English. He claimed to be the rightful owner of the original material, maintaining that the Mexican Senate had given it to him in 1828 in exchange for services, but that shipment had inexplicably been delayed for five or six years.

The tale sounds most improbable. The edition certainly conveys the impression that Baradère put it together out of Kingsborough's compilation, adding some material of his own and of other writers and artists.

Castañeda's drawing on the left and the photograph below are of Zapotec urns found by the Dupaix expedition in the cities of Zaachila and Quilapa. Dupaix comments: "It was found some time ago, together with four others of similar size, shape and substance, in ploughing a piece of ground near the rector's house. For what purpose could it have been designed? ... Perhaps the box was used to hold jewels or incense ... I should in vain attempt to explain the various designs in relief with which the figure is embellished, since they are too complicated and too fanciful for my comprehension."

Relief from a pillar of the "Palacio" in Palenque.

This spacious palace is situated in what is probably the most magnificent ruined city of Mexico. Again it is clear that Dupaix and Castañeda saw more than survives today. No wonder, for the early investigators had no way to remove the rampant jungle vegetation except by burning over the site. The fire damaged even the hard building stone – how much more harm must it have done to the fragile stucco reliefs and terra cotta ornaments. After Dupaix's last visit in 1807 the ruins of Palenque were burned over at least four times.

Dupaix comments on the drawing: "Like the structures which contained them, these reliefs are fast hastening to decay ... All that I could do was to cause those which were still perfect to be copied with utmost fidelity, the greater part having merely left an impression on the wall ... These statues were painted with vermilion, minute particles of which, as well as occasional patches, are still visible in the narrow folds of the drapery."

"I was carried in a litter by several Indians,

and escorted by a dragoon who had been assigned to me for my journey to Uxmal." His presence, wrote Jean Frédéric Maximilian, Comte de Waldeck (1766–1875), struck terror in the Indians and when he appeared they laboured all the harder at clearing the jungle growth away from the ruins.

After Dupaix and Kingsborough, Waldeck was the third European who threw himself heart and soul into the exploration of Middle America's past – at a period when the world cared nothing for it. Yet he became a legendary figure in his lifetime, if only because he lived to be 109. He had grown up in pre-Revolutionary France – the era which Talleyrand later called the only one worth living in; he survived the Terror, outlived Napoleon, saw the Restoration, the Second Empire, and at the age of 105 the Franco-Prussian War. Waldeck was the descendant of a noble family which had emigrated from Germany to France. He began as a painter and pupil of Jacques-Louis David, and took part in the Napoleonic invasion of Egypt. But with the routing of the French, he did not pull out like all the other members of the

303

Scientific Commission, but undertook a private adventure up the Nile as far as Aswan. All turned out well on this trip. Shortly afterwards, however, he tried unsuccessfully to cross the Sahara and reach Portuguese East Africa with a number of others. On this venture – as with Niebuhr's ill-fated party (see page 202) – all his companions perished.

In 1821 Waldeck visited Guatemala for the first time. The following year he went to London, where he prepared the illustrations for Antonio del Río's book describing the ruins of Palenque. In London he met Kingsborough, and the two men engaged in such fierce discussions that they became fast friends. Waldeck maintained that the Mexicans were descended from the Egyptians; Kingsborough, as we have mentioned, was convinced of their Israelite origin. Nevertheless, Kingsborough financed Waldeck's subsequent expeditions from 1832 to 1836, and the count named a Mexican pyramid after him.

Palenque, the temple city in the jungle,

was Maya, not Aztec. Maya civilization is the only advanced one known which subsisted without the plough, the wagon and domestication of animals. Regulated by the rigid patterns of a highly developed calendar that had a singular importance for them, the Maya culture was peculiar in a number of respects. There was no middle class; the caste of nobles and priests lived in strict isolation on the backs of ignorant, characterless masses of peasantry.

If the present correlation between Maya and Christian chronology – on which scientists are at last more or less in agreement – is correct, Palenque was founded in about A.D. 100 – later than Uaxactún, Tikál, Copán, Piédras Négras and Naranjo. The age of the Maya state has not yet been determined. Before it, and sometimes contemporaneously with it, there were other states, the most widespread of which has been called "Toltec", for lack of a more definite name.

At present the origins of the Maya are lost in obscurity. Some people used to call the Toltecs "the Sumerians of Middle American culture", on the theory that they introduced writing, knowledge of the stars and the first laws.

Our panorama is of relatively recent date (1896–9). Right foreground is the *Palacio;* behind it, from left to right: the Crucifix Temple, the Temple with the Altar, the Temple of Trophies or the Sun Temple, the Temple with the Bas-Reliefs, the Temple of Inscriptions. Although the drawing is highly schematic, it conveys the sense of enchantment felt by all who came upon these ornate places of worship in the heart of a primeval jungle.

With Kingsborough dead, Waldeck was unable to raise the money to publish the results of his explorations. Finally, he appealed to Prosper Mérimée and other members of the French Academy. Assistance was granted. In 1866, when he was 100 years old, his account of Palenque was published.

"If I had come to Uxmal only a year later",

writes Waldeck in regard to this reconstruction, "I should not have been able
to reproduce this monument so completely, for the middle had sunk, several
stones necessary for the stability of the centre having meanwhile been removed.
In order to prevent the entire structure from collapsing, I attempted to replace
the missing stones, and even intended to take one or two masons along on my
second expedition in order to repair the damaged place properly and thus
preserve the ruin in the interests of future travellers ... I have named this pyramid
'Lord Kingsborough' because it seemed to me, of all the buildings in Yucatán,
the worthiest of immortalizing the memory of that noblest of all great gentlemen, to whom the world of scholarship is indebted for that redoubtable book
about Mexico."

306

Cortés passed by the ruins of Palenque

unaware. The jungle had grown so thickly over them that even the natives in the immediate vicinity knew nothing about them. The incendiary methods of the early expeditions fought back the jungle but at the same time furthered the destruction of the buildings. In 1787, when Antonio del Río examined the ruins, he reported with pride that "we left not a window nor a door walled up; we did not fail to tear down every partition wall; we did not fail to undertake excavations of two to three ells depth into every room, corridor, courtyard, entrance or underground corridor".

Here is the Temple of the Sun, also called the Temple of Trophies, a wholly unique piece of architecture. Our illustration shows a model now in the American Museum of Natural History in New York.

Middle American archaeology was really born in 1842.

In that year the investigations which had hitherto been carried forward quietly and privately suddenly began to stir the public imagination. Waldeck's *Voyage pittoresque* ... had appeared in Paris in 1838 without making much impression. But in 1842 John Lloyd Stephens's book *Incidents of Travel in Central America, Chiapas and Yucatan,* illustrated by Frederick Catherwood, was published in New York and aroused intense interest. The bizarre, magnificent and monstrous relics of the Middle American civilizations suddenly burst upon the consciousness of all literate people.

Stephens (1805–1852) practiced law in New York for eight years before he took up archaeology. He travelled in Egypt, the Near East and Greece. In Egypt he struck up a friendship with Catherwood, the artist who had been a member of the unfortunate Robert Hay expedition (see page 99). In 1839 he took Catherwood with him into the jungles of Central America and began his explorations near the city of Copán in Honduras. Then, one day, after unspeakable hardships, when the two men had already begun to lose faith in the native tales which had led them on, they found themselves confronting a statue in the jungle earth. It was a pillar in human form, ornamented with such barbaric magnificence, carved in such alien forms, that it took their breath away.

Our illustration shows a drawing by Catherwood of one of the many sculptured pillars they found in Copán. Stephens's accompanying text reads:

"Monument 'T', a buried image. It was one of the most beautiful in Copán and in workmanship is equal to the finest Egyptian sculpture ... It stands at the foot of a wall of steps, with only the head and part of the breast rising above the earth ... When we first discovered it, it was up to the eyes. Arrested by the beauty of the sculpture and by its solemn and mournful position, we commenced excavating. As the ground was level up to that mark, the excavation was made by loosening the earth with the machete, and scooping it out with the hands. As we proceeded, the earth formed a wall around and increased the labour. The Indians struck so carelessly with their machetes, that, afraid to let them work near the stone, we cleared it with our own hands. It was impossible, however, to continue; the earth was matted together by roots which entwined and bound the monument. It required a complete throwing out of the earth for 10

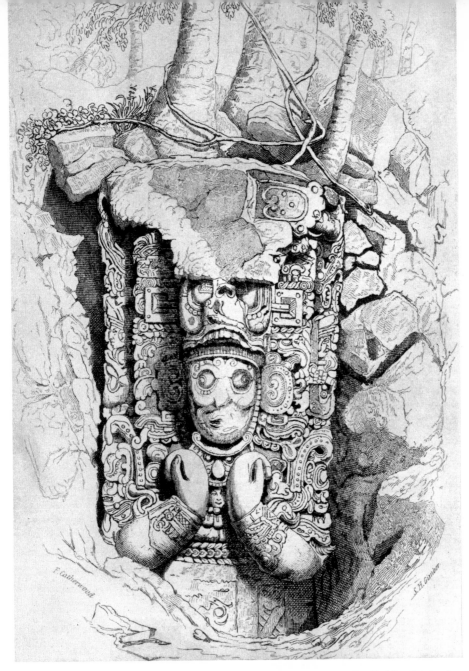

or 12 feet around; and without any proper instrument and afraid of injuring the sculpture, we preferred to let it remain, to be excavated by ourselves at some future time, or by some future traveller. Whoever he may be, I almost envy him the satisfaction of doing it.''

Today the Maya stelae stand behind barbed wire.

On the right is a photograph of a stele from Quiriguá, near Copán. On the left Catherwood's drawing of another stele, of which Stephens says: "This statue had suffered so much from the action of time and weather, that it was not always easy to make out the characters, the light being in all cases very bad and coming through irregular openings in the branches of trees."

The drawing is a masterpiece of exact representation. The fourteen hieroglyphs are copied with surpassing accuracy – a task all the more difficult because at the time designs such as these were utterly novel to the European eye.

Moonlight in Izamal.

A drawing by Catherwood which shows his highly romantic treatment of
jungle ruins. For archaeologists, it is important as the only reproduction of a
vanished work of art: a colossal mask on the outer wall of the wrecked step
pyramid at Izamal, Yucatán. In the foreground Dr. Cabot, the young physician
of the expedition, is about to take aim at a puma, while a native looks on.

Stephens supervises the moving of a sculptured stone door-jamb

from Kabah in Chiapas. The pillar is now in the American Museum of
Natural History in New York.

After having smashed valuable stones in several earlier attempts, Stephens
thought of another way to preserve these extraordinary monuments for science.
He obtained permission to have plaster casts made. A specialist then worked
for several years, in Copán and Quiriguá especially, constantly struggling with
the terrible climate, the trackless jungle and the wildly luxuriant vegetation.
Today these casts stand in New York and London – blackened by a century's
metropolitan soot, but as impressive as ever.

noticed by few, stood a sprinkling of ancient American art and documents which had come into the possession of the French state. Monsieur de Long-périer, the curator of the collection, kept another hoard of vessels and sculptures in his own office because he was refused any more room for exhibition.

We learn of this lamentable state of affairs from Abbé Charles Etienne Brasseur de Bourbourg (1814–1874), who sacrificed his career in order to dedicate himself to studying the antiquities of Middle America. A scholar as well as an adventurer, he made several vital discoveries among dusty books. Two of the documents he found must be reckoned among the most important sources on ancient American civilizations.

Brasseur studied philosophy and theology. In 1845 he was ordained priest, and went to live in Canada. In 1852 he published a history of that country. But he felt an unconquerable urge to study the cultures of Middle America, for he saw that no real scholar had engaged on the task which must precede all proper historical writing: the digging up, accumulation and inter-pretation of all available documents. He had held a teaching position in Canada and at thirty-two was made vicar-general of Boston. Renouncing that high office as well as the certain prospect of further advancement, he ac-cepted a post as priest in the Indian village of Rabinal in Guatemala.

First of all he learned Quiché, the Maya tongue which was still spoken in his village. Then he gave up his priestly duties, and began travelling, visiting many ruins, but constantly returning to the libraries of America and Europe to search for documents. To pay for all this, he first sold his property, then began writing highly successful historical novels under various pseudonyms. He was able to undertake new journeys and researches. He discovered what is prob-ably the most important surviving text on Maya religion.

The so-called *Popul Vuh* is the sacred book of the Quiché Indians, written down in the middle of the sixteenth century by an unknown Quiché loyal to the traditions of his tribe. The original has been lost, but the contents were preserved in a copy made by Francisco Ximénez between 1701 and 1703. He, too, wrote in the Quiché language, rendered in the Roman alphabet.

Brasseur discovered this copy at San Carlos University in Guatemala, and

published a facsimile edition along with a French translation. Thus, he put at the disposal of scholars incomparably valuable information on Maya religious customs, as well as material on the textile arts of the Maya.

Our photograph shows a Maya ruler at prayer; it is a detail from a relief stele from Yaxchilán (Chiapas), probably carved in the seventh or eighth century A.D. The embroidery-like designs on the ruler's garment are composed of parts of various hieroglyphs which mean *union*, *fire*, and *heaven*. This "magic armour" is strongly reminiscent of the magical bee and wasp patterns which are spoken of in the section of the *Popul Vuh* quoted on the following page.

The two damsels

who played the chief part in the following story
from the *Popul Vuh* may have looked like this.
At any rate they were probably dressed like these
two, who are pictured in the *Codex Ríos*.

The fable goes that the Quiché Indians felt
that they could no longer endure the high exac-
tions of their gods. The wizard priests Balam-
Quitzé, Balam-Acab, Mahacutah and Iqui-
Balam were making innumerable human sacrifices to the gods Tohil, Avilix and Hacavitz.
The tribes held a council and discussed what they
might do to protect themselves.

" 'How shall we overcome the gods?' they asked.

" 'This shall be our way ... Since they have the appearance of youths when
they let themselves be seen in the water, then let two maidens who are really
beautiful ... go and provoke in them the desire to possess them', they said.

" 'Very well, let us go then; let us find two beautiful maidens,' they exclaimed,
and then they went to find their daughters. And truly beautiful were the
maidens. Then they instructed the maidens: 'Go, our daughters, go to wash
clothes at the river, and if you see the three youths, undress before them, and
if their hearts desire you ... then you shall say: "Give us a token of yours."
And if after they have given you something, they want to kiss your faces,
really give yourself to them. And if you do not give yourself to them, we shall
kill you ... When you have the token, bring it here, and this shall be proof,
in our judgment, that they were joined with you.' ... And the two maidens,
Xtah and Xpuch, were sent to the river, to the bathing place of Tohil, Avilix
and Hacavitz. This is what was decided by all the tribes ... And the girls
became embarrassed at the moment when Tohil came, and did not speak
to him. Thereupon he questioned them: 'Where did you come from?' ...

And they answered: 'The lords have sent us to come here. "Go look at the faces of Tohil and speak with them", the lords told us; and "then bring proof that you have seen their faces", they told us.' Thus the two girls spoke, making known (that is, giving away) the purpose of their coming. Well, what the tribes wanted was that the two maidens would be violated by the incarnation of Tohil. But Tohil, Avilix, and Hacavitz, speaking again to Xtah and Xpuch, as the two maidens were called: 'Very well, with you shall go proof of our conversation. Wait a little and then you shall give it to the lords,' they said. Then they held council with the priests and sacrificers, and they said to Balam-Quitzé, Balam-Acab, Mahacutah, and Iqui-Balam: 'Paint three capes, paint on them the symbol of your being, in order that it may be recognized by the tribes when the maidens who are washing carry them back.' ... At once the three began to paint. First, Balam-Quitzé painted a jaguar; the figure was made and painted on the surface of a cape. Then Balam-Acab painted an eagle on a cape; and then Mahacutah painted bumble-bees and wasps all over, figures and drawings of which he painted on the cloth. And the three finished their paintings, three pieces they painted. Then they went to give the capes to Xtah and Xpuch, as they were called, and Balam-Quitzé, Balam-Acab and Mahacutah said to them: 'Here is proof of your conversation; take these before the lords. Say to them, "In truth, Tohil has talked to us; here we bring the proof." Tell them, and have them dress themselves in the clothes which you will give them.'

"... When they (the maidens) arrived, the lords were filled with joy to see their faces and their hands, from which hung the things the maidens had gone for. 'Did you see the face of Tohil?' they asked them. 'Yes, we saw it,' answered Xtah and Xpuch. 'Very well, and you bring the token, do you not?' the lords asked, thinking this was proof of their sin. Then the maidens held out the painted capes ... At once the lords felt a desire to put them on.

"The jaguar did nothing when the lord threw the first painting on his back. Then the lord put on the second painting, with the figure of an eagle. The lord felt very well wrapped within it. And he turned about before all of them. Then he undressed before all and put on the third painted cape. And now he had on himself the bumble-bees and wasps which were on it. Instantly the bumble-bees and wasps stung his flesh ... Thus they were overcome ..."

One fine day the Maya people left their cities behind them, abandoned their homeland, and set up a new state for themselves in the northernmost corner of what is now Yucatán – with new cities and new temples. The reason for this unique, apparently arbitrary mass migration has not yet been determined.

Chichén-Itzá became the centre of this Maya "New Empire". It was a gigantic city, a complex of bizarre temples, step pyramids, an observatory, a vast "ball ground", and a palace. That indefatigable searcher of libraries, Brasseur, dug up in Madrid an account of this city by a sixteenth-century ecclesiastic, and published it in 1864. Immediately, a storm broke; the ecclesiastic was suspected of having been a teller of tall tales, if not a deliberate liar. He was a Franciscan, Diego de Landa (1524–1579), one of the great zealots of the age. His zeal in burning "heathen" documents had won him the rank of bishop of Mérida, the capital of Yucatán. It is no longer possible to say what caused this fanatic to undergo a sudden change of heart, and work for the preservation of surviving Indian documents, or what impelled him to study seriously the mores and customs of the Maya people, or what finally made him devote his attention to the altogether un-Christian Maya calendar. Thus, when his *Relación de las cosas de Yucatán*, edited by Brasseur, was reissued, people put little credence in its stories and interpretations. But there was one man who as soon as he became acquainted with the bishop's writings took them at their word, believed them quite literally, as Schliemann had the *Iliad*. And his instinct proved to be as right as Schliemann's. This was the American explorer and archaeologist Edward Herbert Thompson. Our picture shows the Sacred Well of Chichén-Itzá, from whose muddy depths Thompson fetched the treasures which Diego de Landa had said were there.

The bishop related that the "well" of Chichén-Itzá had been a place of sacrifice. Every year in the dry season the people threw young girls, prisoners and gems into the well to appease the rain god. Thompson took lessons in diving, and descended into the dark waters. The "well" is in reality a big basin of water, approximately circular in form. The depth is considerable, and has not yet been exactly measured. At its widest point the hole is some 187 feet across. Steep limestone walls, some fifty feet in height, frame the entire basin.

Thompson began to dredge. No luck. Then he hired some sponge-divers from the Bahamas, himself donned a diver's suit, and went down into the well. The things he brought to the surface were a tremendous vindication of the bishop. There were skeletal remains and gold work of the finest sort – the very offerings to the rain god of which he had spoken. The golden ornaments Thompson salvaged – some of these are reproduced overleaf – are precious for their rarity as well as their metal. Gold was what the Spanish conquistadors were seeking in El Dorado; that was what had led them to the country, and for gold they conquered, pillaged and killed. To them, the value lay in the metal, and therefore they melted jewelry, finely-wrought utensils and beautiful vessels, into gold bars – these being easier to ship. Thus almost all the Maya works of art in gold vanished in the melting pot – but at the mud-level of the well that Thompson reached, eighty feet under water, such treasures lay intact. We would never have had them but for Thompson's courageous action. Yet we cannot regard him as a really serious interpreter of his finds. He was by nature

a visionary. Moreover, his diving had injured his health; later he became lame and partially deaf, which may sometimes have affected the tone of his reports. These are not always organized with precision and clarity.

The gold objects he found (above are parts of a gold mask) were not only interesting, but full of surprises for scholars. For the most part they were not pure gold, but alloys – evidence of advanced metallurgical techniques on the part of the makers. Furthermore, most of them were imports; this was proved by chemical and technological studies. This in turn indicated a continent-wide commerce whose existence had not been remotely suspected.

Unfortunately, this adventure put an abrupt end to Thompson's delvings in Mexico. The Mexican government accused him of theft of national property, demanded a fantastic sum in compensation, and confiscated the property he had bought in Yucatán . . . Feeling, with some justification, that sinister forces were closing in upon him and that he was in real danger, this adventurous archaeologist took swift action. He chartered a half-finished schooner. His party consisted of twenty-six persons, and he had food aboard for only eleven: moreover he had no nautical instruments. After a perilous thirteen-day voyage he reached Cuba. He never again set foot in Mexico.

Upon the death of Eduard Seler in 1922,

the museum at Mexico City closed its doors for three days as a sign of mourning. When Seler (1859 –1922) was a young man of twenty he went down with a dangerous gastric disease. It left him so ravaged that he had to abandon his plans for a career as a teacher; the authorities considered him physically unfit and refused to rehire him. Forced to find some other way to earn his living, he translated a book on American prehistory, and thus found his way into the field in which he was to be a leader and path-finder for forty years.

Seler went to work as an assistant in the Berlin Ethnological Museum; later he became director of the Americanist department. With his wife (daughter of the physician who had saved his life), he set out in 1887 on his series of great explorations. Seler's contributions to knowledge of the religions, the languages and the arts of Central America, are inestimable. A piece of good fortune came his way in his meeting with the Duc de Loubat, who owed his title to conquests in the realm of the intellect; it had been given him by the Pope for important research in the Vatican archives. Loubat, an immensely rich man, established the first substantially-endowed chairs for Americanist studies in Paris, New York and Berlin – where, in 1899, Seler became its first occupant. Loubat also stood sponsor for those great congresses of "Americanists" at which Seler took the leading role for many years.

In his time Seler was also the foremost student of Middle American languages. The smallest scraps of his translations serve as bases for further research today. He was the first to make something of the mysterious Maya texts; he also grasped the system of the Aztec calendar. As a scholar, he never departed from the actual evidence. Speculation, even somewhat too audacious hypotheses, he abhorred. Consequently, with all his vast knowledge, this man never gave thought to the question of possible cultural links between Asia and America.

the strongest proof of a connection with Near Eastern and Egyptian cultures? Not only the pyramids but also certain linguistic forms, certain divinities and a large number of other peculiarities of the Middle American civilizations virtually drove scholars to assume cultural transfusion or imitation. We have already mentioned the theory that the Indians were descendants of the ten lost tribes of Israel who were expelled from Assyria by Sargon in 721 B.C. That thought cropped up early in post-Columbian history, and was enunciated by a Jewish traveller, Aaron Levi de Montezino, when he returned to Amsterdam in 1644. Eleven years later the idea was developed with messianic overtones by Rabbi Menasseh ben Israel in his book *Piedra gloriosa* (The Glorious Stone), published in 1655, with illustrations by Rembrandt.

There were other views: that the Indians were Hindus, whom St. Thomas had once set out to convert. Or they were descendants of one of the sons of Noah. To a man of strict scientific mind like Seler, all such notions seemed dilettante nonsense. And yet as Seler and like-minded scholars went about their tasks of collecting material and arranging it, new facts emerged bearing on the old problem.

Grafton Elliot Smith, the anatomist and investigator of mummies (see page 144), revived the question in 1924 with a flourish. The title of his essay gives us a hint of his approach: *Elephants and Ethnologists*. On the right, we reproduce one of the drawings he released for publication in the *Illustrated London News* – unmistakably an elephant with raised trunk from a stone relief from the palace at Palenque. Any keen-eyed observer could see such elephants among the reliefs of the pyramids at Copán and Palenque, as well as in Maya manuscripts. Since there were certainly no elephants in Middle America in historical times, *someone* must have brought with him to America at least a mental image of

an elephant. That, for Smith, was the only logical explanation. Some cautious
scholars, it was true, circumambulated the elephant by suggesting that the animal
pictured might be a rendering of the tapir, that small relative of the rhinoceros
native to Mexico and South America. But Smith simply laughed at them.

The foremost champion of the most recent theory of "diffusionism" – which
now holds that Indian cultures originated as a result of influences via China and
Indo-China – is the Austrian scholar Robert von Heine-Geldern (born 1885).
It must, however, be emphasized that the problem is far from solved. But during
1949 a discovery was made which demolished one of the favourite arguments of
the opponents of diffusionism.

Advocates of the independence of the American cultures had always maintained that the similarities between Mexican and Egyptian pyramids were
purely superficial. (Above, a model of the Pyramid of Tenayuca which
reveals the growth, layer by layer, of the vast structure.) One had only to compare their purposes for the fundamental difference to be instantly apparent.
For the Egyptian pyramids were tombs, mighty structures raised around the
burial chambers of the pharaohs. The Mexican pyramids, on the other hand,
were terraced structures serving the sole end of raising a temple above the
jungle and lending it commanding size and height.

This argument from function was persuasive. In fact none of the known
Mexican pyramids gave any indication of having been used as a tomb. Occasionally small chambers were discovered inside them, but since these were
empty, they were disregarded. Then, in 1949, a Mexican archaeologist discovered inside a pyramid a vault which was not empty.

When Alberto Ruz began excavation

of the Temple of the Inscriptions at Palenque (above, a cross-sectional drawing made after the excavation was completed), he attacked a shapeless hill covered by green jungle growth. After laborious digging archaeologists identified what had been an eight-stepped pyramid.

325

Inside the temple, which stood upon the top platform, the entrance to a staircase was found. It was carefully constructed and in a good state of preservation. Descending the forty-five steps, the scientists came to a landing from which two shafts opened out; these must once have admitted light and air. After a further twenty-one steps, the excavators came across a horizontal passage which had been closed by a wall. They broke through this obstacle and found, scattered over the floor, pots, objects of jade, and a pearl. These finds, so reminiscent of the funeral furnishings of Egyptian tombs, stirred the scientists to feverish excitement, which reached its height when, close by, they found skeletons – the bones of several young men and one woman. Behind this corridor a chamber opened out. A burial vault? It lay 80 feet below the floor of the temple, 6 feet under the base of the pyramid, and was 30 feet in length by 13 in width. Stucco reliefs adorned the walls. In the centre of the chamber stood a low stone structure which was though to be an altar. Its top was a slab of stone 12 feet long by 6 feet 6 inches wide by 10 inches thick, covered with reliefs and bordered by an indecipherable inscription.

When Alberto Ruz had this stone slab raised, he encountered something that shook the firm opinions of two generations of Maya scholars. What had looked like an altar was a sarcophagus. The hollow base contained the skeleton of a man between the ages of forty and fifty. Jade ornaments lay untouched in their original position. There were large earrings inscribed with Maya hieroglyphics, a diadem, a mosaic mask, a necklace of beads in the form of fruits and flowers, rings for all ten fingers, and many other objects. On both sides of the skull two enormous pearls were found. There could be no doubt about it: Ruz stood before the mortal remains of a Maya ruler. And was it not highly probable that the skeletons at the entrance were those of sacrifices offered to the ruler?

A complete scientific interpretation of this find is not yet possible. But opponents of the diffusion theory can no longer say that Mexican pyramids never served as burial chambers, as the Egyptian pyramids always did. In at least one case a Maya pyramid was *also* a mausoleum.

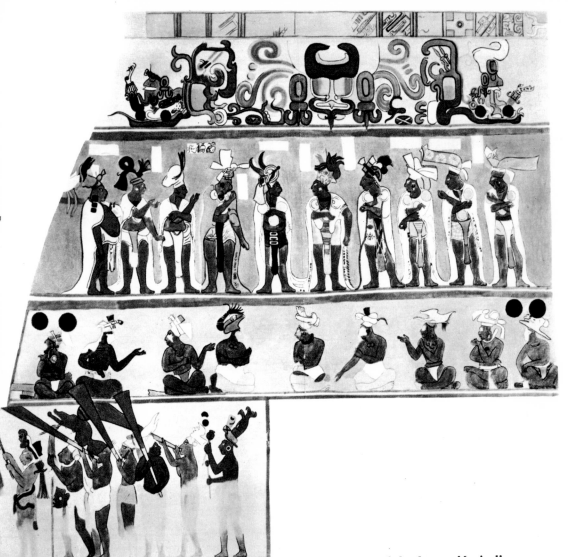

The territory of the Lacandón indians,

a dying branch of the Maya people in south-eastern Mexico, is a god-forsaken region visited by white men only when they are seeking mahogany trees or chicle, the raw material for chewing gum. Here, in 1946, came an American film unit commissioned by the United Fruit Company to produce a documentary film, *The Mayas in the Course of the Ages*.

The natives, extremely primitive, are the one Maya tribe which has never been

Christianized. The unit did its best to establish friendly relations and Mr. Giles G. Healey won their confidence to such an extent that they showed him their most sacred mystery: the "Coloured Walls". Healey became the first white man to see a sight of priceless value to archaeologists.

A considerable number of "Coloured Walls", that is frescoes, were already known. But those previously examined had pictured only religious subjects, gods and symbols. Here in Bonampak, however, on the walls of three rooms inside an ancient building, overgrown by vegetation, were found pictures of the daily life of the old Maya unparalleled in beauty and richness.

After Healey published an account and photographs of these paintings, a Mexican, and two years later an American, expedition went to Bonampak. But although complete lighting equipment was transported on muleback through the jungle, and although the best photographic apparatus was employed, all the photographs proved to be but feeble reproductions of the paintings. It is curious that in this age of the camera the scientists had to return to the methods of the nineteenth century. Two artists were engaged to copy the paintings as exactly as possible. Aided and advised as they were by professional archaeologists, their series of paintings, now exhibited in the National Museum of Mexico and in the Peabody Museum at Harvard University, are the most faithful of renderings. They had the dramatic effect of shocking archaeologists into awareness of all they did not know about the Maya. The meaning of the various figures, who are obviously presented in a certain order of rank; the costumes, which were undoubtedly determined by ritual; the still indecipherable Maya hieroglyphs – all these things presented riddles. Moreover – but we must put this tentatively – the style of the paintings is in a startling way reminiscent of Egypt. The figures are arranged in rows, and the heads and feet of most of the persons represented are shown in strict profile.

In the jungles of Middle America lurk many mysteries whose very existence we do not yet suspect. But one by one they will yield to man's endeavours. The day will come when we shall be able to write the history of Middle American civilizations with as much specific knowledge as we have long possessed in regard to Mediterranean cultures. And if the most recent attempt at deciphering the Maya hieroglyphs, offered by the Russian scholar Knorosov in 1955, proves valid, we shall soon know how those civilizations arose.

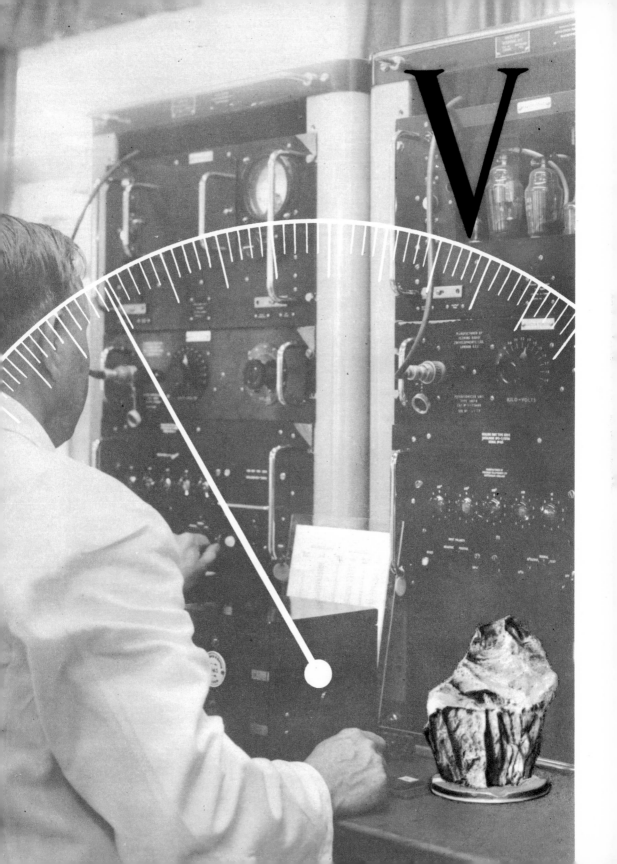

Book V

THIS BOOK has shown in 326 illustrations Western man's awakening to awareness of his own past, his extension of awareness into detailed knowledge and his distillation of knowledge into historical insight. Thus we have learned – or shall we say, are still learning – to understand our place in history. "The historian is a prophet turned backward", Friedrich Schlegel said. Western man's journey into the past was inspired by the spirit of humanism. Naturally enough, then, he first sought out the nearby world of Greco-Roman antiquity. Then he travelled further, into those civilizations with which we are connected by the Bible, and finally struck back to those primeval times in which civilization was first taking shape.

Since then this journey has assumed wider, global meanings. Not only do we seek our own beginnings; we search out alien roads as well. The historian finds that he must look to archaeology to understand the development of the world, of humanity in general. That is, archaeology has joined hands with prehistory, anthropology, and half a dozen other sciences. It is impossible to present even a bird's-eye view of the archaeological work that is going on today, as these lines are written, in China and South America, in Cimmerian Russia and in the former Holy Land. To mention a few names would be to omit arbitrarily far too many others. That revolutionary discoveries are still possible today (indeed, that we must hold ourselves in readiness for them), is illustrated by the chance finding of the Dead Sea scrolls – those Old Testament texts which must lead to a revision of many passages in the Bible. The photograph above shows G. Lancaster Harding, British director of archaeological research for the kingdom of Jordan, sorting fragments of the scrolls. Then, too, there are the latest excavations in Jericho, where foundations have come to light of cities that are probably older than any we have hitherto known. Or again, as in the case of the Hittites, we are suddenly in a position to write the history of old empires of whose existence we knew but dimly until recently. Perhaps a similar revelation will be forthcoming before long, in regard to the still mysterious Indus culture.

331

The pioneering age of archaeology is past. But it would be wrong to assume that archaeology's tasks have been diminished by a wealth of accomplishment. New developments in science have enriched the apparatus and methods of the archaeologists. The spade may remain the symbol of the excavator; but modern archaeology also makes use of airplanes, diving gear, and atomic physics.

Underwater photograph of a diver

bringing the neck of an antique amphora to the surface.

In 1900 the Greek sponge diver Elias Stadiatis, while returning from the Tunisian coast, was driven by a storm to the nearly uninhabited island of Antikythera off Crete. Descending into its waters after sponges, he came upon the wreck of a ship filled with quantities of bronze and marble statues. He brought to the surface a more than life-size bronze arm, because he justifiably feared that his story would not be believed without evidence.

That find probably marks the birth of underwater archaeology.

Sponge divers again, in 1907, called the attention of Maurice Merlin, director of monuments in Tunis, to a wrecked ship which they had found outside Mahdia, a small town on the eastern coast of Tunis. The ship had for cargo some sixty marble columns, as well as capitals, great marble torsos and busts, fauns, nymphs, statuettes of bronze. With the help of the French navy, Merlin worked from 1907 to 1913 to raise these treasures.

Ancient shipping in the Mediterranean was chiefly coastal. It is not surprising, therefore, that wrecks took place close to the land, so that the sunken ships usually settled to their final rest in moderate depths. Since 1925 fishermen of Albenga on the Italian Riviera had known the position of an ancient wreck. Not until 1952 were serious diving attempts undertaken; in twelve days some 500 perfectly preserved ancient amphorae were brought to light.

There was one trouble with all of these diving enterprises: they required too much equipment and were too costly for an always impoverished science. Archaeologists could not lavish private or public funds like Mussolini, who had half Lake Nemi pumped out to salvage the legendary galleys of Caligula.

332

During the nineteen-thirties an Austrian and a Frenchman pioneered entirely new methods of diving. Using no complicated apparatus, Hans Hass, the Viennese naturalist, began his undersea adventures with sharks. The French naval officer Jacques-Yves Cousteau further developed "skin" diving; he invented the aqualung, and achieved dives of up to two hours to depths of 300 feet. Archaeology seized on this technique as a means for recovering treasures buried in the sea. Today underwater maps of the French and Italian coasts have been drawn up which mark the precise positions of numerous ancient wrecks. The holds of these wrecks may yield up wondrous things.

This Roman road, easily recognizable to the airman,

is invisible to anyone on the ground. Père Antoine Poidebard (died 1954) of the St. Joseph University, Beirut, was the first person to assess fully the value of aerial observation and photography for archaeology. "We had reason to be-lieve that the Romans had built a fortified network of roads on their frontier, consisting on the one hand of radial highways, on the other of roads which followed the border along the edge of the desert. There was scarcely any sense in searching for unknown roads at ground level, since the borders had often shifted during the Parthian wars and the struggles with the Sassanids. I realized that we would be able to see the roads we sought only from the air." (Our picture shows the Gebel Seys, the road to the East, in Syria; it was taken on Oc-tober 17, 1930. The track seen dimly on the far left is the modern motor road.) Aerial archaeology was a war baby. During the First World War the British, French and Germans began photographing the terrain of the Near East for purposes of military observation, and discovered that the camera saw what the terrestrial observer could not. In the past two decades the English landscape in particular has been thus surveyed; countless traces of old roads and forti-fications, the outlines of vanished Roman buildings, have suddenly been made visible. Osbert Guy Stanhope Crawford, who until his death in 1957 was supreme in the field of aerial archaeology, called the surface of every ancient civilized land "a palimpsest, a document that has been written on and erased over and over again".

Archaeology has meanwhile also profited by the discoveries of modern physics. The method of "radiocarbon dating", based on the disintegration of the isotope

Carbon 14, enables the scientist to make extremely accurate estimates of age wherever organic substances are available for analysis. Thus, independent of archaeological finds, philological connections and historical points of reference, there is an almost exact criterion for the age of a charred bone, of a piece of wood from a bier, a flower found in a king's grave. We have already said that the pioneering age of archaeology is over. But only one who feels reality to be incompatible with romance and adventure could say that archaeology has therefore ceased to be a romantic adventure. History is always romantic, in the sense that we can only apprehend it through sensitivity and imagination. Flinders Petrie's noble words are still valid: "Imagination is the fire of discovery." Or, as the thought was put by that great historian Theodor Mommsen:

"Imagination, mother of all poetry, is likewise mother of all history."

In the selection of dates no strict method has been followed. A lecture was often more of a milestone in the development of archaeology than the several tomes on the subject which might be published ten years later; and as a rule the actual excavation usually proved more important than the first traveller's report, the first scouting expedition or the first sampling, even though this sampling led to the discovery. The decision on the most significant dates is a highly subjective matter. I have attempted here, by my brief notes, to bring the dates to life – but I cannot carry this too far. A chronology must be a précis, not a full-scale review. I have also deemed it best to deal more exhaustively with earlier developments in the field at the risk perhaps of stinting contemporary ones. Here assessments are still tentative and such vast quantities of new material are being amassed so rapidly that proper evaluation of these must remain the task of professional journals. May I hope, therefore, that the many first-rate scholars who are currently at work in the field, making discoveries of vital importance, will forgive me for being unable to mention their names here.

1119 and 1162 Decrees are published in Rome to protect the columns of Trajan and Marcus Aurelius from damage.

circa 1150 Henry, Bishop of Winchester, acquires classical statues in the course of a journey to Rome, and sends them to England.

1337 Petrarch visits Rome for the first time. He studies classical Latin, collects antique coins, and writes lives of classic figures. He is perhaps the first person to read classical writers critically.

circa 1400 The architect Filippo Brunelleschi organizes the first excavations in Rome. As was often the case with excavators up to the nineteenth century (and not always without reason), he is suspected of treasure-hunting.

1420–1427 The philologist and poet Francesco Filelfo learns Greek in Constantinople.

Back home in Italy, he becomes one of the most prominent teachers of Latin and Greek, and a rallying-point for the first humanists.

1435–1436 and again in *1443–1447* the merchant Cyriacus of Ancona travels about methodically collecting antiquities.

circa 1450 Poggio Bracciolini laments that less than a dozen of the sculptures of ancient Rome are left. According to an old inventory, fourth century Rome had 3,785 bronze statues, 22 equestrian statues, 73 gold and ivory images of gods and 80 gilded images.

1471 Pope Sixtus IV begins collecting ancient statuary in Rome. The collections of this period were only first steps toward future museums. They were amassed planlessly, at random, and were not made accessible to the public.

337

1485 Twenty thousand people in Rome flock to see the well-preserved mummy of a Roman girl discovered by chance in a tomb on the Appian Way.

1506 The *Laocoön* group is discovered; for more than two centuries the aesthetic interpretation of this work influences Europe's conception of the nature of classical art, and of art in general.

1520 Albrecht Dürer is in Brussels at the time the first examples of Aztec art are put on exhibition. He sets down his reaction to them in his diary.

1565 Johannes Helffrich visits the pyramids and the Sphinx in Egypt. In 1579 he publishes his journal.

circa 1566 Bishop Diego de Landa writes his *Relación de las cosas de Yucatán*.

1568–1648 The lifetime of Ixtlilxochitl (baptized Fernando Pimental, called Fernando de Alva), Chichimecan prince, whose chronicles of the Toltecs and Maya, based upon old texts and oral traditions, were given little credence until quite recently.

circa 1569 Bernardino de Sahagún, a missionary in Mexico, completes the first version of his book on the Aztecs, the most important source for the cultural history of Old Mexico.

1574 What is probably the first drawing of an Egyptian mummy to be published in Europe appears in an herbal by Joachim Strüppe.

1580–1765 The span of the lives of three travellers of the French nobility, N. C. Fabri de Peiresc, Bernard de Montfaucon, and the Comte de Caylus. In numerous books and pamphlets and thousands of letters they contribute such hoards of material on classical antiquity that sifting and interpretation become inevitable.

1605 The *Aldobrandine Wedding* is found, a Roman mural based on an Hellenistic prototype. Today it is considered a representation of the sacred wedding of Dionysus.

1614 Pietro della Valle sets out on his travels through the Orient. In 1621 he sends from Persepolis the first five cuneiform signs to reach Europe.

1615 Lorenzo Pignoria compares Mexican representations of gods to those of Euro-Asiatic antiquity, thus founding the science of comparative religion.

1617 Garcia de Silva Figueroa is the first to recognize the ruins of Persepolis for what they are. His results are not published until 1661.

1622–1623 Cardinal Ludovico Ludovisi assembles, within a single year, a collection of more than 300 antiques, including many Greek originals.

circa 1635 The Jesuit Athanasius Kircher begins the first systematic collection of antiques at the Collegium Romanum in Rome.

1640 Lord Arundel begins a similar collection in England.

1666 The Royal Society in London urges investigation of the ruins of Persepolis. The jeweller Chardin brings back the first detailed reports.

1674 Jacob Spon, a physician, travels through Asia Minor and Greece. He returns with descriptions of what he actually saw, critically set against ancient accounts. He is also the probable father of the term "archaeology".

1685 The physician Engelbert Kämpfer visits the site of Persepolis. He brings back numerous drawings and the first cuneiform text of any length to reach Europe.

1701–1703 Father Ximénez compiles the *Popul Vuh*, the sacred traditions of the Quiché Indians.

1714 Publication of a pamphlet by Cornelis de Bruin, in which he joins issue with his predecessors in regard to Persepolis.

1733 Foundation of the Society of Dilettanti in London, which actively supports collecting and excavations.

1734 The Capitoline Museum in Rome, by acquisition of the Albani Collection, becomes one of the earliest museums of antiquities.

1735 The *Antinous* relief is found; as with the *Laocoön*, aesthetic interpretation of this relief establishes an idealized conception of antiquity in the public mind.

1737–1742 R. Pococke travels through Egypt, Arabia and Greece. His works are published from 1743 on.

1748 Excavations begin in Pompeii under the direction of Alcubierre.

1749 R. Dalton makes the first reliable drawings of the Parthenon sculptures.

1751 J. Stuart ("Athenian Stuart") and N. Revett visit Athens. They publish in 1762 *The Antiquities of Athens Measured and Delineated.*

1753 Uncovering of the Villa dei Papiri in Herculaneum. Scrolls are found and Piaggio succeeds in unrolling a number of these.

1753–1759 Foundation and opening of the British Museum.

1761 G. B. Piranesi's evocations of Roman architecture are published. His romantic conception stirs general interest in antiquity.

1762 Carsten Niebuhr reaches Arabia. Later, as sole survivor of his expedition, he publishes a travel book which Napoleon is to find useful during his Egyptian expedition.

1764 J. J. Winckelmann publishes his *Geschichte der Kunst des Altertums* (History of Ancient Art), commonly considered to mark the beginning of modern archaeology.

1771 William Jones discovers the relationships among the Indo-European group of languages. His discovery is the foundation of modern linguistic science and, for archaeology, of many future decipherments.

1772 Sir William Hamilton sells his famous collection of vases to the British Museum.

1787 Antonio del Río undertakes first investigations of the ruins in Mexico. His work is published in 1822.

1788 Publication of Abbé Barthélemy's *Voyage du jeune Anarchasis en Grèce*, a much-translated book which popularized an idealized picture of Greece.

1793 The Louvre is opened as a French museum, with 117 antiques. In 1815 it contains 384 pieces. An innovation: the public is admitted free of charge.

1796 Napoleon includes a special article in the armistice of Bologna, which requires the delivery of numerous ancient monuments and documents to France. "Legitimate" pillage of art by such treaties remained the rule up to very recent times.

1797 Georg Zoëga, after innumerable bungling attempts by others, for the first time undertakes a serious study of the Egyptian hieroglyphs. He recognizes the significance of the cartouches.

1797–1799 Friedrich Hölderlin's *Hyperion* is published, presenting an idealized Hellenism as the goal of romantic longings.

1798 Bonaparte embarks at Toulon for Egypt. The researches and collections of his Scientific Commission form the foundation of modern Egyptology.

1799 In the Nile city of Rosetta the trilingual Rosetta Stone is found, the basis for the decipherment of the Egyptian hieroglyphs.

1800–1803 Lord Elgin succeeds in transporting the most important parts of the Parthenon frieze to England.

1802 G. F. Grotefend deciphers the Persepolitan cuneiform script. His discovery is scarcely noticed by scholars.

1803 The first book on ancient Egyptian architecture is published by A. C. Quatremère de Quincy. (It had been written as far back as 1785.)

1804 Lord Elgin requests the sculptor A. Canova to assume the task of restoring his Greek sculptures. Canova refuses; he argues that works of such quality should not be touched. Restorations had hitherto been customary; this was the first clear proclamation of respect for the originals.

1805–1807 Captain G. Dupaix and L. Castañeda travel in Mexico. Their extensive collections of material on Old Mexico are not noticed until 1831.

1807 Claudius J. Rich travels through Mesopotamia. In 1811, employing ten workmen, he undertakes the first excavations in Babylon.

1809 Disguised as "Sheik Ibrahim", Johann Ludwig Burckhardt begins his travels through the Near East.

1809–1822 Publication of the *Description de l'Egypte*, the scientific harvest of Napoleon's expedition.

1814 The British Museum buys the great *Frieze of Bassae*. This, added to earlier acquisitions, makes the museum the greatest storehouse of antiquities in the world.

1815 By this time numerous travellers have combed the entire area once dominated by Greco-Roman civilization: E. D. Clarke, E. Dodwell, W. Gell, J. P. Gandy, F. Bedford, G. R. Cockerell, J. Foster, O. Bröndsted, G. Koes, Baron von Stackelberg, Haller von Hallerstein, J. Linckh. These men have visited and brought to the attention of the public the ruins of Tiryns, Mycenae, Bassae and many other places.

1818 Ker Porter meets Claudius Rich in Baghdad. Porter's drawings, which he brings back from his adventurous journeys, are far superior to all those of his predecessors in reliability.

circa 1820 A farmer in Melos finds fragments of a statue of Aphrodite of Parian marble. As the *Venus of Milo* it becomes the most popular of all the sculpture of classical antiquity.

1820 G. B. Belzoni's account of his Egyptian excavations is published.

1820–1829 The R. Hay expedition explores Egypt. Its vast gleanings remain to this day in manuscript in the collection of the British Museum.

1821 Publication of W. M. Leakes's *Topography of Athens* – the first purely topographical description of an ancient city, divorced from a description of travel.

1821–1826 In the course of the Greek revolt the Acropolis of Athens is twice bombarded. The west front of the Parthenon and the Erechtheion are damaged.

1822 J. F. Champollion, utilizing the Rosetta Stone, deciphers the Egyptian hieroglyphs.

1825 William Lane, with the aid of the camera lucida, begins his meticulous drawings of Egyptian monuments.

1825 Eduard Gerhard begins collecting Etruscan figurines.

1826–1830 Publication of J. I. Hittorf's *Architecture antique de la Sicile*. Hittorf is the first to assert that classical sculpture and architecture were painted all over.

1827 In Corneto (Tarquini) the first coloured Etruscan murals are discovered in tombs. Soon after, similar discoveries are made in Chiusi, Veii, Cervateri and Orvieto.

1828 The Duc de Luynes examines the ruined temples of Metapont on the Bay of Tarento.

1828 Tombs are discovered in Vulci containing incredible quantities of painted vases. The owner of the property, Prince Canino, employs 100 workmen daily for the excavations. In 1831 Gerhard publishes the first account of these finds.

1829 J. J. Dubois and Abel Blouet dig at the Temple of Zeus in Olympia. They send the Louvre several reliefs which show distinct traces of painting.

1829 First session of the Istituto di correspondenza archaeologica in Rome, under the direction of Gerhard and attended by the sculptor Thorwaldsen.

1830 Paul Dubrux discovers near Kerch in the Crimea rich hoards of the gold of Scythian rulers.

1830 Publication of Karl Otfried Müller's *Handbuch der Archaeologie*, a bold summary of the work accomplished up to that time. For years to come this "Handbook of Archaeology" remained a standard work on the subject.

1831 The first volumes of the *Antiquities of Mexico*, Lord Kingsborough's vast collection of material, are published.

1832 In this and succeeding years Charles Fellows travels through Asia Minor and becomes one of the first to describe the ruins of Lycia. After 1842 he directs excavations.

1832–1836 Count Waldeck travels in Mexico. He names the Maya pyramid at Uxmal after his patron, Lord Kingsborough.

1833–1837 Charles Texier explores Asia Minor. He is the first to describe the Hittite capital of Hattuses (Boghazköy), although without suspecting what it is.

1834 Gottfried Semper's *Vorläufige Bemerkungen über bemalte Architektur und Plastik bei den Alten* is published. In this book he joins issue over the "white as plaster" conception of the classical world, and shows that the Greeks lived in a world full of colour.

1835 H. C. Rawlinson is transferred to Persia. Independently of Grotefend, he deciphers cuneiform script again.

1835 Block by block, parts of the Temple of Athena Nike are removed from the bastion into which they had been incorporated during the siege of the Acropolis and, under the direction of Ludwig Ross, are put together again to restore the temple.

1836 F. Chesney's attempt to use steam vessels on the Euphrates ends with the total loss of his ship, the *Tigris*. But his experiment is useful for all later archaeologists who wish to transport heavy sculpture.

1837 Colonel Howard Vyse uses gunpowder to blast entrances into the Egyptian pyramids.

1842 John L. Stephens publishes his *Incidents of Travel in Central America* . . . the first extensive account of the discovery and excavation of Maya cities.

1842 Paul E. Botta begins his excavations at Kuyunjik and Khorsabad. His work is crowned by extraordinary success; he uncovers the Palace of King Sargon and, with it, the first masterpieces of Assyrian sculpture.

1842–1846 Richard Lepsius conducts an Egyptian expedition. He extends existing knowledge of the Egyptian Old Empire back to the fourth millennium B. C., brings the number of known pyramids to 67, and investigates some 130 of the hitherto unknown mastabas.

1843 Blind W. H. Prescott publishes his *History of the Conquest of Mexico*. This book is followed in 1847 by *The Conquest of Peru*.

1845 H. A. Layard begins his excavations in the vicinity of ancient Nineveh.

1846–1847 F. C. Penrose draws the outline of the Parthenon at Athens and proves the existence of the so-called "horizontal curves".

1849–1850 Layard finds in Nineveh significant portions of King Assurbanipal's clay tablet library.

1851–1854 Jules Oppert investigates the ruins of Babylon.

1851–1855 Near Memphis Auguste Mariette excavates the Serapeum, the graves of the sacred Egyptian bulls. Later he founds the present Cairo Museum and thus helps to protect Egypt against further looting excavations.

1852 Ernst Curtius gives a lecture in Berlin designed to arouse public interest and participation in an excavation of Olympia. His fund-raising brings in only 787 marks.

1852–1854 Hormuzd Rassam digs in Nineveh and discovers more of Assurbanipal's library, including parts of the Gilgamesh epic.

1853–1859 Publication of H. Brunn's *Geschichte der Griechischen Künstler* (History of the Greek Artists). Brunn sets forth the fundamentals for understanding the laws of form in classic art. In 1888 he publishes the first number of *Denkmäler griechischer und römischer Skulptur in historischer Anordnung* (Monuments of Greek and Roman Sculpture in an Historical Arrangement).

1857 Publication in London of the pamphlet containing the translations of Rawlinson,

Talbot, Hincks and Oppert, proof that these men have correctly read the cuneiform script.

1857 C. T. Newton excavates the Mausoleum at Halicarnassus, one of the Seven Wonders of the ancient world. He completes the Amazon frieze, parts of which had already been taken to the British Museum in 1846.

1858 In Cnidos, Newton for the first time lays bare the ground-plan of an ancient city.

1859 C. Lenormant digs in Eleusis.

1861 Napoleon III acquires the Villa Farnese in Rome. Pietro Rosa uncovers the palaces of emperors. (In 1869 the wall-paintings in the House of Livia are found.)

1861 Georges Perrot's Galatian Expedition starts. Although his task is to study inscriptions on the Temple of Augustus in Ankara, he also undertakes explorations of Anatolia and brings back word of "Hittite" monuments.

1861 In Madrid, B. de Bourbourg finds notes by Diego de Landa which provide a first key to a tentative understanding of Mexican hieroglyphs.

1865 Palma di Cesnola begins the excavation and collection of antiquities on Cyprus which he exhibits in New York in 1872.

1865 Karl Humann pays his first visit to Pergamon.

1866 The centenarian Count Waldeck's account of the Maya pyramids at Palenque is published.

1869 Schliemann goes to Troy for the first time. (See the tables on pages 50–52.)

1869–1874 J. T. Wood locates the Temple of Artemis near Ephesus, another of the Seven Wonders of the ancient world. Out of marshy terrain he brings to light marvellous remains of the temples.

1870 A. Conze determines the "geometric style" of vase ornamentation, thus revealing the importance of ceramics for chronology.

1872 W. Wright sends squeezes of the Hittite hieroglyphs in Hamath to the British Museum.

1872 George Smith announces he has found in the British Museum, among the clay tablets assembled by Rassam, a pre-Biblical Flood legend, part of the Gilgamesh epic.

1873 Smith searches the library of Kuyunjik for the tablets missing from the Gilgamesh epic. After a week's search he finds them.

1873 A. Conze begins excavations at Samothrace. This is the first official archaeological undertaking on the part of Austria since Prince Metternich forbade all archaeological work.

1874 Foundation of the German Archaeological Institute in Athens.

1875 Beginning of the excavations in Olympia under Ernst Curtius. First excavation financed by a government in a foreign country (to the extent of 600,000 marks) in spite of the stipulation that all finds should remain at the site. W. Dörpfeld distinguishes himself on this expedition. The Olympia excavation serves as a model for up-to-date field archaeology. The best known single find of this excavation, noteworthy also for clarifying, by its position, the whole plan of the site, is the *Hermes* of Praxiteles.

1877–1879 Théophile Homolle digs out the Temple of Apollo on Delos. Under various directors the digging is continued until 1894, then resumed in 1902.

1877–1881 In Tello Ernest de Sarzec finds the first works of Sumerian art.

1878 J. Humann begins the excavations in Pergamon (continued 1880–1881, 1883–1896). In 1879 he excavates the last, ninety-seventh piece of the *Gigantomachia*. The altar, packed in 462 boxes weighing a total of 35 tons is shipped to Berlin and housed in a special museum.

1880 At Knossos M. Kalokairinos uncovers the remains of walls which, it is supposed, were part of the Labyrinth.

1880 W. Flinders Petrie begins his work in Egypt, and continues until 1935. His work comprises the most extensive research in modern Egyptology.

1880 In London A. H. Sayce gives a lecture asserting that an empire of the Hittites existed in the second millennium B.C.

1881 In a cave at Der-el-Bahri Emil Brugsch finds the mummies of forty kings: Sethos I, Ramses II, and others.

1881 Gaston Maspero discovers the first inscriptions in the pyramids of Sakkara – some 4,000 lines.

1882 W. Dörpfeld begins his collaboration with Schliemann. He introduces system into the excavations at Troy.

1882–1890 Demetrios Philios digs at the Sanctuary of the Mysteries in Eleusis.

1885–1886 Marcel Dieulafoy brings sculptures from Susa to Paris.

1887 By chance, with no scientists present, the clay tablet archives of Tel-el-Amarna are found.

1887–1910 Eduard Seler explores Middle America, studying the archaeology, ethnology, religions and languages of the region. He becomes the founder of modern Americanist studies.

1888 K. Humann and F. von Luschan begin excavation of the Late Hittite city of Zinjirli. By the second day of work they find twenty-six orthostats (carved slabs).

1888 Under the direction of Peters, the American Oriental Society expedition begins digging in Nippur. (Work continues 1889 –1890, 1893–1896, 1898–1900.) Strictly scientific methods are not followed until the fourth excavation under Hilprecht. Rich finds of cuneiform inscriptions are made.

1891 H. Brugsch brings some 3,000 rolls of Egyptian papyri to Europe.

1892–1894 O. Puchstein and R. Koldewey investigate the temples of southern Italy and Sicily, in particular Selinunte.

1893 Adolf Furtwängler undertakes to classify by artists the vast amount of ancient statuary which by now has been collected.

1893 Under T. Homolle's direction excavations in Delphi begin.

1895 K. Humann begins to uncover the city of Priene. (This work is continued by Wiegand and Schrader.) This excavation marks a shift in archaeological interest from single objects to relationships; archaeologists turn their attention from *finds* to *history*.

1899 Robert Koldewey begins his eighteen years of excavation at Babylon, one of the greatest excavations of all times. Germany grants a total of 2,000,000 marks in support of this work.

1899 Max von Oppenheim devotes his own wealth to excavations at Tel Halaf and displays finds and sculptures of three millennia in a museum of his own in Berlin.

1899–1904 Baalbek Expedition under O. Puchstein and B. Schulz.

1899–1914 Theodor Wiegand, after purchasing sizable portions of the city, examines the remains of Miletus.

1900 Arthur Evans begins his work on Crete, which goes on over twenty-five years.

1900 A. Furtwängler publishes his *Antike Gemmen*, a first treatise on the *historical* as well as the artistic value of gems.

1900 Gustav and Alfred Körte open five mound graves in Gordion, the ancient capital of Phrygia.

1900 Sponge divers discover near the island of Antikythera a sunken Roman ship with a cargo of bronze statues.

1902–1904 Christian Blinkenberg and K. F. Kinch explore Lindos on the island of Rhodes. They find inscriptions which enable them to establish more precisely the dates of the sculptor Boethos and of the sculptors of the *Laocoön* group.

1902–1904 Ludwig Borchardt deduces the general plan of the tremendous area of pyramids at Abusir.

1902–1904 Rudolf Herzog digs on the island of Cos.

1903 W. Andrae starts his excavations at Assur and charts the development of the city over a period of more than 3,000 years.

343

1905 Hugo Winckler and T. Macridi-Bey travel in Anatolia. In 1906 they begin to uncover the clay tablet archives of the Hittite city of Hattusas (Boghazköy).

1907 Sellin begins excavations near Jericho; his finds extend from the neolithic to the Byzantine age.

1910 John Garstang, after travels in Asia Minor, publishes *The Land of the Hittites*, the first important attempt to write Hittite history.

1911 Amadeo Maiuri begins to probe Pompeii and Herculanum in a scientific manner.

1911–1914 D. G. Hogarth, C. Leonard Woolley and T. E. Lawrence begin excavations in the Late Hittite city of Carchemish.

1912 On the plateau around Cuzco, Peru, Hiram Bingham discovers the old Inca fortresses of Machu Picchu and Vitcos.

1912 Julius Jordan begins excavations in Warka (Uruk, Erech).

1914 Publication of *Mexican Archaeology*, by T. A. Joyce, the first handbook of Middle American archaeology.

1914 Ernst Buschor temporarily writes finis to the excavations at Samos. (Continuation, 1925–1940.)

1915 Friedrich Hrozny publishes his decipherment of Hittite cuneiform script and announces that Hittite is an Indo-European language.

1915 S. G. Morley publishes his fundamental *Introduction to the Study of Maya Hieroglyphs*.

1917 The Carnarvon expedition, directed by Howard Carter, begins digging near Luxor in the Valley of the Kings.

1918 H. R. H. Hall starts excavations in Ur of the Chaldees.

1920 H. E. Winlock finds in Thebes the "mummy of Wah", of which X-ray photographs are prepared for the first time in New York; Elliot Smith had earlier examined mummies by fluoroscope.

1922 Leonard Woolley goes to Ur, where he succeeds in finding royal graves filled with golden treasures.

1922 Howard Carter discovers the entrance to the tomb of Tutankhamen.

1922–1927 John Marshall digs in Mohenjo-Daro in India. He discovers the hitherto unknown Indus culture, as old as the Sumerian, possibly older.

1922 Elliot Smith revives the question, often raised earlier by amateurs, of a possible relationship between the cultures of the Mediterranean and Asia and those of Middle America.

1925 Publication in Germany of the fundamental work on Attic red-figure vase painters, by John D. Beazley, who had examined some 10,000 pieces of ceramic. The English edition does not appear until 1942, by which time Beazley has studied 15,000 pieces.

1926 H. E. Winlock finds at Der-el-Bahri on the Nile a mass grave containing sixty half-mummified soldiers of the period *circa* 2000 B. C.

1926–1937 Oliver G. Ricketson investigates Maya cities, especially Uaxactún.

1927 T. Wiegand resumes the interrupted work at Pergamon.

1929–1939 Claude F. A. Schaeffer digs in Ras Shamra, "Ugarit", the principal port city of Syria in the second century B. C. The many layers of the site afford significant information on the chronology of the Near East and Egypt. Schaeffer's *Stratigraphie comparé et chronologie de L'Asie occidentale* (1948) is a fundamental book on the subject. Schaeffer resumes excavations in 1948.

1931 The Mexican archaeologist Alfonso Caso discovers on Monte Albán near Oaxaca the richest gold treasure ever found in Middle America. Almost all the pieces show a high degree of artistry.

1931 Kurt Bittel (with Rudolf Naumann) begins systematic excavations at the Hittite capital of Hattusas, near present-day Boghazköy. He finds more than 6,000 clay tablets, among them bilingual seals by which H. G. Güterbock is able to confirm a number of hypothetical readings of Hittite hieroglyphs.

1930–1932 The Semitic expert Hans Bauer performs an amazing feat of decipherment. He proves the alphabetic character of the clay tablet script from Ras Shamra and immediately deciphers seventeen signs correctly.

1933 André Parrot begins his investigations of the ruins of Mari, which are to continue for some twenty years. His most important find is the state archives, including some 20,000 clay tablet inscriptions. Decipherment of these dictated a new date for the reign of Hammurabi.

1935 Sir Leonard Woolley digs up the capital of the Yarim Lim near Alalakh (Atchana).

1936 Werner Jaeger publishes *Paedeia.*

1937 S. N. Kramer begins a study of the cuneiform finds from Nippur and discovers a hitherto unknown chapter of the Gilgamesh epic.

1938 K. Lehmann resumes excavations at Samothrace (and again in 1947–1948).

1941 The Carnegie Foundation completes its seven-year restoration work in Copán. The government of Honduras assumes the task of protecting the ruins.

1945 Helmut T. Bossert fixes his attention upon Karatepe, where in subsequent years he discovers numerous reliefs in a Late Hittite citadel, as well as a Phoenician-Hieroglyphic Hittite bilingual which enables him to decipher the Hittite hieroglyphic script.

1946 Dhorme in Paris offers a tentative decipherment of the proto-byblic script which was used in Byblos, northern Phoenicia, around 1000 B. C.

1946 Photographer G. G. Healey, a member of a motion picture expedition, is led by Lacandón Indians to a temple near Bonampak wherein are coloured frescoes portraying the daily life of the ancient Maya.

1947 Out of fragments of cuneiform script brought from Nippur by H.V.Hilprecht around 1900, F. Steele pieces together a law book of King Lipit-Ishtar which is older than the laws of Hammurabi.

1947 A Bedouin finds in a cave near Kumran, north of the Dead Sea, Hebrew scrolls stored in clay vessels; among them is a scroll of Isaiah dating from the second century B. C. and the first century A. D. Since then numerous other finds seem to necessitate a revision of the existing text of the Bible, and throw new light on the sect of the Essenes and its relationship to New Testament origins.

1949 The Mexican archaeologist Alberto Ruz begins excavations at the Temple of the Inscriptions at Palenque. Inside the pyramid he discovers the tomb of a ruler, thus producing the first proof that the Maya pyramids, like the Egyptian pyramids, *could be* used as mausoleums.

1950–1952 Leonhard Schultze-Jena continues the work of Seler, retranslating the greater part of Sahagún's *Historia.*

1952 Williard F. Libby published his method of radiocarbon dating; a technique for determining the age of organic substances; this constitutes the most significant contribution physics has hitherto made to historical science.

1952–1956 Homer Thompson completely excavates the Stoa on the Agora at Athens, and at a cost of 2,000,000 dollars erects a mighty reconstruction.

1953 The architect Michael Ventris deciphers Cretan Linear Script B and finds that Old Cretan was a Greek dialect.

1953 Madame Halet Çambel, formerly assistant to H. T. Bossert at the Karatepe excavations, with the aid of Italian specialists, begins restoration of the Late Hittite sculptures from Karatepe.

1954 Zakkaria Goneim discovers a new step pyramid near Sakkara, and in the interior of it an untouched sarcophagus – which, however, is empty.

1954 Zaki Nour, digging close to the Pyramid of Cheops, turns up the 120 foot long "death-ship" of a Fourth Dynasty pharaoh.

1955 The Russian scholar J. V. Knorozov published a tentative decipherment of the Maya hieroglyphs.

Bibliographical Note

and List of Sources for the Illustrations

Many of the works consulted for this book are noted in the text or in the List of Sources for the Illustrations. The following selection has been deliberately restricted to a few basic works which, in the author's opinion, will supply the essential background for anyone wishing to delve deeper into the history of archaeology. With these books as guides, moreover, the interested reader will be able to pursue the subject as far as he wishes.

The best general survey is *A Hundred Years of Archaeology*, by Glyn E. Daniel (London, 1950). Daniel devotes particular attention to prehistoric archaeology. A more specialized work, which tells the story of Mesopotamian exploration, is Seton Lloyd's *Foundations in the Dust* (London, 1947). A brief handbook of archaeological practice is Kathleen M. Kenyon's *Beginning in Archaeology* (London, 1953). Considerably more comprehensive is Sir Mortimer Wheeler's brilliantly written *Archaeology from the Earth* (London, 1954), which can be most warmly recommended. For Middle American archaeology acquaintance with William Prescott's histories is a prerequisite; then Sylvanus G. Morley's *The Ancient Maya* (London, 1946) and George C. Vaillant's *The Aztecs of Mexico* (London, 1950) will both serve as excellent introductions.

For the reader to whom German is no obstacle, the classical work on the history of archaeology remains, for all its restriction to "art archaeology", *Die archäologischen Entdeckungen des neunzehnten Jahrhunderts*, by Adolf Michaelis (Leipzig, 1906). *Die archäologischen Entdeckungen im 20. Jahrhundert*, by Friedrich von Oppeln-Bronikowski (Berlin, 1931), can be regarded as its continuation. A survey of recent research is provided by Karl Schefold in his *Orient, Hellas und Rom in der archäologischen Forschung seit 1939* (Bern, 1949). The history of ideas is the subject of Max Wegner's *Altertumskunde* (Munich, 1951). Probably the best outline of the problems of decipherment for the reader already grounded in philology is Johannes Friedrich's *Entzifferung verschollener Schriften und Sprachen* (Berlin, 1954).

The list is brief, but the bibliographies in these books will lead the interested reader to the original sources.

List of Sources for the Illustrations

List of Sources for the Illustrations

List of Sources for the Illustrations

List of Sources for the Colour Plates

I Zeus abducting Ganymede. Peloponnesian terra-cotta, about 470 B.C. Fragments of the group were found scattered in various places at Olympia by German expeditions active there between 1878 and 1952. The sculpture, which shows unmistakable traces of having once been coloured, now stands in the Olympia museum. *(Photo Prof. Max Hirmer)*

II Greek Temples were Coloured. Entablature of the Parthenon in Gottfried Semper's coloured restoration. Hand-coloured engraving from Sempers *Über Anwendung der Farben in der Baukunst*, Dresden, 1836. *(Specially photographed)*

III Vase Painting. Athene bearing Arms. Greek vase painted in Athens (late 6th century B.C.). *(By perm. of the Tr. of the Brit. Mus.)*

IV Roman Woman playing the Cithara. Wall painting in a villa at Boscoreale, near Pompeii (1st century A.D.). *(By perm. of the Metrop. Mus., New York)*

V Egyptian Death-Ship. Model carved in wood, probably from Thebes (Eleventh Dynasty, about 2000 B.C.). At the head and foot of the boat stand the protective goddesses Isis and Nephthys (see also p. 176). *(By perm. of the Tr. of the Brit. Mus.)*

VI Pharaoh Tutankhamen. The golden lid above the mummy of Tutankhamen (Eighteenth Dynasty, about 1350 B.C.). Found in the pharaoh's tomb in the Valley of the Kings by Carnarvon and Carter. *(Photo George Allan, Esq.)*

VII A Dead Man's Prayer. The dead man praying under a palm tree. Wall painting in the tomb of Pashedu at Der el-Medineh (Eighteenth or Nineteenth Dynasty, between 1580 and 1200 B.C.) *(Photo George Allan, Esq.)*

VIII Entrance to the Tomb of an Egyptian Queen. The anteroom of the tomb of Queen Nephertari at Thebes. The paintings are executed in slight relief against a stucco background. (Nineteenth Dynasty, thirteenth century B.C.) The tomb was discovered in 1904 by an Italian expedition. *(Photo Prof. Max Hirmer.)*

IX Goat at the Tree of Life. Known as "The Ram caught in a Thicket". Polychrome figure on wooden core (approx. 2500 B.C.). From Ur of the Chaldees, the home of Abraham. *(By perm. of the Tr. of the Brit. Mus.)*

X Model of Persian War-Chariot (fifth to fourth centuries. B.C.). From the "Oxus Treasure", found 1877. *(By perm. of the Tr. of the Brit. Mus.)*

XI Persian Drinking-Horn (fifth century B.C.). From the "Oxus Treasure", found 1877. *(By perm. of the Tr. of the Brit. Mus.)*

XII Head-Dress of a Queen of Ur. Golden ornaments of Queen Schub-ad. From the royal graves at Ur (about 2500 B.C.). Leaves were the favourite ornamental motif of the period. Brit. Mus., London, from the finds of Sir Leonard Woolley. *(By perm. of the Tr. of the Brit. Mus.)*

XIII Aztec Skull overlaid with Mosaic. The overlay consists of bits of turquoise and obsidian; the eyes are of iron pyrites. (Aztec, between A.D. 1324 and 1521. Typical of the rich tradition of mosaic work among the Aztecs (see also p. 280). *(Photo Irmgard Groth-Kimball, by perm. of the Tr. of the Brit. Mus.)*

XIV Ritual Axe from Middle America. Olmec axe; human face and cat face merged; highly typical of the Olmec style. *(Photo Irmgard Groth-Kimball, by perm. of the Tr. of the Brit. Mus.)*

XV Maya attacking their Neighbours. Copy of a wall painting from the Maya city of Bonampak in Central America (between A.D. 317 and 987). Discovered by an American film expedition. *(By perm. of the Peabody Mus., Harvard Univ., Cambridge, Mass.)*

XVI Aztec Shield with Feather Mosaic. Representation of a prairie wolf. (Between A.D. 1324 and 1521.) Gift from Montezuma to Emperor Charles V (through Cortés). *(Photo Conzett and Huber, Zurich, by perm. of the Mus. f. Völkerkd., Vienna.)*